Clinical Prediction in Psychotherapy

Leonard Horwitz

Clinical Prediction in Psychotherapy

Jason Aronson   *New York*

Library of Congress Cataloging in Publication Data

Horwitz, Leonard, 1922-
    Clinical prediction in psychotherapy.

    Bibliography: p.
    1. Psychotherapy--Cases, clinical reports,
statistics. 2. Psychoanalysis--Cases, clinical reports,
statistics. 3. Prediction (Psychology) I. Title.
[DNLM: 1. Prognosis. 2. Psychotherapy. WM420 H824c]
RC480.H66   616.8'914   74-6949
ISBN 0-87668-149-6

The Psychotherapy Research Project of the Menninger Foundation was supported by the Public Health Service Research Grant MH 8308 from the National Institute of Mental Health, the Foundation's Fund for Research in Psychiatry, and the Ford Foundation.

CONTENTS

Foreword   XIII

Author's Introduction   XIX

I.   The Overall Research Design   1
       A Naturalistic Study, 3
       A Process and Outcome Study, 4
       Patient Selection, 5
       Quantification of Variables, 6
       Controls, 8
             Systematic Data Collection • Convergent Data •
             Hypothesis-Testing
       Summary, 12

II.   The Prediction Study   15
       Formulating the Predictions, 17

Converting the Predictions, 19
Confirming and Disconfirming Predictions, 22
The Form of Results, 25
Critique of the Prediction Study, 28
   Incorrect Initial Assessments • The Weighting of
   Explanatory Factors • The Linkage Between the
   Prediction Proper and the Assumption
Summary, 32

III.   **Anxiety and Defense**   35
The Uncovering Process, 36
Countertransference and Uncovering, 39
Disruption of Defenses and External Stress, 41
Termination of Treatment, 42
Family Pressures, 45
Treatment Induced Stress, 47
Resistance, 50
Environmental Outlets, 52
   Behavior Outside Treatment • Pre-existing Neurotic
   Interactions
Hierarchical Ordering of Defenses, 56
Summary, 58

IV.   **The Uncovering Process**   61
The Major Transference Assumption, 62
Infantile Wishes in the Transference, 64
Alloplastic Resistances, 65
Conscious Sense of Guilt, 67
Multiple Determination of Behavior, 68
*Reciprocity Between Transference and Environmental
   Outlets, 69*
Regressive Effects of Psychoanalysis, 70
Summary, 74

V.   Indications and Contraindications for
      Psychoanalysis   77
      Psychotic Potential: Borderline Personalities, 80
      Oral and Narcissistic Fixation, 86
         Narcissistically Defended Patients • Passive-Dependent
         Patients
      Phallic Conflicts, 92
      Masochism, 97
      Anxiety Tolerance, 99
      Motivation, 103
      Summary, 109

VI.   Conflict Resolution and Behavioral
      Change   113
      The Assumption of Proportionality, 115
         Medical Specialist • Tantrum Woman • Phobic
         Woman • Snake Phobia Woman • Adoptive Mother •
         Divorced Teacher • English Professor • Phobic Girl
      The Assumption of Necessity, 129
      The Assumption of Stability, 134
      Summary, 136

VII. Adjunctive Supports to Psychotherapy   139
      Destructive and Self-Destructive Symptoms, 140
      Fostering a Therapeutic Alliance, 145
      Enhanced Expressiveness of Treatment, 150
         Hospitalization as an Adjunct to Psychoanalysis •
         Hospitalization for Greater Expressiveness in
         Psychotherapy
      Summary, 155

VIII. The Therapeutic Alliance   157
      Need Gratification, 159
      Capacity to Perceive a Good Object, 165
         Predictive Assumptions • Postdictive Assumptions
      Summary, 177

IX.   Effects of Supportive Aspects of
       Psychotherapy   179
       Selection of Improved Cases, 181
       *Summaries of Treatment Techniques and Patient
           Changes, 184*
           Predictions Based on Supportive Psychotherapy •
           Bohemian • Playboy • Obedient Husband • Thespian
           Predictions Based on Expressive Aspects of Psychotherapy
           • Phobic Girl • Fencer • Involutional Woman •
           Claustrophobic Man
           Predictions Based on Psychoanalysis • Historian •
           Travel Phobia Woman
       Extent of Supportive Techniques, 200
       Extent of Improvement and Limitation, 204
       *Significant Changes in Expressive Treatments Based
           Upon Supportive Factors, 208*
           Adoptive Mother • Prince • Heiress
       Summary, 214

X   Stability of Change with Supportive
       Treatment   217
       Overall Change Scores, 219
       *Stable Change Without Continuing Therapeutic
           Contact, 221*
           • Bohemian • Playboy • Obedient Husband • Fencer
           • Thespian
       *Stable Change with Continuing Therapeutic
           Contact, 231*
           Partial Irregular Contact • Phobic Girl • Involutional
           Woman • Patients Requiring Regular Therapeutic
           Contact • Historian • Travel Phobia Woman
       The Unstable Transference Cure, 238
       *Follow-up Improvement in Two Additional
           Cases, 240*

Covert Addict • Movie Lady
Summary, 243

XI.   The Curative Process: Summary and
       Reformulation   247
       Working Assumptions of Psychoanalytic
       Psychotherapy, 248
       Major Findings of Study Bearing on Curative
       Factors, 249
       Internalization of Therapeutic Alliance, 255
       Negative Transference as a Barrier to
       Internalization, 262
       Degrees of Successful Internalization, 264
       Critique of the Structural Change Concept, 271

       Appendix 1
       Diagrams of the Hierarchical Organization of
       Assumptions, 277
       A Expressive Aspects of Psychotherapy, 278
       B Supportive Aspects of Psychotherapy, 279
       C Common Core, 280

       Appendix 2
       Predictive and Postdictive Assumptions, 281

       Appendix 3   349

       Glossary of Terms   349

       References   363

FOREWORD

From its beginning in 1954, all through to the present, the Psychotherapy Research Project of the Menninger Foundation has been centrally a longitudinal and prospective study of the processes and outcomes of psychoanalysis and psychotherapy. Inherent in this perspective, whether considered from within a strictly scientific or strictly clinical framework, has been the concept of prediction. For, as we have emphasized throughout the project's conceptualizing process, we have felt the scientific study of prediction to be "not only consonant with the clinical viewpoint but, even more, a logical and systematic extension of what is at least *implicitly* a constant and integral part of ordinary diagnostic and therapeutic clinical practice—the making of clinical predictions by clinician judges" (Sargent, *et al.*, 1968). Or considered from the side of prediction as both a scientific principle and tool, we have, again, stated that it "deals with issues equally relevant and crucial to the advancement of analytic knowledge along whatever path, whether the classical method of the consulting room, clinical observation and analytic case study, or the formally organized research program aimed at systematizing knowledge through generalization and abstraction across a population of cases" (Wallerstein, 1964).

This then is the early stated intent and credo of the overall project and specifically of its Prediction Study component. The tracing however from that point to this present final report by Leonard Horwitz, *Clinical Prediction in Psychotherapy*, has been a painstaking although often exciting and always rewarding incremental effort. The conceptualization of prediction in its salient role, as principle and as tool, in both the clinical enterprise and the research enterprise, and therefore as especially central to the clinical research enterprise that this project is, we owe to the late Helen D. Sargent, creator of the original philosophical and methodological base of the Prediction Study. We are indebted to her as well for the original devising of the system, anchored in the rules of formal logic, for the translation of discursive clinical predictive judgments, embedded in the usual clinical context and clinical qualification, into formalized and testable predictions in accord with a tripartite (if-then-because) logical model. The statement of both the conception and the planned methods for its implementation was first made —briefly, but comprehensively enough so that one could foresee the whole of the later greatly elaborated development—in one of Helen Sargent's (1956) original cluster of articles in the project's first publication.

The relating of this understanding and this use of prediction by the project to its place and its possibilities within the developmental fabric of psychoanalysis as a history and as a theory, and especially to its potential for linking the data of psychoanalytic therapy more systematically and more precisely to the theory of psychoanalysis (and thereby using it as a wedge by which to test and to extend the theory) has been delineated in detail by me in a theoretical exposition from the work and the thinking of the project (Wallerstein, 1964). And, together with Lewis L. Robbins, I had the task over the first four years of the life of the project, 1954 to 1958, of carrying out the comprehensive clinical diagnostic and prognostic studies of each of the forty-two project cases at the initial point in time, which included in each instance not only the assessment of the range (twenty-four in all) of variables of personality function- ing deemed relevant to treatment planning and prognostication, but also the clinical predictions and prognoses regarding the prospective treatment course and outcome, together with the supporting reasons for these predictive statements, reasons based on the assessment of the relevant patient and situational variables in conjunction with the theoretical assumptions con- cerning the nature of change and of the theory of therapy against which the observations on the variables were grouped and juxtaposed. The predictive process was so much the heart of this research endeavor that there was strong pressure within the project to call the whole Initial Study of each of the patients, the clinical bedrock of the entire enterprise, the *Prediction Study.* (It was decided however to reserve that designation for the study of just the specific individual predictions made on the cases within the project, followed in each instance from their inception through to their testing, and the then-strengthening or revision or discarding of the theoretical propositions on which they were based.)

It is for that major phase of the overall task, the full elaboration of the methods and design of the Prediction Study, the actual work of transformation of the clinical predictive statements on all forty-two project cases into testable hypotheses in accord with the various instruments devised to fulfill the requirements of the tripartite (if-then-because) model, and the subsequent Confirmation Studies of detailed inquiry

into the fate—confirmation or refutation, complete or partial—
of the average of fifty discrete predictions for each of the forty-
two cases—it is for that very considerable undertaking that
Leonard Horwitz early joined in partnership with Helen Sargent and which, following her untimely death, he undertook to
complete, together then with Ann Appelbaum who had, in turn,
joined him in partnership.

The first fruit of those partnerships and the presented
distillation of the shared thinking that infused them was the
monograph jointly authored by Helen Sargent, Leonard Horwitz, Ann Appelbaum, and myself (Sargent *et al.*, 1968). The
scope was ambitious, with chapters that (1) described the role
of prediction in psychological research and presented our
rationale for its employment in our efforts, (2) outlined our
design and our procedures, including the detailed description of
the various forms developed for the formal restatement of
clinical predictions and for their subsequent testing for verifica-
tion, (3) gave an account of the various philosophical and
methodological vicissitudes we traversed and of the decisions
made at the various choice-points in the construction of the
formal model for stating predictions in a form which paralleled
the familiar scientific model of classical experimental design,
(4) presented the entire detailed schema, the complete manual
of instructions for the translation of the informal and discursive
clinical diagnostic and prognostic statements into formal testable predictions, (5) gave a full case illustration, the Prediction
Study for Mrs. X, including the entire body of *clinical*
assessment and prediction, and then all of the derived *formal*
predictions, each stated in the devised if-then-because tripartite
form, and (6) finally followed with the detailed *Confirmation
Study* on the same case, giving a condensed account of the
treatment process and outcome, and reporting the fate of each
of the individual predictions and their associated assumptions.

So much then for the prologue and context of the present work. What follows is Leonard Horwitz's comprehensive realization of the high promise set forth in the earlier monograph and in the associated writings. In this present work, Dr. Horwitz has taken the *whole corpus* of the Prediction Study, the fate of some two thousand discrete individually studied predictions across forty-two cases, their individual confirmation or refutation, together with the elucidation of the assumptive bases of these outcomes into strengthened or revised or weakened theoretical propositions that together constitute our theory of psychoanalytic therapy. He has rendered the whole into a comprehensible survey and exposition grouped as to the major areas of theoretical concern, the governing assumptions of psychoanalytic, of expressive psychotherapeutic, and of supportive psychotherapeutic work, all as conceptualized and guided within the psychoanalytic theoretical framework. In accomplishing this task, Dr. Horwitz has wisely, I think, chosen a more clinical, rather than a tabular statistical, approach to the organization of his data and his findings, in order to better portray the larger and more significant issues, letting thereby many individual trees sink back into the highlighted massed effects that convey the characteristic, in part expected, and in part quite unanticipated, emergent configurations of the overall forest.

Many of his findings and conclusions are sufficiently unexpected to raise thoughtful questions and issues, not only for the psychotherapy researcher in his quest to add to the body of theory that constitutes his science but at least equally for the psychotherapeutic and psychoanalytic therapist in his quest to improve his clinical effectiveness in pursuit of his humane goal of alleviating human suffering. In this sense, this book can be taken to represent some recompense from clinical research which has one-sidedly lived on the questions fashioned by the problems of clinical practice, as now feeding back new insights and new perspectives that can perhaps in their turn begin to influence and modify clinical practice.

ROBERT S. WALLERSTEIN, M.D.

REFERENCES

Sargent, Helen D. (1956), "Design." In "The Psychotherapy Research Project of the Menninger Foundation: Rationale, Method, and Sample Use," *Bulletin of the Menninger Clinic,* 20:234–238.

Sargent, Helen D., Horwitz, Leonard, Wallerstein, Robert S., and Appelbaum, Ann (1968), "Prediction in Psychotherapy Research: A Method for the Transformation of Clinical Judgments into Testable Hypotheses," *Psychological Issues,* Monograph No. 21, Vol. 6:1–46.

Wallerstein, Robert S. (1964), "The Role of Prediction in Theory Building in Psychoanalysis," *Journal of the American Psychoanalytic Association,* 12:675–691.

INTRODUCTION

  This work represents the culmination of fifteen years of collaborative research with many Menninger Foundation colleagues. My affiliation with the Psychotherapy Research Project started in 1957, when Helen Sargent invited me to assist her with the Prediction Study. Our task at that time was to convert clinical predictions into testable hypotheses using a detailed and sophisticated method which she had devised. After her death in 1959, with much of the preliminary work out of the way, I assumed responsibility for carrying the Prediction Study to completion. For a brief period I was assisted by Dr. Helene Gerall, now at Tulane University, and in 1963 Dr. Ann Appelbaum joined me in the confirmation phase of the study.

  It is difficult now to convey the excitement of working both with the predictions and later with their confirmation. In some ways it recaptured my experience as a weather forecaster in the military service. In that situation the feedback concerning one's accuracy was almost immediate and usually unequivocal, especially from disgruntled pilots. But each forecast presented a challenge to one's understanding and mastery of the principles of meteorology.

In a similar way, the more protracted work of studying a detailed set of predictions about a patient's treatment aroused one's curiosity about how each case would really eventuate. This was especially true of those cases where stepwise, "critical" predictions were made. For example, a patient first had to reach the crucial insight that he was indeed an alcoholic before any further progress could be made in his analysis (he didn't). Or, a woman had to recognize the impossibility of a marriage in which the partners were incompatible before making further progress with her depressive symptoms (she did). Each case generated its own exciting questions: how would these lives really unfold, would therapist and patient avoid the pitfalls envisioned for them, would the predictors' optimism be borne out, or would the Cassandra-like forecasts for some be averted? Imagine, then, the excitement of opening the research team's write-up of a completed case as part of the confirmation phase of the work.

The scientific reward of this study was not expected to be derived from the scoreboard of predictive success and failure. Rather, we wanted to know what the predictions for a particular case had to teach us about the scientific base of psychotherapy. If predictions were confirmed, did it strengthen the underlying assumptions, or were some other explanations in order? Or, more important, if predictions went awry, what were the implications for the theory that had been used?

Most psychotherapy researchers have lamented the fact that investigations into psychotherapy have not penetrated or influenced clinical practice. Bergin and Strupp (1972) recently evaluated the feasibility of attempting a wide-scope study involving a comparison of the leading approaches to psychotherapy as a way of eventually finding answers which could have an influence on treatment techniques. Their feasibility study convinced them that a project of this magnitude could not be undertaken at this time.

Although difficult to prove, I would venture to say that the Psychotherapy Research Project had an influence on the practice of psychotherapy and psychoanalysis at the Menninger Foundation both in large and small ways. One definite finding which I believe infiltrated into our thinking and practice was the importance of a careful diagnostic study before embarking upon treatment, particularly psychoanalysis. Despite the current popularity of the new briefer therapies, there is still considerable conviction at our institution, reinforced by the present study, that analysis is an unrivaled method for the alteration of deep-seated character problems. But the research impressed upon us the great care that must be taken in the selection of cases for such treatment lest we expend much effort, time, and money to no avail. For example, the reasoning advanced by some that patients who do not fulfill the exacting criteria for analysis but who require this modality if they are to have a chance for remission of symptoms—the "heroic" indication—did not stand up under research scrutiny. Other cases taught us that significant ego defects should rule out analysis and, furthermore, that psychological testing is the best method for detecting such weaknesses. Even if this general understanding existed prior to this study, I believe that a refinement of the criteria for successful analysis gradually grew as we studied a number of analytic cases and this knowledge permeated our clinical practice. For example, in contrast to the preresearch years, not a single patient at the Menninger Foundation today begins analysis unless first given a battery of psychological tests.

The study has also yielded rich educational benefit to our staff and students. Numerous seminars and study groups have taken advantage of the project's intensive case studies, probably the best teaching cases available in our setting. Whether the focus be a detailed study of a treatment process, or the inference-making process in psychological testing, or simply an instance of initial diagnostic study—the extensiveness of the data available, both cross-sectional and longitudinal, is difficult to match.

For the future, there is still much treasure to be mined from these highly detailed case studies. They constitute an unusually rich reservoir of psychotherapy cases studied in great depth, systematically covering the relevant clinical variables, including both quantitative assessments and detailed qualitative descriptions. Many clinical questions and hypotheses, not already asked by our project members await study by interested researchers with the wisdom to scrutinize this data further.

Dr. Helen Sargent was mentor, colleague, and friend. She had an abiding interest and talent in research methodology and was probably the greatest single contributor to the planning of the various phases of the project. Despite a lifelong physical handicap and health which was beginning to fail, she never forsook her role of scientific conscience and articulate spokesman for combining sound research methods with good clinical thinking. I am in her debt for the opportunity to work on this project, for the general direction of the work, and for her encouragement and challenges during our work together.

Dr. Robert S. Wallerstein carried the heavy burden for many years of captaining a large and diverse interdisciplinary team. Most of us were part-time researchers who had to struggle against letting the demands of clinical responsibilities encroach on our research efforts. His administrative approach was more carrot than stick, but he never let any of us lose sight of the ultimate objective of bringing this ambitious long-term project to completion. He had to enlist the cooperation of therapists whose work came under the exacting scrutiny of a research team despite a universal, and understandable, reluctance to being thus exposed. I am grateful for his able direction, as I am to Dr. Lewis L. Robbins who was his codirector until he left Topeka in 1958. Since Dr. Wallerstein's departure in 1966, Dr. Otto Kernberg with his considerable energy, enthusiasm, and scholarship helped the various research groups complete their part of the work.

The person who collaborated with me most closely during the latter half of the Prediction Study work was Dr. Ann Appelbaum. More than any other individual, her contributions are represented throughout the pages of this book. Her clinical acumen and clear thinking were exercised in generous measure on every case we scrutinized together. During our many years of collaboration she helped to sharpen case formulations, devised assumption statements to express succinctly an explanatory generalization, and contributed to a logical organization of these many statements. It is impossible to acknowledge all of the clinical and theoretical ideas she originated as we hammered out formulations and conclusions concerning each case. In addition, she did a most thorough reading of the entire manuscript and helped to refine the final version.

I am indebted to several colleagues for their critical reading of parts or all of the manuscript: Dr. Stephen Appelbaum, Dr. Esther Burstein, Dr. Lolafaye Coyne, Dr. Otto Kernberg, Mr. Arthur Mandelbaum, Dr. Irwin Rosen, Dr. Howard Shevrin, and Dr. Robert Wallerstein. Mrs. Virginia Eicholtz did a careful and creative job of editing the manuscript.

The loyal and efficient secretaries of the project, Mrs. Sarah Heil Hunt, Mrs. Gloria Smith, and Mrs. Mary Patton were invaluable helpers over the years. More recently, Mrs. Hazel Bruce has applied her talents, versatility, and dedication to producing a readable manuscript.

Finally, my wife's willingness to endure the presence of a demanding competitor in our home made my task more congenial than it might have been.

L.H.

CHAPTER 1

THE OVERALL RESEARCH DESIGN

The Psychotherapy Research Project of the Menninger Foundation had its inception in 1954, after approximately two years of discussion and planning by a committee of senior clinicians. During the early fifties the issues being raised by the scientific community, both within and outside the psychoanalytic group, were centered more on *how* psychotherapy and psychoanalysis worked, than on *whether* this kind of treatment was of significant value. Eysenck (1952) was just beginning to seriously question the validity of dynamically oriented therapy, but he was a lone voice in the wilderness at that time. Not until the sixties did opposing points of view and opposing technologies, like the behavior therapies and the innovative group therapies, begin to gain prominence and demand attention as rival forms of treatment.

Therefore, the design of the project was much more concerned with answering questions raised by psychoanalytic practitioners than responding to attacks by critics. We were not really interested in establishing the validity of the method nor were we interested in comparing analytic therapy with other methods. The only "rival," and one that was even then beginning to wane, was Rogers' nondirective or client-centered approach. Existential therapies were just beginning to appear on the horizon. We were interested in finding answers to two basic questions: what kinds of changes take place in analytic treatment, and how do such changes occur?

No analyst was so naive as to believe that every patient responded favorably to any or all of the analytic therapies. In fact, the first of our questions included such considerations as what kinds of patients responded best to what kinds of treatment. Is expressive treatment capable of producing more extensive and more stable change than supportive treatment? When is psychoanalysis indicated and when not; if indicated, does it produce more definitive changes than psychotherapy? What are the patient characteristics that are significant in determining assignment to a given modality, and how do these variables affect the process and outcome? Finally, how do situational variables affect treatment? The supports and obstacles, both in the patient's usual environment and those engendered by treatment (like hospitalization), will both foster and limit the change made possible by psychotherapy.

The second group of questions consisted of those relating to the more difficult problem of discovering how change comes about. Analysts have written extensively about the mechanisms of personality change in a treatment process but there was scant research data on this question. What is the role of insight? Does insight precede or follow behavioral or symptom change? What is the role of identification with the therapist as a change agent? How significant is the skill and personality of the therapist in the various modalities in contributing to therapeutic change?

These questions lead to a rather complex design which has

been described extensively elsewhere (Wallerstein *et al.*, 1956, 1958). In this introduction to the results of the Prediction Study we shall summarize sufficient details of the overall design to make possible an understanding of the study design (Chapter 2).

Briefly, the Psychotherapy Research Project was an intensive, in-depth study of forty-two patients whose primary treatment was analytically oriented psychotherapy or psychoanalysis, half by the former and half by the latter. The patients were studied at three points in time, initially, at termination, and at a two-year follow-up point. Three major dimensions were investigated at the appropriate times: patient variables, treatment (therapist) variables, and situational variables.

Within this broad framework, a number of significant strategies were adopted which formed the design of the overall project.

A NATURALISTIC STUDY

The plan emphasized the need to minimize the research team influencing or distorting the treatment process. This meant that neither the patient nor the therapist should know that they had been selected for study until the treatment had been terminated. The entire procedure of patient examination and assessment, treatment prescription, assignment to a therapist, and carrying out of treatment was done independently of the research team. All clinical decisions and procedures were executed with no reference to the researchers.

This approach had obvious shortcomings in terms of the Prediction Study. The initial evaluation of the patient by the Initial Study team of the project was limited to the data collected by the evaluating team. Fortunately, most patients in the Menninger Clinic setting underwent a uniform initial examination which included psychiatric interviews, a social history based on interviews with the patient's family and/or spouse, psychological tests, and a physical examination. Documents of previous psychiatric contacts were obtained. But the research team was unable to have direct contact with the patient and thus could not use their own clinical impressions in assessing the patient. Neither could they pursue directly with the patient questions raised by the special task they were confronting.

A PROCESS AND OUTCOME STUDY

Although the naturalistic study made it necessary to forego data collection during the course of treatment, one research team (the Treatment Variables Group) studied *both* the treatment course and the outcome and attempted to reconstruct the major elements in the treatment process. Clinic policy at that time required that monthly progress notes be kept by the therapist. Cases treated under supervision, mainly the analytic cases, often had daily process notes. Therapists also were required to write annual summaries of treatment as well as a final discharge summary at termination. Therapists (and supervisors, where available) as well as the patient at termination were interviewed by the researchers. Among other questions, the interviewees were asked to describe as much of the significant events of the treatment process as they could recall. Usually the patients were seen at least twice, as were the therapists, in lengthy interviews. The Situational Variables Group had similar interviews with the patients as well as with the significant figures in their lives in order to assess the impact of the environment on change and vice versa.

Thus, even though there was no data collection during the course of treatment, an effort was made at the conclusion of treatment to collect as much data as possible bearing on the treatment process. Monthly process notes, annual summaries, and discharge summaries were the main written sources of data; and the retrospective reconstruction of both patient and therapist in detailed and searching interviews contributed to fleshing out the recorded data.

PATIENT SELECTION

The major criterion for selection of patients was that the patient's major modality of treatment should be psychotherapy and he should not, for example, be hospitalized for a prolonged period during his psychotherapy. Another requirement was that he be a late adolescent or adult. Only those cases were included whose therapists were beyond their training period (psychiatric residency or postdoctoral psychology training). Mental defectives, neurologically impaired, and overtly psychotic patients were eliminated.

One requirement which probably influenced our research results adversely, particularly the psychoanalytic cases, was that the case not be a "restricted" one: this meant that all patients who were members of the Topeka psychiatric community, mainly the professional staff and their families, were excluded. This group, comprising some 30 percent of our therapy caseload and an even higher percentage of our psychoanalytic cases, was usually considered to be composed of our best psychoanalytic patients in terms of motivation and ego strength. It was necessary to eliminate them from the study because of the large number of professional staff working on this project and the likelihood, because of the relatively small professional community, that some of the research subjects would eventually develop professional or social relationships with the research staff.

QUANTIFICATION OF VARIABLES

All researchers in the behavioral sciences face the dilemma of quantification: the variables which lend themselves to easy quantification are usually not the most clinically relevant and meaningful. Our research group attempted to resolve this dilemma by selecting those variables (patient, treatment, and situational)[1] which they deemed important, regardless of their amenability to being rated or quantified. The research teams described in qualitative, discursive form, their judgments and observations regarding these variables. In this way the richness of the clinicians' thinking and judgment was retained.

But the clinicians' qualitative write-ups were then subjected to further processing by another group of judges. The variables which lent themselves to quantification were singled out and a numerical score was obtained for each patient for each selected variable based on a comparison with the other patients in the population. There were twenty-four patient variables (anxiety tolerance, level of psychosexual development, ego strength, core conflicts, self-concept, etc.); only eleven of the twenty-four could be positioned on a linear scale while the others remained in qualitative form.

[1] There were 24 patient variables, 19 treatment variables, and 7 situational variables. See Wallerstein *et al.* (1956).

The conversion to quantified form was based on an adaptation of the Fechnerian Paired Comparisons Method devised (1967) by Helen Sargent. Briefly, each patient was paired with several other patients and one of the pair was rated as higher or lower on that variable. Through a carefully devised system of overlapping batches, each patient eventually emerged with a quantitative rating comparing him with the other forty-one cases.

These ratings were quasi-cardinal numbers and as such had the limitation of being only relative, not absolute, ratings. The numbers did not tell how much absolute change each subject showed on a given variable. The highs had relatively more than the lows, but we did not know the extent of absolute change, for example, which these patients achieved.

There were three scales which provided absolute ratings. They all consisted of global, overall ratings of functioning or change. One was the Health-Sickness Rating Scale devised by Luborsky (1962), consisting of a detailed hundred-point anchored scale of overt functioning; each patient was rated by the respective research teams studying them at the three points in time. Another absolute measure was devised by the Situational Variables Group and consisted of two five-point scales: one was symptom change and referred to changes in the level of overt functioning from initial to termination, while the other was a rating of essential change in which the focus was on internal shifts in psychic organization. The third rating was made by the Prediction Study Group and was called Absolute Global Change, an overall change measure combining overt and intrapsychic functioning. It was a five-point rating scale: 1—worse, 2—no change, 3—slight change, 4—moderate change, 5—marked change with conflict resolution. These change ratings were made for initial to termination, initial to follow-up, and termination to follow-up.

The quantitative ratings, mainly the paired comparison

data, provided the basis for a number of statistical and other data-processing methods and included a factor analytic study of the variables, analysis of variance, and the application of Guttman's method of facet analysis. The results of these quantitative approaches have been described in a monograph by Kernberg *et al.* (1972).

CONTROLS

The hallmark of a research effort is the use of controls, in order to minimize errors, omissions, biases, and contaminations which characterize uncontrolled observation. The term "control" may be employed in the broadest, most inclusive sense as any method that enhances the validity of one's conclusions, or it may be used in the strictest sense of a design in which the null hypothesis regarding a particular proposition is tested. The latter approach is usually applied by means of comparing an experimental and control group, like treated versus nontreated groups. This approach was not applicable to our study since we were not posing the question of the validity of psychotherapy per se. The issue rather was to evaluate the kind and extent of patient change and to account for such change or the lack of it. Of course, one could argue that a control group would have permitted a more accurate assessment of how much the treatment actually contributed to the extent of change and how much was derived from nontreatment factors. But considering the difficulty of obtaining a matched control group, even this method would not have afforded a definitive answer to the source of observed change.

The design of this study included a variety of means to limit observer bias covering a broad spectrum of rigor ranging from

systematic data collection and classification (including quantification) to controls approaching an hypothesis-testing design.
These methods fell into three categories.

Systematic Data Collection

Optimal completeness of data collection was assured by
specifying in advance the variables (patient, treatment, and
situational) to be studied, described, and quantified. Other
safeguards involved the use of judges who were not directly
involved in the clinical work under scrutiny. While our judges
may have had a positive bias toward analytic theory and
treatment, they were not invested with viewing any particular
treatment in a positive light as a therapist might.[2] A further
safeguard was the practice of not only using our most senior
clinicians on the research teams but also of requiring that
clinical judgments regarding each of the variables be made by a
pair of judges. In some instances, the judgments (like the
Paired Comparisons ratings) were first made independently by
each member of the pair, while for the majority of variables the
research clinicians worked together to form consensus judgments. The Prediction Study team, on the other hand, first
independently recorded their judgments regarding the various
facets of each prediction and then met to form consensus
judgments.

Convergent Data

To the extent that judgments bearing on the same variables
are derived from different sources of observation, the validity of

[2] A study by Harty and Horwitz (1973) clearly establishes that therapists in this
project almost universally viewed the treatment they rendered more positively than did
the patient or the research clinicians judging the same treatment.

the final judgment is enhanced. If ego strength is judged from interview data and then independently from psychological test data, the convergence of such diverse material (or the lack of it) adds an extra source of strength to one's conclusions. Thus, judgments about patient change were not only derived from interviews with patient and therapist, but the Situational Variables Group made independent assessments of patient change by examining the patient's "life space." These judgments were derived in part from interviews with the patient, but were supplemented by interviews with members of the patient's family. Second, and even more cogent, were the independently made psychological test studies in which the psychologist performed a relatively blind evaluation of the patient using a standard test battery at initial, termination, and follow-up points. A comparison of these three test records provided the basis for independent assessments of patient variables as well as changes in these variables over time. The psychologist had a minimal amount of information available to him regarding the patient's treatment at termination and follow-up, mainly derived from the patient's comments in the course of testing.

Hypothesis-Testing

The most rigorous control is one in which the null hypothesis is given a maximum chance to be operative. Such hypothesis-testing was not done in this study although the Prediction Study to some extent approached such a design.

Each patient was used as his own control in the sense that he became an experiment to test a series of explicated hypotheses regarding psychoanalytic therapy. These hypotheses were applied to each patient in the form of predictions concerning the process and outcome of his treatment. A confirmation of the prediction and the underlying assumption affords a strengthening of that assumption. A disconfirmation of a prediction and assumption generally constitutes an invalidation of the underlying assumption. But in order to achieve a clearly positive result we need a test of the null hypothesis in which the independent variables were permitted to cover a range of instances.

To illustrate, let us examine one of the major hypotheses of our study—that patients in psychoanalysis with good ego strength and high motivation are able to resolve their core conflicts. When applied to patients with the requisite qualities, each confirmation would produce some strengthening of the hypothesis while a single disconfirmation would invalidate or disprove it. The null hypothesis, however, would only be tested where patients with both low and high ego strength and low and high motivation were given psychoanalysis. If there was a statistically significant difference between the high and low groups with respect to changes associated with psychoanalysis, then the null hypothesis (that ego strength and motivation were not essential variables) would have been disproved and the assumption would have been markedly strengthened.

We approached true hypothesis-testing in those instances where inadvertent control occurred. On a few occasions the patient, because of practical circumstances like geography or finances, could not follow the prescribed treatment and underwent, for example, a less-expressive therapy than the predictors believed he needed. Or, in cases where the predictors' judgment differed from that of the treatment team, the patient was placed in a modality not considered the treatment of choice by the predictors. In these instances we approached a null hypothesis test in that the independent variables were being permitted to range widely (like a patient with low ego strength being given psychoanalysis).

The prediction method is one of the major controls used in this study and the results of the Prediction Study are the focus of this book. We did not use a rigorous hypothesis-testing method but undertook it insofar as disconfirmations constituted disproof and, even further, we approached a test of the null hypothesis in those instances of inadvertent controls.

The Prediction Study, described in detail in the next chapter, was an effort to systematically set down detailed predictions of the treatment developments and results in each case. In addition, the predictors were asked to explicate their assumptions in making their forecasts, and we thus have a clear-cut description and application of the psychoanalytic theory of therapy as applied to forty-two patients. The success and failure of these predictions and their implications for the theory of treatment constitutes the substance of this volume.

SUMMARY

1. The Menninger Foundation Psychotherapy Research Project attempted to answer two basic questions: what kinds of changes take place in analytic treatment, and how do such changes occur?

2. The project was an intensive, in-depth study of forty-two patients whose primary treatment was analytically oriented psychotherapy or psychoanalysis. The patients were studied at three points in time: initially, at termination, and at a two-year follow-up point.

3. Three major dimensions were investigated at the appropriate times: patient variables, treatment (and therapist) variables, and situational variables.

4. A naturalistic design was adopted in order to minimize possible distortions of the clinical process by research scrutiny. Although this policy limited data collection by the researchers

prior to the beginning of treatment and during its process, the research teams attempted to reconstruct the process and assess the outcome of treatment at termination and follow-up by reference to the existing clinical record and by in-depth interviews with the patient, therapist, and significant others.

5. Patients selected for this project were late adolescents or adults, being treated by a therapist beyond the training period, not handicapped by intellectual or neurological defects, not overtly psychotic, and who were not part of the local psychiatric community.

6. While preserving the qualitative richness of the clinician's observations, the variables of the study which lent themselves to quantification were rated for each patient through a special paired-comparisons technique. In addition to these quasi-cardinal ratings, we used three other rating scales of absolute overall functioning or overall change.

7. The controls in this study ranged over a wide spectrum of rigor. First, the research judges studied a predetermined set of variables with pairs of senior clinicians used to form clinical judgments. Second, convergent data were gathered mainly by doing independent psychological test studies. And third, a hypothesis-testing method was approached by the prediction method which allowed us to invalidate hypotheses which were disconfirmed when their associated predictions were negated. Tests of the null hypothesis were approached even more when inadvertent instances of nonrecommended treatment occurred.

CHAPTER 2

THE PREDICTION STUDY

By formulating predictions about the treatment course and outcome of each case, we were moving the level of the study from hypothesis finding toward a more rigorous examination of assumptions about dynamically oriented psychotherapy. Analytically oriented psychotherapy and psychoanalysis have been practiced since the turn of the century with increasing knowledge and skill being accumulated about theory and application. The theory of psychoanalytic psychotherapy is better developed in certain areas than in others. Those conceptions concerning a theory of personality functioning were relatively well advanced. Propositions concerning the relationship between anxiety and defense or the repetitive nature of the infantile neurosis in the form of transference and resistance and the factors which intensify or dampen such reactions have been relatively well established during the decades of psychotherapeutic practice. But, as Rapaport (1960) pointed out, a major defect in psychoanalytic theory, and one which particularly weakens its theory of psychotherapy, is the paucity of knowledge (and theory) about how learning or personality change takes place. Even though a number of hypotheses exist about the curative factors in psychotherapy, it still remains the area in which clinicians have not attained either clarity or agreement.

However unclear certain parts of the theory may be, a failure to explicate the hypotheses which did exist and to test them in the crucible of clinical practice would indeed have represented a missed opportunity. Those involved in the Prediction Study, and particularly Helen Sargent, whose painstaking work (1968) on this particular phase of the research fashioned most of its design, were aware that most clinical work including diagnosis, treatment recommendations, and even psychotherapy itself, involved making implicit predictions. When we perform a diagnostic study of an individual and conclude, for example, that psychoanalysis is the treatment of choice, we are not only saying that we expect the patient to be able to uncover and resolve certain inhibiting intrapsychic conflicts, but we are also implying the expectation that the patient has sufficient ego resources to withstand the regressive pulls of the analytic process without experiencing severe personality disorganization on the one hand, or extreme defensive rigidity and distance on the other. Since clinicians are constantly using a predictive method, often without being aware of it, why not turn this activity to maximum advantage in these intensively studied cases? The major difference between actual clinical work and this research endeavor would be in the self-conscious conversion of the implicit to the explicit. In brief, the predictors were asked not only to record their expectations concerning process and outcome, but they were asked to carefully provide the assumptions, the theory of psychotherapy, which led them to their conclusions.

The rationale of the prediction method as well as the details of the present study have already been presented in a previous monograph (Sargent *et al.*, 1968). In this chapter we shall summarize the major features of the design and include a retrospective critique of the method based upon our experience in applying it.

FORMULATING THE PREDICTIONS

The Initial Study Group consisted of two senior clinicians who studied all of the documents relevant to a given case. These usually included the psychiatric examination, a social history done by a social worker with significant figures in the patient's life, psychological testing using a standard battery, records of previous psychiatric treatment (when applicable), and a physical examination. On the basis of this material, the Initial Study Group described the patient in terms of twenty-four patient variables including such items as level of anxiety, ego strength, extent of desired change, quality of relationships, etc. They then formulated in discursive essay form their predictions regarding the patient's probable response to the modality of treatment for which he was recommended. Where it was expected that the patient's treatment might be changed, alternate predictions were made. Other kinds of contingencies were also considered, like situational pressures or major situational changes (death of a family member, divorce, loss of job, etc.). The items covered in this detailed predictive statement included: treatment recommendations, nature of problems expected to arise in psychotherapy, anticipated changes in symptoms, impulse-defense configurations and manifest behavior patterns, structural changes in the ego, and the acquisition of insight in its relation to changes in attitudes toward the self and others. As mentioned, the predictors attempted to carefully delineate the considerations which led to their conclusions.

The Initial Study Group performed a few other operations in order to explicate as clearly as possible their expectations concerning a patient's treatment. Mainly, they completed two sets of inventories which we refer to as the Core Evidence Form and the Individualized Evidence Form. Both consist of rather extensive true-false questions relating both to process and outcome. The Core Form contains statements and questions pertinent to all treatments and the same form is applied to every case. The questionnaire covers such areas as the length of treatment, whether or not adjunctive treatments were used, the extent to which transference developed and was used by the therapist, the fate of the patient's major symptoms and defenses, etc. The predictors were asked to complete the inventory as they expected it would be completed by the researchers at the end of treatment, and thus they committed themselves in advance to expressing at least some of their predictions in a form which allowed for easy and definite comparison to another team's judgments at termination.

Obviously there were individualized predictions not covered by the Core Form which required similar processing. Thus, an individualized, tailor-made inventory was composed for each patient based upon all of the predictive statements made about that case. This true-false inventory was composed by a Prediction Study Group and was based upon the predictions made by the Initial Study team. Approximately half the statements were arranged to be true and half false, and the inventory was then submitted back to the Initial Study Group for them to "answer," once again from the vantage point of a termination judge. Since the Individualized Evidence Form was based upon the predictions made by the Initial Study Group, the statements included all of the areas covered in the original prediction essay.

The two inventories described above constituted objective evidence to which the predictors committed themselves in advance. When the research judges, at termination and at follow-up, responded to the same inventories, we expected a fairly accurate means for assessing the confirmation or disconfirmation of the predictors' judgments. By having the predictors as well as the termination and follow-up judges respond to the same comprehensive inventories, one is provided with a more direct measure of agreement and disagreement than having to infer more indirectly from the predictions of the Initial Study Group to the observations and descriptions of the Treatment Variables Group at later points in time.

Further precision was added to the predictive validation process by means of the Health-Sickness Rating Scale, a hundred-point anchored scale of overt functioning devised by Luborsky (1962). It provided a global measure of the extent to which the person is free of symptoms and inhibitions and the extent to which he is able to "work and love." Not only was the Initial Study Group asked to rate the patient at the beginning of treatment but they were also asked to predict the Health-Sickness Rating for the termination point.

CONVERTING THE PREDICTIONS

In discussing the Individualized Evidence Form and how it was devised, we mentioned that a Prediction Study Group was involved in performing certain operations on predictions after the Initial Study Group had finished with them. Essentially these operations may be described as converting the predictive essay into a series of testable statements.

The first step in this process consisted of carefully sifting through the predictive essay and gleaning each individual, discrete predictive statement. Although many of the statements for a given case were interdependent and interrelated, we attempted to separate the statements into small, simple units in order to be maximally clear and unambiguous about what was being confirmed and disconfirmed.

When interdependencies did exist, we encompassed those by our contingency clauses. All contingencies were the "if clauses" in an if-then statement. The universal contingency applicable to each prediction was the treatment modality for which the prediction was being made. The major treatment contingencies consisted of the four major modalities (psycho-analysis, expressive, supportive-expressive, and supportive treatments), but there were additional treatment contingencies such as psychotherapy beginning with a period of hospitaliza-tion, or accompanied for a period of time by day hospital or family care treatment. Other kinds of contingencies included certain key developments in the treatment: if the patient overcame his denial of illness, if he was able to develop a solid therapeutic alliance, or if he was able to gain access to his repressed affective life. These statements, of course, would have been the prediction proper of another, prior prediction which then became the contingency for an interdependent set of other predictions. Another class of contingencies included possible situational developments, e.g., loss of a significant figure through death or divorce or some other important life development.

Thus far we have discussed the two important elements of a predictive statement: the *prediction proper*, and the *contin-gency*. There is a third element, equally important, which was added to the other two: the *assumption clause*. The ultimate objective of the Prediction Study is to test the theory of treatment used by our practitioners. The assumptions are those statements which explain the predictors' basis for formulating the prediction, in effect the psychoanalytic theory of psychotherapy. The addition of the assumption clause produces a tripartite prediction statement with an "if-then-because" form.

We attempted to achieve uniformity of language in our assumption statements. Wherever the same theoretical base explained more than one prediction, we used the same language for the assumption. Where the assumption had not been used before, we wrote a new statement and, as we progressed through the forty-two cases, we accumulated a fairly complete set of assumption statements representing the theory of psychoanalytic therapy. Typical assumption statements are[1]

> To the extent that patients have good ego strength and strong motivation to effect psychological change in themselves, they are able in expressive psychotherapies to resolve their intrapsychic conflicts with a concomitant remission of symptoms as well as characterological changes.
> Patients with marked oral fixations who rely primarily upon externalizing defenses such as projection, somatization, and denial are unable to achieve major intrapsychic change.
> Reality aspects, both in the treatment situation itself and in the patient's current difficulties, play a more prominent role early in expressive psychotherapy and become subordinated later to the more internal fantasy-dictated, genetically prior aspects of the patient's difficulties.
> Patients who derive gratification of infantile needs in the supportive aspects of the treatment situation experience a reduction of symptoms associated with this gratification without a resolution of the conflicts.

As we accumulated assumption statements we observed that many of them were interrelated and, in fact, stood in some kind of hierarchical relationship with each other. In writing an

1. The complete list of theoretical assumptions, predictive as well as postdictive, arranged in hierarchical order, may be found in Appendixes 1 and 2.

assumption statement we had a considerable degree of latitude concerning the level of generality appropriate for the assumption. For example, a patient referred for psychoanalysis was expected to experience only a partial success because of the intensity of her oral fixations which were likely to lead to an insoluble transference neurosis. One could write a statement concerning the limitation of results in terms of the intense oral fixation or one could attempt to generalize more broadly and refer to the intensity of libidinal fixation at all levels being a limiting factor (also true). In this instance, it is actually possible to write both statements, with the former being subsumed by the latter in a hierarchical ordering. In this way, if a statement at the lower level of the hierarchy is confirmed, it also helps to strengthen the statements at a higher level.

A second dimension of hierarchical ordering is one which involves causality. There is, for example, a whole series of causally linked statements describing the process of expressive treatment. To put this in a highly skeletonized form: a patient attains insight into his unconscious conflicts *because* he develops a regressive transference neurosis which gets interpreted *because* elements of the analytic process (free association, recumbent position, rule of abstinence, etc.) contribute to a libidinal regression. Thus the hierarchical organization of our assumption statements was determined both by a generality-specificity dimension and by a causal dimension.

CONFIRMING AND DISCONFIRMING PREDICTIONS

The Prediction Study team not only converted predictions into testable form but they also assessed the correctness and incorrectness of each prediction. As mentioned above, each prediction was composed of three component parts (contingen-cy, prediction proper, and assumption clause), and each of the component parts was evaluated separately on a four-point scale of true, partly true, partly false, and false.

First, the two members of the Prediction Study team read the complete write-up of the research teams at termination and follow-up. The Treatment Variables Group produced qualita-tive descriptions of the twenty-four patient variables, including any observations of change from initial to follow-up. The assessment of change was partly made by using the patient descriptions of the Initial Study Group as a point of reference. The Treatment Variables Group also wrote an extensive description of the treatment process and outcome. They described the major problems which arose during the course of treatment, the kind of unfolding of transference paradigms which emerged, the therapeutic techniques relied upon by the therapist, changes which ensued, and factors which both facilitated and deterred therapeutic change. In addition, the impact of the therapist's skill and personality upon the treat-ment was described. Another team, the Situational Variables Group, assessed seven life situational factors which either influenced the treatment or were influenced by the treatment. Descriptions done at termination and repeated at follow-up provided the background material for the Prediction Study team in the confirmation process.

It will be recalled that the true-false inventories or evidence forms had been keyed by the Initial Study Group as they had expected them to be answered at termination. These forms, now also answered by the Treatment Variables Group, the Situa-tional Variables Group, and the therapist, became the major source of data used by the Prediction Study team for assessing the accuracy of the predictions. The Individualized Evidence Form, in particular, provided specific data for judging the accuracy of each prediction.

As mentioned earlier, every step of the research which involved clinical judgment was performed by at least two clinicians or two judges, first working independently and then meeting together to reach a consensus. This procedure was applied in the Prediction Study; the independent judgments were preserved in most instances and provided the basis for our reliability data.

An important facet of the confirmation process is the question of whether a disconfirmed prediction negates the theory or simply reflects an incorrect initial assessment. The structure of the assumption statements consists of two major elements: (1) the interaction of certain patient, treatment, and sometimes situational variables (2) leading to a particular patient response, either of a process or outcome nature. Thus, the usual assumption statement is as follows: patients of a certain type, in a given life situation, who undergo a particular set of treatment interventions, manifest a certain result; for example, "patients with good ego strength and motivation to achieve significant change, when treated by psychoanalysis, are able to achieve the resolution of their core unconscious conflict." (See Appendix 2)

A major point is that the test of a theoretical assumption statement is dependent upon the correct assessment of the relevant variables. In the instance of the proposition about psychoanalysis, one is obviously unable to test the assumption with an instance in which the patient was erroneously assessed as having good ego strength when actually it was weak. Whenever a predicted event does not occur as expected, one must ascertain whether the variables involved were correctly assessed before one may assert that the theory was disconfirmed or weakened. One must also guard against the ever-present danger of post hoc reasoning, in which one automatically decides that the variables were inaccurately assessed if the expected result did not occur, i.e., that the patient could not

possibly have been of good ego strength if he was unable to
undergo a successful analysis.

When the contingencies occur and variables are correctly
assessed and still the predicted event does not occur, the theory
has to be discarded, revised, or supplemented. These revisions
or additions were called postdictive assumptions, new assumption statements written to explain a predictive failure. Thus,
when one of the predictions and its accompanying assumptions
is judged as incorrect, we are left with an explanatory void and
an additional statement constructed retrospectively or postdictively is required.

The negation of a single assumption statement is sufficient
to require a postdictive correction because all of our propositions are general laws rather than aggregate ones, using
Bakan's (1955) distinction. He observed that probability or
aggregate statements about how a given class of individuals is
likely to respond to a certain intervention are not useful to a
clinician with a particular case. Rather, the clinician ideally
attempts to find groups narrowly enough defined so that his
theory has universal application to that class of patients. The
two patient variables cited for successful psychoanalysis are
ego strength and motivation and presumably there would be no
exceptions to that general law. Of course, there are many facets
of ego strength which must be spelled out in lower (more
specific) parts of the hierarchy. A general proposition may be
negated by only a single disconfirming instance and would
require modification.

THE FORM OF RESULTS

Following the confirmation process, our findings were
organized and further processed in three different ways: (1)

confirmation summaries for each case, (2) a tabulation of the fate of each assumption statement and, (3) a reorganized hierarchical ordering of the assumption statements.

1. Confirmation summaries were written upon the completion of the confirmation process for a given case, that is, following the consensus conference between the two members of the Prediction Study team. We did not follow any particular outline for this summary although our greatest emphasis was focused upon the single major prediction which we called the Overall Prediction—the summary statement which encompassed the predictors' expectations regarding the extent of success or failure in a given treatment. When the Overall Prediction was confirmed, the underlying assumptions were usually strengthened, though not always. Exceptions occurred when a treatment outcome happened as expected but for reasons different from those explicated by the predictors. Where a predictive failure occurred, not only were the assumptions often called into question or disconfirmed, but very frequently new assumptions to explain the unexpected event (postdictive assumptions) were written. The data giving rise to these postdictive assumptions were described in the confirmation summary. Although the major emphasis was on the overall prediction, the fate of the less central predictions, particularly when they were disconfirmed, was also discussed in terms of implications for theory.

2. A second product of the confirmation process was a tabulation of the fate of the assumptions. This tabulation provided a convenient summary of how each assumption fared when tested in a number of different cases. The tabulation included the case involved, the prediction number, and the "scores" for the three elements (contingency, prediction proper, assumption) of the prediction.

3. Finally, the hierarchical ordering of the assumption statements, which was done initially following the assignment

of assumptions to each prediction, had to be redone at the conclusion of the confirmation process. Approximately 350 assumptions comprised the initial group written for some 2,000 prediction statements. At the end of the confirmation process we had an additional 50 postdictive assumptions which required insertion into the hierarchy, but these statements sufficiently altered the original overall structure as to require a major revamping of the entire hierarchy.

In presenting the findings of the study, these three kinds of data will be used extensively. The revised hierarchy will be used in order to cluster the assumptions into coherent, related wholes. The various segments of the hierarchy are divided into nine parts which comprise the nine chapters on results. The assumption tables, of course, became our primary source of data in describing the confirmation or disconfirmation of particular assumptions or groups of assumptions and the implications. The confirmation summaries became an important point of reference for us with regard to each case as a whole, and to the genesis of the postdictive assumptions in particular.

Since we are dealing with general, not aggregate, propositions, we shall not emphasize a scoring or percentage of hits and misses. While such numbers may be of incidental interest, our major focus will be a qualitative discussion of confirmations and disconfirmations, particularly the latter. Our greatest scientific yield, we believe, should develop from the predictive error which disconfirms an assumption. Such an instance will be discussed in detail and a corrected or postdictive assumption will be offered in its stead with all of the observational data presented to support the new assumption.

Both our original and revised hierarchies of assumptions divided themselves largely into three groups of assumptions: expressive aspects of treatment, supportive aspects, and a set of assumptions common to all treatment. The book is organized around these three segments: Chapter 3 deals with a variety of anxiety-defense propositions belonging to the third (common-core) category. In the next three chapters (4 to 6) we treat the expressive aspects entitled The Uncovering Process, Indications and Contraindications for Psychoanalysis, and Conflict Resolution and Behavioral Change. Chapters 7 through 10 are concerned with the supportive aspects of treatment and are divided under the headings of: Adjunctive Supports, Therapeutic Alliance, Effects of Supportive Psychotherapy, Stability of Change with Supportive Treatment. The final chapter (11) on the Curative Process presents a summary of the major findings of the Prediction Study.

CRITIQUE OF THE PREDICTION STUDY

There were a number of limitations, partly inherent in the design of the study and partly a result of the subject matter of the research, which the reader should bear in mind as he examines our results.

Incorrect Initial Assessments

Approximately 50 percent of our assumption statements could not be tested because either the initial assessment of the patient was incorrect or the treatment contingency was not fulfilled. A fairly frequent error of assessment consisted of judging a patient's ego strength to be higher than it actually was. This led to a number of incorrect assignments to psychoanalysis, but the failure of the patient to profit from psychoanalysis could not be attributed to a failure of the theory about indications for or results of analysis. The theory required a minimum of ego strength for a successful analysis and, at some point following the initial assessment, the patients incorrectly assigned to analytic treatment were found to be deficient in the necessary ego resources. Their treatments failed, as did the prediction of successful outcome. In fact, this kind of result provides an indirect, negative confirmation of the theoretical statement; that is, postdictively we discovered that the patient did not possess the required attributes to respond in the predicted way and hence it strengthened the assumption that such attributes were necessary. These negative confirmations are weaker than the positive confirmations since they are postdictive and are always subject to the dangers of circularity.

We observed in Chapter 1 that the naturalistic feature of the research design probably contributed to the high number of incorrect initial patient assessments. The failure of the predictors to use the usual clinical procedure of direct interviewing and the need to rely upon "filtered" observations contributed to some degree of inaccuracy in the assessment process. The original diagnostic studies used by the Initial Study Group were not always done by senior, experienced clinicians, thus erecting an unstable tower of judgment piled upon judgment. A further factor was a deficiency in some instances in the completeness of the initial work-up. For example, five patients were not given psychological tests at the initial point, and a few others did not have the benefit of a complete social history.

In retrospect the advantage of the naturalistic feature of the design probably did not offset the disadvantages of data limitation at the initial point. Clinical experience suggests that despite the carefulness of an initial work-up, important modifying data often emerges in the first three to six months of the

2. A study by Appelbaum and Horwitz (1967) indicates that predictive accuracy increases in relation to the extensiveness of the initial work-up and that the social history in particular greatly enhances accuracy.

treatment to alter the clinician's original assessments. During this extended evaluation period, not only the patient's ego strength and his motivation for treatment but also important features of the history which the patient may have consciously or unconsciously withheld until the treatment process was launched will significantly alter the picture of the patient. A design which included an early reassessment of the initial picture would have made it possible to effect many more tests of assumptions than occurred in the present study.

The Weighting of Explanatory Factors

The research design was predicated on the basic notion that clinical judgment should be the primary data for the study. We believed that a patient variable like ego strength, for example, was too complex and multifaceted to be measured accurately by a simple objective questionnaire or test. We still believe that clinical judgment—based upon skillful interviewing, testing, and a social history—provides the most accurate means available for patient assessment. But despite its superiority to other available methods, it is still as fallible and imperfect as other human endeavors which have to sift through, organize, and comprehend a plethora of facts, impressions, and other data.

One would expect greater agreement among the judges concerning the question of *what* changed (and how much) than there was concerning *how* the change occurred. The latter question involved more reliance upon inference-making and involved a greater distance from observable data. These judgments about the "how" of change were probably less reliable than other kinds of clinical judgment but it is questionable that our design could really have been altered to improve this situation. Our hypotheses regarding the mechanisms of change, the curative factors of psychotherapy, are still relatively undeveloped and hence these questions were explored with less precision than were those elements where hypotheses were more advanced.

More specifically, the clinician-judges were constantly plagued by questions of how much weighting or significance to allow for significant explanatory factors. A patient failed to make significant progress in psychoanalysis and, judged in retrospect, his narcissistic personality organization was a severe deterrent. But the analyst's countertransference, his tendency to be overly respectful of the patient's narcissistic needs, and too formal and distant in his manner, were also significant contributing factors to the limitations of the treatment. The inevitable question in cases of treatment failure, almost always present in day-to-day clinical work, continued to plague us in this study; could the treatment failure have been avoided if a different therapist (more skilled and less hampered by countertransference) treated the patient? This question is not easily answerable either in clinical work or in clinical research. Using only the most skilled therapists might reduce this particular problem but it certainly would not eliminate it.

The Linkage Between the Prediction Proper and the Assumption

We have already noted that there is no constant, unvarying linkage between the prediction proper and the assigned assumptions. If the prediction proper is confirmed, the assigned assumptions or reasons for that occurrence may or may not be the ones that apply. Similarly, in the instance of a negative predictive outcome, the assigned assumptions may or may not be negated by the predictive failure. This kind of inconsistent, and sometimes tenuous, linkage was not sufficiently appreciated when the research was designed. Although the connection between predictive outcome and the fate of the assigned assumption could usually be determined from the write-ups of the research teams examining the treatment process, a more precise way of tapping directly into the observations and reasoning process of the research teams would have been to have included the assumptive statements as part of the individualized evidence form. For the most part, these forms included only questions concerning the prediction proper. We had the erroneous idea that the prediction proper would be sufficient for the assessment of the validity of the assigned assumption.

SUMMARY

1. Detailed predictions regarding the course and outcome of the patient's treatment were formulated by a team of senior clinicians who had access to all of the initial documents relating to the patient's initial diagnostic assessment. The predictors' write-up included not only expected future developments but also the relevant assumptions, based on the psychoanalytic theory of psychotherapy.

2. The major controls to assure the correct assessment of the Initial Study Group's predictions were the Evidence Forms, the Core Form being applied to all the patients in the study and the Individualized Form written and tailor-made separately for each patient. These forms were true-false questionnaires which the predictors were asked to answer in terms of how they thought the research teams at the termination point would respond.

3. The Prediction Study team converted the Initial Study

Group's predictive essay into single and discrete predictive statements. These statements had a tripartite form and consisted of a contingency, the prediction proper, and the associated assumption being tested by the prediction or, if-then-because.

4. The assumption statements, after being written for all of the cases and comprising some 350 statements, were organized into a hierarchical network based upon causality and generality.

5. The three elements of each prediction underwent a confirmation process by the Prediction Study team using all of the data assembled by the research teams at termination and follow-up.

6. The confirmation process resulted in the writing of a number of postdictive assumptions to account for predictive errors and unanticipated results, a revamping of the original hierarchy, and, cutting across all the cases, a tabulation of the fate of each test of each assumption.

CHAPTER 3

ANXIETY AND DEFENSE

A cornerstone conception in psychoanalysis is that anxiety serves a signal function in the psychic apparatus. When unacceptable impulses threaten to emerge into consciousness, small quantities of anxiety are sufficient to mobilize the person's defenses. Conversely, when defenses are weakened, for whatever reason, the person begins to experience anxiety. This overall conception gives rise to numerous corollaries and special instances in relation to a theory of psychotherapy. Thus, the uncovering process associated with expressive psychotherapy and psychoanalysis encourages the experience and verbal expression of previously repressed impulses. The expressive aspects of psychotherapy tend to heighten anxiety and the resulting unfreezing makes possible a realignment of impulse-defense configurations; the supportive aspects of treatment, on the other hand, seek to enhance the efficacy of the patient's defenses by anxiety reduction rather than mobilization. Thus, the anxiety-defense conception is basic to a psychoanalytic theory of psychotherapy and findings based upon predictions using various aspects of this segment of theory will be discussed in this chapter.

THE UNCOVERING PROCESS

We used about a dozen assumptions describing with varying degrees of specificity how the uncovering-expressive method in psychotherapy and its attendant anxiety result in a number of defensive operations characteristic of the patient. When anxiety is heightened the patient calls upon intellectualization, somatization, premature behavioral change, "flight into health" to cope with internal and external pressure. This series of assumptions was applied in eighty-seven instances and was tested only thirty-six times. The major reason they were not tested was that the treatment contingency, in this instance the expectation that the patient would receive psychoanalysis or expressive psychotherapy, was not fulfilled. A secondary factor leading to inconclusive tests was an incorrect initial assessment of the patient. If a patient was viewed initially as an intellectualizer and this turned out to be a diagnostic error, the assumptions regarding intellectualizing patients applied in this case would not be tested. It is mainly in regard to the reassessment of initial diagnoses where a loophole of circularity becomes a danger. When a patient fails to behave in treatment as predicted, either the theory behind the prediction or the validity of the original assessment is called into question. Our only means of warding off this hazard was to remain constantly aware of it.

However, in the thirty-six instances where the series of assumptions were tested, all yielded confirmation or partial confirmation. The majority of these assumptions possess what amounts to a face validity, even to nonanalytic theorists. For the most part the assumptions merely elaborate the central notion that a person's character traits, defenses, and symptoms become mobilized in the face of threats engendered by the treatment process.

The strengthening of most of these assumptions was neither surprising nor of great scientific interest. Had the assumptions been negated, however, we would have been faced with an important challenge to a firmly entrenched part of the theory. There were instances, however, in which some of these assumptions were applied postdictively, i.e., to explain an unpredicted development, and these findings may throw light on unexpected pitfalls in the treatment process. Of particular interest to the therapist is the patient who resorts to a "flight into health" in order to avoid confrontation with unacceptable aspects of his personality makeup. The outcomes of two cases were wrongly predicted for reasons associated with unanticipated premature behavioral change. Both started in psychoanalysis but showed significant ego weakness in the form of low tolerance for anxiety. One patient (*Peter Pan*) sought to avoid an intense dependence-independence conflict in the transference by developing a normal-appearing heterosexual relationship, behavior which was very difficult for her prior to her treatment. But this relationship was only superficially mature and actually was being used as a vehicle to express infantile and narcissistic needs in addition to helping her avoid confronting her neurotic difficulties in the treatment. The other case (*Travel Phobia Woman*) was simply unable to free associate and ultimately had to be switched to a more supportive treatment modality. She neither had the curiosity nor the "courage" to delve into intrapsychic forces impinging on her. When alone it was necessary for her constantly to play a radio to avoid her own thoughts. Her unswerving orientation during treatment was to seek the analyst's advice, guidance, and approval by presenting him with achievements in her everyday life designed to impress him. In both cases the patients' inability to tolerate unacceptable aspects of the self led either to premature termination or to behavioral change which interrupted the uncovering process.

A development of particular interest in this series was an assumption comparing analysis with a more supportive approach which was tested unexpectedly. On a few occasions the predictors attempted to compare the fate of individual symptoms, given psychoanalysis as opposed to other less intensive forms of treatment. Naturally, it was almost impossible to test any of these expected differences because a true test would consist of the patient being exposed to both treatment modalities, a virtual impossibility.

In the case of one patient (*Obese Woman*), the presenting symptom of obesity was expected to yield somewhat to psychoanalytic treatment but the predictors did not expect the symptom to abate as effectively in analysis as in some other form of psychotherapy in which the therapist and patient focused more clearly upon the symptom. The assumption underlying this prediction was stated as follows: "Treatments that encourage the giving up of symptoms in order to please (or displease) the therapist are more effective against individual items of symptomatic behavior than treatment attempting to uncover the underlying unconscious conflicts." The patient underwent psychoanalysis and achieved some degree of improvement, she developed a better modulation of sadomasochistic patterns of interaction and acquired better impulse control, but her obesity was changed only to a small extent. However, during the follow-up process it was possible to demonstrate the effectiveness of the patient's wish to please the therapist as a vehicle for more effective weight reduction. Several months after the termination of the analysis the patient began to make plans to revisit the analyst, who by that time had moved to another city. The plan for this visit was several months in the making and, by the time it occurred, the patient had shed more weight than ever before. The conclusion drawn by the research team was that the patient's wish to please the therapist, operative during this follow-up visit, was more effective in this symptomatic improvement than was the analytic process itself which ranged widely over a gamut of problems.

COUNTERTRANSFERENCE AND UNCOVERING

In some instances a therapist's unconscious needs and wishes may significantly color his understanding of the patient. One prominent manifestation of countertransference distortion is the tendency to understand the patient exclusively in terms of a single guiding transference paradigm rather than in terms of a variety of transference manifestations. Two cases illustrate the tendency of the therapist to overemphasize the positive libidinal wishes of the patient to the relative neglect of either the patient's hostility or his more infantile wishes.

The *Obese Woman* was an analytic case whose deep-seated sadomasochistic conflicts were only partly uncovered and resolved. One of the major factors accounting for the limited result in this case was the therapist's tendency to perceive love where he should have seen hate. The underlying dynamic of the patient's personality organization was a hostile tie to a sadistic mother resulting in excessive dependence upon that parent, obesity, impulsive behavior, and masochistic sexual perversions. In the opinion of the research team, the analyst rather consistently interpreted her anger as a defense against positive, loving wishes. While such a dynamic constellation undoubtedly existed, he underplayed the role of the sadistic-aggressive impulses which formed a core of the patient's pathology.

The second case (*Phobic Girl*) was that of an infantile

young woman also characterized by a tendency to obesity, multiple phobias, and, in the early stages of treatment, pronounced promiscuity. The predictors expected the therapist to experience difficulty in perceiving her erotization of the transference as an expression of oral dependent wishes since she expressed underlying oral drives in genital form. Since the patient was not in analysis, the therapist would be expected to have particular difficulty in understanding the fantasies underlying her overt behavior, but the predictors expected that most therapists would err to some degree in the direction of understanding the transference in terms of more mature sexual wishes based upon common countertransference propensities. Actually, the transference was not colored significantly by erotization inasmuch as the patient's acting out with a variety of sexual partners offered considerable displacement opportunities. But we confirmed the part of the prediction that the therapist would tend to underplay the significance of the infantile aspects of her sexual behavior.

Another form of countertransference lies in the therapist's tendency to overestimate the patient's assets, particularly with those who present fairly good facades despite evidence of personality weakness. One might question whether this kind of diagnostic error could be attributed to countertransference growing out of anxieties associated with personal needs or whether it represents technical insufficiency. We can only say that since these errors were made by people who were well trained and experienced, they therefore may be understood as a product of some personality factors in the therapist. There were at least two cases in which the research team thought that the patient's facade conspired with the therapist's willingness to ignore available facts about the patient's ego weakness to produce an underestimation of the patient's pathology. In these cases treatment was attempted either outside a hospital structure or the patient was discharged from the hospital prematurely, even though there were fairly clear indications for more support and control than psychotherapy alone could provide. The best example of such an error was in the case of a young woman (*Hypochondriac*) whose frequent temper tantrums and paranoid outbursts would be occasionally interrupted by charmingly coy and seductive behavior. Although she obviously was unable to function outside a hospital, her persistent and persuasive demands upon both her therapist and husband eventuated in a discharge which only produced increasing chaos in the psychotherapy and in her life outside. The other case demonstrates in a somewhat less dramatic form the failure of the therapist to insist upon the hospital structure as an adjunct to the psychotherapy. For example, the pressure from the hospital staff was a significant additional factor in the therapist's decision to continue treatment with a patient who obviously needed hospitalization but who could not be hospitalized for certain external reasons.

It is impossible to generalize about the kinds of counter-transference factors which enter into the decision to follow a course which contradicts one's better judgment. In view of the overall tendency in this project for diagnostic errors to be made in the direction of overestimating strength, assets, and health, one could speculate that therapists generally have a need to minimize the presence of pathology in their patients.

DISRUPTION OF DEFENSES AND EXTERNAL STRESS

When some form of external stress is exerted on the individual, particularly one which triggers an intrapsychic conflict, the individual will react with anxiety and his characteristic defenses. In other words, "To the extent that external factors trigger intrapsychic conflicts there is a proportional enhancement of painful affects and defenses." Again, this is a fairly axiomatic statement and one with almost face validity. From our vantage point, it seems to be a commonsense proposition. It was tested eight times in six cases and in each instance the assumption was strengthened.

Perhaps the most interesting observation to be gleaned from these predictions is not the fact of confirmation but rather the uniqueness of the conflict triggers. "The flame which melts the butter hardens the egg." Reduction of stress was predicted for a woman (*Bohemian*) who was expected to give up a very stressful marriage, while increased anxiety was anticipated from another woman (*Divorced Teacher*) whose shaky marriage at the beginning of treatment suggested a good possibility of divorce. Similarly, departure from the hospital mobilized anxiety for one patient (*Prep School Boy*) while the very fact of being hospitalized was a conflict trigger for another (*Alcoholic Heir*) who denied any illness and insisted that he be permitted to leave the hospital prematurely.

The majority of tests of this general proposition, however, were made with regard to specific treatment developments: the pressures of termination, family pressures, and the loss of certain adjunctive treatment modalities which we shall now examine.

TERMINATION OF TREATMENT

A common assumption regarding termination of treatment is that it is a stressful experience for most patients in psychoanalysis or long-term psychotherapy. In particular, it was assumed that patients with pronounced dependency conflicts *or* those whose dependency was ego-syntonic would be especially prone to difficult termination reactions. One might say that such patients experience the dependency which treatment inevitably fosters as a "side effect" in the same way as an addiction may develop where bromides are used for the relief of a painful medical condition. This side effect often produces a number of special termination phenomena: depression, exacerbation of character defenses or symptoms, as well as a clinging to the treatment relationship.

Interestingly enough, predictions of this kind were made for half the research subjects. In all there were 49 predictions regarding termination reactions made for 21 patients, and related assumptions were used. A relatively large percentage of assumptions (8 out of 21, or 37 percent) were disconfirmed. We were faced with the interesting problem of why this group of assumptions had such a high rate of disproof.

The most general way of explaining the high negative outcome of these assumptions is that the treatments were not as "gratifying" as expected. The predictors failed to consider an unsuccessful or ungratifying outcome as a factor which could mitigate anxiety or depression at termination. But even some of those who benefited from treatment often welcomed termination because of certain fears which outweighed their dependent attachments.

Six patients were initially expected to show difficult termination reactions but they actually were eager to stop the relationship and did not show the expected response. None of them experienced the therapeutic relationship as predominantly gratifying either of their dependency or of other psychological needs. One patient (*Dancer*) left the hospital prematurely and could not be helped by psychotherapy alone; another (*Silent Woman*) experienced the entire analytic procedure as frustrating and the analyst as lacking in warmth. One form of nongratification was an ever-present fear of the relationship: two patients (*Suspended Student, Covert Addict*) experienced considerable paranoid fear of their therapists and hence were only too happy to terminate. Another (*Obedient Husband*) was working strenuously to ward off aggressive feelings to the controlling mother-figure he saw in his therapist and, even though he benefited by the treatment, he welcomed the termination. The last patient (*Movie Lady*) in this series suffered from a pathological sense of guilt about her hostility toward father surrogates, and managed to duplicate this relationship with her therapist. She proved unamenable to interpretation or confrontation of this repetitive neurotic pattern and was therefore not averse to bring therapy to a conclusion.

Most important is the finding that in the cases mentioned above, the dependency conflicts were usually correctly assessed and, hence, the difficult termination phase might well have been expected were it not for the preponderance of other affects which outweighed their dependency wishes.

We may now ask if there is evidence that special termination effects *do* indeed occur as predicted (partial return of symptoms) when other special factors are not present. There were a few cases where the special termination effects were prominently in evidence. The *Divorced Teacher* showed considerable depression during the termination phase of a rather long analysis. Her depression was exacerbated by the loss of her husband and two children during treatment as a result of divorce. Another patient (*English Professor*) experienced a partial return of his phobic symptoms during the termination process, but the major reaction was that of loneliness and feelings of loss. His fantasy of eventually finding the overidealized good parent was finally being shattered, and he later reported this period as one of the most anguished times of his life. The termination phase proved to be a most helpful part of his treatment since he had to face the reality that he was never going to be magically cured.

A less decisive instance of a special termination reaction occurred to the *Claustrophobic Man*. He did not experience a return of his earlier phobic symptoms but he did begin to show an exacerbation of his reactive defenses against dependency. Mainly, he set his own termination date and showed other signs of hyperindependence.

An interesting case was the patient (*Medical Specialist*) whose termination reaction was probably forestalled by a gradual tapering off of the treatment. This procedure was atypical since he was an analytic case but it was used by the analyst because a return of addictive symptoms (alcohol and drugs) would have been quite damaging to the patient's professional reputation as it had been prior to the start of treatment.

The above cases were instances of confirmation of the usual termination assumptions. They were cases where the patient's dependency conflict or his ego-syntonic dependency led the predictors to expect a noteworthy termination reaction. All cases should show these reactions to some degree, but the predictors confined their statements to those with the greatest dependency conflicts.

In summary, even though numerous instances of termination reactions occurred, a number of special conditions arose during treatment which overrode the patient's expected reaction to the loss of his therapist during the termination process of long-term psychotherapy. A lack of gratification in the relationship based upon a constant, paranoid-tinged fear of the therapist or a pervasive lack of fulfillment of needs, or a sense of guilt about one's own destructive effects seemed to neutralize any of the usual termination phenomena.

FAMILY PRESSURES

A special external pressure which is probably necessary for effective psychotherapy (not true of hospital treatment) is the presence, if married, of one's spouse and children in the treatment environment. The absence of one's immediate family permits the patient to avoid and deny the existence of significant conflict-laden interactions and creates an artificial cocoon-like situation for the patient. The family's absence protects him from the anxiety, and hence the motivation, necessary for effective treatment.

Such a deterrent to treatment was expected in two cases and was partially confirmed in one (*Script Writer*), but could not really be tested in the other (*Hypochondriac*) because treatment was disrupted too early. In the first case, the patient's denial of domestic problems, particularly her own hostility to her husband and children, was fostered by geographical separation. Indeed, she was subtly helped by the treatment to neglect her obligations to her family so that the treatment situation not only fostered avoidance of anxiety but also contributed to a perpetuation of her narcissistic attitudes toward them.

There were at least two other cases which *postdictively* confirmed the assumption that treatment is hindered by such separation. The *Divorced Teacher* took a longer period than expected to discover the role she had in provoking marital discord because the treatment was conducted at a considerable distance from her spouse. By the time she grasped awareness of her contribution it was too late to save the marriage. The *Snake Phobia Woman* underwent analysis living apart from her husband, except for weekend visits home. She had an unhappy marriage and lived in an isolated, hyperreligious country town in which she felt like an outsider. This feeling was enhanced during the course of her treatment as she achieved a college degree, enjoyed life in Topeka during the week, and lived as a weekend wife with her family. Throughout her psychoanalysis she led a "double life" which was ego-syntonic and free of guilt. The gratification involved for her in escaping from her husband, children, and the hated hometown was great enough to prevent her from fully examining some of her unrealistic transference expectations.

TREATMENT INDUCED STRESS

Even without the uncovering process, the treatment situation itself tends to produce anxiety insofar as it stimulates expectations which cannot be entirely met and encourages intimacy which may be threatening. These conflictual situations may produce intense reactions in patients whose internal conflicts are especially stimulated by the role of being a patient. When the patient is highly intolerant of his dependency needs or must deny his illness, he will experience considerable frustration in treatment.

We were able to test the predictions on three patients who were expected to show considerable conflict generated by their intolerance of dependency wishes. Interestingly, all three came to treatment mainly because of addictive problems. The two who were expected to show the most intense reactions (*Salesman, Alcoholic Heir*) broke off treatment before a successful termination could occur, while the third (*Medical Specialist*) showed a somewhat milder reaction to the conflict and finished his treatment quite successfully.

The *Salesman* was described by the predictors as showing intense contradictory strivings, a strong bipolar conflict involving childlike dependency countered by extreme intolerance of these wishes manifested by hypermasculinity and impulsive, reckless behavior. It was mainly his intolerance for his dependency which led him to disrupt his treatment after a period of about a year. (Interestingly enough, the researchers who studied this case at termination and at follow-up concluded that his weak motivation as well as his intense dependency conflict made him essentially untreatable even under ideal conditions.)

Similarly, the *Alcoholic Heir* was caught in the difficult bind of wishing to comply with the demands of authority figures and to please them while needing to cling to the self-concept of self-sufficiency and independence. The latter was expressed by his denial of illness or his need for therapeutic help despite crippling alcoholism. He was hospitalized and entered analysis under the threat of divorce. The predictors believed he had better than an even chance of eventually overcoming this conflict, of being able to reach the stage of accepting himself as needing help for a severe disturbance. But the conflict was too intense and the patient disrupted the treatment after eight months.

The *Medical Specialist* experienced a similar problem in analysis but on a much more manageable scale. He was characterized by the predictors as a man with a strongly ingrained feeling that he should be able to manage his problems by himself. A difference between him and the preceding patient was that he recognized a psychological disability in himself but was loath to acknowledge that he could not overcome the problem on his own. The other patient did not concede, to others or to himself, that a disturbance existed. The *Medical Specialist*'s difficulty with dependency was manifested by a slow-starting analysis, one in which little movement occurred for the first year and a half, and where the major transference paradigm at the outset was an attempt to bore the analyst, in effect to put him to sleep, so that he could escape from his prying and meddlesomeness.

One other patient, the *Good Son*, was expected to experience much difficulty in treatment owing to an internal struggle between compliance and need to control. The analytic situation, as predicted, produced considerable stress insofar as he wished to do as the analyst instructed but free association was quite alien to his need to inhibit, suppress, and compulsively order his impulse life.

An instructive predictive error was one expecting the *Prep School Boy* to experience depression whenever he successfully deflected the goals of treatment by his intellectual competitiveness with the therapist. His strong need to comply and win approval was expected to run directly counter to an equally strong need to be intellectually superior to his therapist. This kind of process prediction was not easily tested in the present study but, insofar as one could determine, the patient did not manifest such a response. We would be inclined to explain the predictive error on the basis of the patient's superficial involvement in a treatment which was prematurely terminated. He remained substantially aloof and did not permit himself sufficient investment in the relationship to develop a feeling of concern about his hostility toward the therapist. Conflictual feelings about a relationship occur only when a patient's narcissistic aloofness is overcome.

Let us now turn to the postdictive assumptions which were required to account for an unexpected development in this area. The *Thespian* began treatment as a rebellious, impulse-ridden adolescent, with a chaotic sexual life and strong homosexual leanings. The predictors expected a number of negative and hostile responses to the therapist. They expected her to see him as a critical, nagging parent, uninterested and disrespectful of her needs. In turn, they expected her to depreciate him. None of these negative transference developments actually eventuated even though the researchers believed that the patient had a potential for such reactions. She was a primitively organized person who tended to view herself and others in terms of black and white, good and evil, perfect or impossible. She developed an overidealized image of the therapist as omnipotent and all-giving. The researchers believed that the patient's homosexual behavior, which became more crystallized during treatment, was the outlet for her anger at the bad-mother introject. Thus, the anxiety of a close relationship involving primitive longings and intense fear and hatred led this patient to protect herself against her destructive wishes by the mechanism of splitting in which the therapist was preserved as all good and others were seen as bad.

The price of this splitting mechanism was a carefully circumscribed relationship with the therapist. She could not permit herself to express the powerful negative side of her ambivalence and hence could find only limited gratification from the relationship. This was significant insofar as the predictors expected the patient to give up her homosexual behavior because of the oral nurturance she would experience from the therapist. Apparently, such nurturance cannot emanate from the "good" therapist when his goodness is bought at the cost of suppressing negative views of him, when he is a part object rather than a whole object.

RESISTANCE

As one might expect, the general resistance proposition that characteristic defenses are brought to bear by the patient as anxiety rises was by and large confirmed. In those instances where the prediction of the specific event was not confirmed, the assumption was judged not to be affected and the original assessment of the patient was cast into doubt. We had hoped that certain derivative assumptions which specified an application of this general principle might yield some interesting tests. For example, there was an assumption that markedly masochistic people seek out forms of treatment that will either be ineffectual or harmful. Unfortunately this assumption was applied to only one patient (*Spinster*) and the judges considered it untested. The predictors believed that she would *not* seek out analysis, even though recommended and indicated, because of her self-defeating tendencies; but during her psychotherapy she revealed enough ego weakness to make the recommendation of analysis dubious. Another patient (*Passive Student*) confirmed this assumption postdictively by not seeking out a more intensive, expressive treatment in order to overcome his deep-seated passivity and his sexual impotence. In other words, there was no impressive evidence to support or to negate the assumption.

An assumption in this series with a rather high degree of validity in terms of clinical experience and observation is the one pertaining to the emergence of anxiety and other affects when alloplastic behaviors are given up. More precisely, "To the extent that alloplastic behaviors come under control in psychotherapy, patients experience the disturbing affects and ideation formerly warded off by that behavior." Two related assumptions were that (1) the interruption of alloplastic behaviors mobilizes anxiety, and (2) the interruption of alloplastic behaviors will lead to the development of autoplastic symptoms. These two assumptions were used in eight instances but only confirmed three times. There was disconfirmation once, and the assumptions could not be tested on four occasions mainly because alloplastic symptoms rarely came under control in our population. Most of the alloplastic symptoms referred to were addictive, like alcoholism, and these patients were among our least successful cases. Another handicap in attempting to test these predictions and assumptions was related to the "process" nature of them. They often required knowledge about detailed aspects of the process, day-to-day developments, and hence were frequently not easily amenable to test by the design of our study.

The one instance of disconfirmation was a female patient in her forties (*Bohemian*) who gave up an unsatisfactory marriage during the course of her treatment. Her discontent with her role as wife and mother led her to seek out a rather Bohemian existence which involved separating herself from her family geographically for months at a time. The predictors expected that during the course of treatment she would develop a conscious sense of guilt associated with this history of hostile behavior directed toward her husband and their adopted son. This prediction was made with the idea that the patient's alloplastic life-style would be considerably modified, leading to the experience of affects associated with her behavior rather than acting to dissipate these affects. Although the alloplastic behavior was indeed modified, there was little, if any, experience of conscious guilt. An important facet of the patient's character makeup i.e., her narcissism, had been overlooked. The predictors believed she had more concern for significant persons in her life than she actually had. Her narcissistic orientation prevented her from experiencing concern and guilt despite the fact that her alloplastic behavior was to a large extent interrupted.

ENVIRONMENTAL OUTLETS

Behavior Outside Treatment

The anxiety which accompanies and gets generated by the treatment process frequently spills into the patient's life outside of the treatment sessions. The assumption "increments of anxiety induced by the therapeutic process produce increased reliance upon characteristic symptoms and behavior in the patient's life outside the therapy" was used thirty-three times for twenty-two patients. It was confirmed fourteen times, not tested nineteen times, and never disconfirmed. Although applied to over half the research population, it was particularly applicable to those patients with prominent alloplastic defenses. Usually they were the patients who experienced the therapy as frustrating their oral wishes and expectations; they had a low tolerance for frustration and expressed the inevitable aggression by some behavioral deviation. In some cases there was antisocial acting out, including the writing of bad checks; several others manifested excessive indulgence in alcohol.

An instructive error was one in which the predicted acting out apparently did eventuate, but not for the anticipated reason. The *Raconteur* was a borderline psychotic individual whom the predictors thought—and they were subsequently proven correct —should not have been assigned to analysis because of his weak ego. He had a history of no substantial achievement since his graduation from high school, had been addicted to alcohol for many years, was grandiose and megalomanic, and had poor control over hostile paranoid outbursts. His pathology was not seen accurately by the evaluating team, and psychoanalysis was recommended by the hospital staff. The predictors foresaw a lack of fit between the patient and the prescribed treatment and expected his latent psychosis to grow worse because of the anxiety generated in response to free association. They believed that the further emergence of primary process material would unleash instinctual forces already threatening his beleaguered ego. His response would be further withdrawal, alcoholism, and outbursts of rage. These events did occur but, according to the researchers, not because of anxiety associated with the emergence of primary process content. Rather, they believed that the patient's "free association" was in the service of his narcissism, consciously and unconsciously designed to impress the analyst and actually quite pleasurable to the patient. The acting out was the result of the encouragement he experienced in the relationship to indulge himself freely in gratifying activities, to say not only what came to mind, but to do whatever occurred to him. He experienced a lowering of a sense of responsibility for his actions and behavior outside the analysis, as though he had now turned such responsibility over to the analyst.

Pre-existing Neurotic Interactions

One assumption in this series stated that displacement of certain transference wishes would occur in the arena of preexisting neurotic interactions. Five cases were expected to show this particular reaction, despite the fact that they were being treated at some distance from their spouses or parents with whom they were involved. The assumption was confirmed in all but one case (*Phobic Woman*), a young married woman who was neurotically tied to her parents and who was seen initially as quite infantile and demanding. She turned out to have considerably more ego resources than anticipated and did not attempt to draw her parents into the arena of her transference struggles. Parenthetically, effective social work with her husband also aided the patient's control of her displacement tendencies.

The predictions for one case (*Obedient Husband*) were made largely on the basis of the vicissitudes of his wife's illness. When she remained incapacitated and dependent on him, the predictors said, he would react positively; if his wife, who was also in psychotherapy, began to improve they would expect him to manifest anxiety and enhanced symptoms of depression and somatization. The predictors believed that he was unmotivated for change in his neurotic equilibrium with his wife. There was, however, more than just the "holding action" expected by the predictors. The patient became more of a breadwinner in the family, loosened himself from his caretaking role with his wife, became appropriately more assertive, lost some of his depressive symptoms, and dropped his somatizations. His wife, in fact, did not change significantly but his treatment mobilized him toward great self-assertiveness with her and others. The research team attributed the predictive error to an incorrect initial assessment of the patient's need for a sick wife and to an underestimate of his initial motivation for change. He entered psychotherapy under some external pressure from his wife's treatment team, but once involved in treatment he was able to use it effectively.

A special instance of displacement of transference wishes is that of "splitting." The predictors used this principle to describe their expectations about one case (*Loner*), a rigid, paranoid man with considerable anger and fear which became mobilized whenever a relationship threatened to become close. The predictors expected him to split the transference into external "enemies" and a benevolent therapist. This forecast was partly correct in that he was eventually able to establish a stable therapeutic relationship, but only after two previous unsuccessful attempts. His third therapist, using the experience of the earlier efforts, deliberately set his therapeutic goals low and was assiduously careful to maintain the distance the patient needed. Even in this latter relationship, the patient seemed to keep hostile fantasies alive toward a variety of other people and institutions from whom he was rather removed. Postdictively, another patient (*Thespian*) also maintained an unswervingly "good" but somewhat distant relationship with her therapist by acting out her negative, depreciating attitudes in her outside life. Her homosexual adjustment had apparently encapsulated her negative attitudes toward men.

HIERARCHICAL ORDERING OF DEFENSES

An important bloc of assumptions involved the idea of a hierarchical ordering of defensive positions which are brought into play depending upon the degree of stress placed upon the defensive organization of the individual. The general statement of this conception is: "Defenses are mobilized in response to increments of anxiety in the sequence, characteristic of the individual, from those involving the least to the greatest reality abrogation." This assumption was applied postdictively for three cases in four separate predictions and in each instance it was confirmed.

Some subsidiary assumptions concerned patients with high and low ego strength and their reaction to the inevitable strains of the treatment process. For example, patients of high ego strength were expected to be able to tolerate the anxiety associated with the uncovering process without engaging in actions which would be disruptive of the treatment. They were expected to confine overt displays of emotion, such as temper tantrums and outbursts of rage, to either the treatment situation or to those with whom they were on intimate terms. These predicted developments, when tested, were confirmed.

A frequently used assumption in this series was the one dealing with the reaction to patients with weaker ego resources. "The less elaborate the defensive structures and the more insistent the instinctual strivings, the more intense the reaction to the frustration of wishes in psychotherapy." This assumption was applied in twenty-two instances for eight cases, confirmed on ten occasions, and disconfirmed once. There were a few instances of untestability because the patient showed better personality organization than expected, at least as assessed postdictively. An even more frequent error which prevented the testing of this assumption was the patient's experience of greater gratification in the treatment than was expected. The predictors generally anticipated a more expressive and less supportive approach than was generally applied. Their predictions often spoke of the "inevitable frustration of oral demands." While these frustrations undoubtedly occurred, the therapists modulated these reactions by means of a more actively supportive approach than expected.

One instance of "support," even in analysis, occurred in the case of the *Raconteur* (described in the preceding section in connection with acting out) who was clearly unable to tolerate the stress of a free association procedure. The predictors expected that the free association process would weaken the repressive boundaries of this already beleaguered individual whose poor control over aggressive impulses, tendencies to excessive drinking, and deviant thinking were prominent symptoms. This was one of the few cases where the clinicians and the research team differed significantly in their treatment recommendations at the initial point. The former did not view the patient as having the kind of ego weakness which would preclude psychoanalysis. But his defense against further decompensation consisted of giving "controlled" associations, thoughts which were produced with the idea of gaining favor with the analyst. During much of this process the patient seemed to be experiencing considerable narcissistic and exhibitionistic gratification from the admiration which he assumed to be forthcoming from the analyst for his productions.

The one instance in which the assumpton concerning the stress of psychotherapy was disconfirmed also was related to the phenomenon of more support than had been anticipated. The predictors expected the *Playboy*, a person with strong sadistic tendencies, to experience chronic rage during his treatment which would manifest itself intermittently in angry outbursts at the therapist (as well as hypomanic acting out in the environment). Actually, during a four-year course of treatment no such outbursts occurred nor was there any evidence of chronic rage. The treatment course was benign with a steady upward trend in his work and marital adjustment. How should we account for this predictive error? Mainly, it was related to the therapist's very sensitive and skillful application of supportive techniques of treatment. When the weakness of the patient's ego resources was apparent, the therapist carefully avoided probing or pushing the patient. He quite consciously lent himself as an ego ideal for the patient and in no way encouraged regressive transference developments. He counseled the patient about appropriate behavior as a husband and as a professional man when he felt the patient could profit from this. As a result, there was a consistently friendly relationship between the therapist and patient throughout the treatment and the predicted rage against the former never materialized.

SUMMARY

1. Propositions regarding the heightening of defenses under the pressure of anxiety, and the arousal of anxiety associated with the disruption of defenses, have the status of axioms in the psychoanalytic theory of psychotherapy and hence were not disconfirmed even when a specific prediction was incorrect. In the judgment of the researchers, the explanation for predictive errors was not to be found in the weakness of this general

theory, but rather was due to either incorrect assessments of the relevant variables or inadequacies in the subsidiary hypotheses.

2. Certain subsidiary assumptions were overthrown and those which fared most poorly pertained to termination reactions. A number of assumptions were applied in which the patient was expected to show a pronounced depressive reaction or a recrudescence of symptoms which had already remitted or a clinging to the treatment or some combination of these. These assumptions were frequently disconfirmed. We concluded that a number of special conditions might arise during the treatment which would override the expected reaction. A lack of gratification in the relationship based upon a constant, paranoid-tinged fear of the therapist, or a pervasive lack of fulfillment of needs, or a sense of guilt about one's destructive impulses seemed to prevent various predicted termination phenomena from occurring.

3. Anxieties in the therapist lead to distortions in their understanding, commonly referred to as countertransference. Treatment errors tended to be based upon the therapist underestimating the seriousness of the patient's pathology. In at least three cases the research team agreed that treatment was incorrectly undertaken outside of a hospital structure, even though there were fairly clear indications for more support and control than psychotherapy alone could provide.

4. Family interactions are an external pressure creating anxieties which supply needed leverage in psychotherapy. A special form of denial and avoidance, induced iatrogenically, occurred in treatment in which the patient was separated from spouse and family. Three cases, one predictively and two postdictively, confirmed the finding that this condition encourages the denial of conflict and makes transference expectations more difficult to resolve.

5. The predictors' expectation that patients who rely heavily upon denial of illness in order to maintain self-esteem would

cling tenaciously to this defense was confirmed in five instances. The three patients who showed a pervasive denial of illness failed in treatment, while the two who denied unacceptable aspects of themselves showed only limited improvement. The predictors expected hostile reactions both within and outside the psychotherapy as a result of the "inevitable frustration of oral demands." Such reactions occurred less often than expected largely because there was less frustration than expected in the therapeutic relationship. The treatment was frequently more supportive than expected by the predictor and the gratification of dependent needs in a predominantly supportive treatment contributed to the abating of such reactions.

CHAPTER 4

THE UNCOVERING PROCESS

One of the axioms of psychoanalytic theory is the proposition that the relationship with the therapist will either be colored or dominated by the patient's early childhood relationship paradigms. The more expressive the treatment approach, the more the therapist attempts to elicit and uncover these transference distortions. The majority of the predictions made about the treatment process in this study dealt with the vicissitudes of transference reactions or of the transference neurosis. Thus, there were many predictions concerning the content of the transference, its resistance to change (its "stickiness" or insolubility), the sequence of its unfolding, the patient's likely response to interpretations, etc.

Although the predictions consisted of statements about process as well as outcome, the design of the study was definitely slanted toward securing outcome information with data about process comparatively more limited. Detailed observations about the process of treatment could not be obtained since the study was designed to be naturalistic and no research intrusions were made during the course of the psychotherapy. Hence, there was a clear limitation on gathering the evidence for assessing many of these process predictions.

THE MAJOR TRANSFERENCE ASSUMPTION

Practically all of the predictions about expected transference contents were based upon the following general transference assumption: "To the extent that treatment aims consistently to uncover unconscious conflict, transference distortions override the realities of the treatment situation, i.e., the patient's reactions to the therapist are more consistent with genetically determined intrapsychic needs that are active at a given time than with the actual behavior and intentions of the therapist."

It is not surprising to us that this *assumption* was never negated in the seventy times it was tested in our study. This is not to say that every transference *prediction* was correct. As a matter of fact, only forty-five were confirmed, with the remainder being untested. If a prediction about transference content was incorrect, the prediction study judges had to determine whether this error was caused by faulty theory or inaccurate assessment of a patient or treatment characteristics. As one might expect, the theory of transference in its general form is too firmly established by years of treatment observations to be seriously challenged by inaccurate prediction. That is, the alternative inevitably chosen by the prediction judges was to attribute the predictive error to an incorrect assessment of a relevant variable.

In a few instances predictive errors pointed up a need for greater precision in our statement of the general transference proposition. Thus, in the case of *Peter Pan*, the predictors expected the patient, during the course of psychoanalysis, to alternate between seeing the analyst as kindly and accepting on the one hand, and stern and forbidding on the other. This prediction did not eventuate during the analysis since a positive image of the analyst was maintained by the patient throughout the three years of treatment. The analyst departed from the expected neutral stance and applied numerous supportive parameters which tangibly demonstrated his interest and concern about the patient, thus helping to suppress a negative image of him. This observation made it necessary for us to make explicit in our general transference proposition the fact that transference distortions override reality when the therapist attempts to uncover unconscious conflict and the first phrase about the therapist's technique was added to the assumption.[1] (Of course, transference distortions may even predominate in supportive psychotherapy as a result of a patient's tenuous hold on reality and his proneness to regression.) Thus, the failure of certain transference dispositions to eventuate could be the result of the application of a more supportive treatment modality than was expected.

In fact, it was necessary to write a new (postdictive) assumption to cover the above-cited case as well as two others in which an accurately assessed transference potential did not materialize because of the supportive nature of the treatment. In one case (*Bohemian*) we expected the patient's relationship to her therapist vis-á-vis her hospital doctor to duplicate exactly the good and bad parent figures she had established for herself in her life situation. She had been neurotically tied to an unhappy marriage and saw her husband as dull and plodding, while her lover had been viewed as cultured and exciting. The predictors believed she would regard the hospital doctor like her

1. This kind of revision was not considered sufficient to be called a postdictive assumption since the conception was a part of the theory which had not been fully explicated in writing the original statement.

restricting husband, and the more neutral therapist could then be viewed as similar to her ex-lover. This eventuality did not occur and, in fact, she saw her therapist very much in terms of his actual personal characteristics—a stable and interested parental figure. Likewise, the *Phobic Girl* was expected to react to her therapist at times as the bad father, distant and critical. Actually, she maintained a mild positive relationship with her therapist throughout treatment.

This instance led to the writing of the following postdictive assumption: "The more supportive the treatment mode, the greater is the tendency of the transference to conform to the actual personality attributes of the therapist."

INFANTILE WISHES IN THE TRANSFERENCE

A special type of transference assumption is based upon clear evidence in the history of someone having been "spoiled": infantilization by parental figures in which childish needs and demands are unduly gratified beyond age appropriate periods. Such people are overindulged, their whims are catered to, and they do not learn to suffer the consequences of their misbehaviors since they are protected and rescued by their parents; they therefore expect their unreasonable demands will always be gratified. One would anticipate that such infantile expectations and demands would be repeated in the therapeutic relationship with some clarity and intensity. The assumption which embodies this idea is: "The more the infantile wishes have been fulfilled, and the reality of infantile fears confirmed, the more peremptory are these wishes and fears in psychotherapy."

This assumption was tested thirteen times and, as one might expect, was confirmed with one exception. Practically all of the predictions concerned intense oral expectations which were highly ego-syntonic.

The one prediction and its accompanying assumption in this series which was disconfirmed concerned the gratification of passive anal wishes in a young female analytic patient (*Tantrum Woman*) whose mother had given her enemas until the age of twenty-four. There had been considerable reality reinforcement of fears of poisoning by fecal products as the mother told her throughout her childhood of the horrors of constipation. The predictors anticipated that these elements would occupy a central place in the analysis and that the analyst would have to pull material from her in order to rid her of the "poison" of her illness, while she would meanwhile stubbornly withhold. This was by no means the case because the analyst never experienced her as stubbornly withholding material. We lack an adequate explanation for the failure of this prediction but since she also showed intense oral fixations, we may hazard a guess that the earlier oral strivings and conflicts in some way left their stamp on all subsequent experiences, so that her constipation was intrapsychically experienced as an oral clamping down and holding on. The first year of the analysis was characterized by intense affect storms in which she would rage and complain and demand that the analyst make her life better immediately. Also, the intensity of her oral demands might have overshadowed the less prominent passive anal paradigm. Thus, an incorrect patient assessment could explain the predictive error.

ALLOPLASTIC RESISTANCES

The predictors anticipated that patients who characteristically dealt with anxiety by predominantly alloplastic means, i.e., behavioral outlets, would give up such behavior only with considerable difficulty. They expected this difficulty to be especially pronounced in analytic treatment where the therapist's neutrality and lack of intervention in the patient's life were maximal. The relevant assumption was "to the extent that a patient's alloplastic defensive modes effectively relieve anxiety, he strongly resists giving up these behaviors."[2]

The assumption was applied mainly to those patients who were addicted to alcohol and drugs or who were prone to impulsive maladaptive behavior. The four alcoholic patients in analysis helped to strengthen this assumption insofar as their treatment failed to bring their drinking under control.

Of interest, however, is one patient (*Travel Phobia Woman*) who suffered from a serious barbiturate addiction. Her symptom was brought under fairly rapid control in the early stages of an analysis begun while she was a hospital patient. The predictors erroneously anticipated a recrudescence of addictive symptoms after the patient left the hospital. What they failed to consider was that this patient might experience her "analytic" treatment as highly supportive. She turned out not to be analyzable partly because of her low tolerance for anxiety and perhaps as a result of a mild organic condition which may have inhibited the development of the necessary psychological-mindedness for expressive treatment. Even more significant was the patient's guiding fantasy that a benevolent figure would nurture and protect her. She developed this kind of gratifying relationship with her therapist even during the one-year attempt at analysis. The postdictive assumption written for this case was: "Patients who enter the psychotherapy situation with the fantasy of being cared for by a benevolent parent, who experience the permissiveness and dependability of

2. Although the assumption is rather general, the predictions usually spelled out in more concrete terms the specific manifestations of these resistances.

the psychotherapy as consistent with this fantasy, and who are able to ward off their instinctual demands toward the therapist, can experience expressive psychotherapy, even psychoanalysis, as gratifying."

The expectation of difficulty with patients given to impulsive behavior was borne out in two other cases, one of whom (*Peter Pan*) engaged in compulsive stealing of food, and another (*Tantrum Woman*) indulged in temper tantrums and affect storms (within the treatment situation). These behaviors at the very least impeded analytic treatment and, in the case of the stealing, could seriously have threatened the treatment situation. However, they were both brought under control in the early stages of treatment by a firm ultimatum from the analyst that such behavior needed to stop if treatment were to continue and have some chance of success. These parameters turned out to be effective in helping the patients control their behavior.

CONSCIOUS SENSE OF GUILT

The predictors forecast that those patients whose behavior had actually been destructive toward significant others in their lives would eventually develop a conscious sense of guilt. The assumption reads as follows: "Patients with a history of hostile and destructive behavior eventually experience a conscious sense of guilt based upon the real destructiveness they have wrought and the guilt feelings associated with earlier hostile impulses."

The assumption was applied in three cases and received equivocal support. One of the patients (*Script Writer*) terminated treatment prematurely and the prediction could not be tested; in another instance (*Snake Phobia Woman*) the expected depression and guilt did occur, but in the third instance the expected guilt did not emerge.

This latter case (*Bohemian*) was of special interest because the patient had behaved in a remarkably callous manner toward both her husband and her adopted son, in effect deserting and abandoning them for a considerable period of time while she pursued an artistic career in the company of a Bohemian-type lover. Although she effected a reasonably successful outcome in her treatment and was able to set up a new and more compatible marital situation, she never developed feelings of guilt concerning the abuse and destructiveness she had inflicted upon her family. She remained too infantile and narcissistic in her character organization to take her past behavior seriously or to feel deeply concerned about the distress she had caused. Hence, the qualifying statement was written to modify the original assumption: "Markedly narcissistic patients with limited ego strength do not develop guilt in psychotherapy."

MULTIPLE DETERMINATION OF BEHAVIOR

Another assumption which is practically axiomatic in psychoanalytic theory and practice is that of multiple determination of manifest behavior and symptoms. A particular behavioral pattern or transference manifestation is characteristically rooted in a number of different layers of psychosexual development and conflict. This proposition was expressed as "whatever the predominant level of conflict manifested in a given transference reaction, elements of conflict at other levels will be present as well."

This assumption was applied to five cases and confirmations were obtained in four with one case being untested because of premature termination. The assumption was invoked to cover multifaceted determinants of the erotized transference of five female patients. In each instance the erotic transference was expected to contain mixtures of phallic aggressive, oral dependent, and other pregenital components, and such expectations were confirmed.

Far less clear-cut was a related assumption concerning the sequential working through of conflicts at different genetic levels. "Before conflicts of a genetically later psychosexual level are completely resolved, it is necessary that the major conflicts at an earlier level be worked through." Although this assumption was applied in a number of cases, it failed to be adequately tested since there were too few instances in our population of analytic resolution of both genital and pregenital conflicts.

RECIPROCITY BETWEEN TRANSFERENCE AND ENVIRONMENTAL OUTLETS

Another strongly held tenet in the psychoanalytic theory of therapy is that a patient will tend to displace his transference reactions onto other figures in the environment when unable to tolerate feelings generated in the therapeutic relationship. Usually the therapist will redirect such behavior into the therapeutic arena by interpretation, depending upon his assessment of the patient's capacity to deal with such feelings and upon the treatment goals. This displacement phenomenon was stated in the following assumption: "There is a reciprocal relationship between the intensity of wishes directed toward the therapist and the fulfillment of psychological needs in the patient's life outside the therapy." Once again, in the thirteen instances in which this assumption was used there were no disconfirmations.

Actually, six out of the seven predictions which could be

tested were confirmed. The single predictive error was that of the *Phobic Girl*, who was expected to erotize the transference in a supportive-expressive psychotherapy. The prediction was made on the basis of the patient's strong oedipal strivings as well as her prominent oral fixation which, prior to treatment, had led to considerable promiscuity. Although the symptomatic promiscuity was brought under control during the early phases of the treatment, the patient continued to act out her transference propensities in a less self-destructive way, and the therapist decided against interpreting the transference implications. The predictive error did not weaken the assumption since the transference wishes were displaced onto the environment. Disconfirmation conceivably could have occurred if this patient had *neither* erotized the transference *nor* engaged in sexual liaisons.

REGRESSIVE EFFECTS OF PSYCHOANALYSIS

A frequent assumption was that patients with weak egos who undergo psychoanalysis experience a further weakening in their adaptive responses both in and out of treatment. "The more primitive the patient's fixations and less adequate his defenses, the more likely is a patient to experience an uncontrolled ego regression in response to the uncovering of unconscious conflicts." This assumption was generally confirmed and strengthened, but there was a sufficient number of variations of regressive responses to warrant further elaboration on these findings.

The clearest instances of ego regression occurred for two of the alcoholic patients whose addictive symptoms grew worse in the course of treatment. The *Alcoholic Heir* denied any serious emotional problems or that his alcoholism was out of control.

He would not free associate, dismissed any reference to transference reactions as silly, refused rehospitalization even when his drinking was out of control, and spent most of his brief eight-month analysis describing crises attendant on his severe marital conflicts. Whether or not the deterioration of his life situation (as well as the treatment situation) was accelerated by the threatened emergence of primary process material is difficult to assess. He obviously needed hospitalization to halt his uncontrolled drinking, but refused to accept it. Although he balked at free associating, he did begin to develop paranoid ideas about his wife as well as some of his friends and these reactions may well have been the result of a silent paranoid transference development which could not be checked.

The *Alcoholic Doctor*, on the other hand, very quickly accepted the invitation to free associate and, within a relatively brief period of time, began to develop intermittent psychotic transference manifestations. Throughout this patient's relatively long analysis he developed a number of bizarre ideas, described earlier, about the analyst and about his parents and during these periods the analyst sat the patient up and attempted to confront him with reality. But the weakness of the patient's reality testing made him unable to tolerate the stressful analytic procedure and the treatment took a steady downhill course.

The regressive effects of analysis were partly offset for certain other patients by the gratification they were able to obtain from treatment. We have already mentioned the *Travel Phobia Woman* who experienced the analytic process as a kind of supportive psychotherapy. Her rigidity and concreteness, partly compounded by a mild organic condition, helped her to avoid viewing the analyst as anything but a benevolent father-figure whom she tried to please.

The *Raconteur* showed a relatively mild regression in his borderline psychotic state during his two-year period of analysis. This was contrary to the predictions, which foresaw an intensification of anxiety as primary process material was released, with the expectation of increased withdrawal, promiscuity, alcoholism, and aggressive outbursts. These symptoms did in fact heighten to some extent but they did not seem to be associated with anxiety generated in his analysis since the patient was not made anxious by what he discussed in analysis. He made "deep" interpretations about his own material, and he enjoyed producing reminiscences and fantasies for the entertainment of the analyst. One can question whether he was really free associating at all since his attitude was that of impressing the analyst and enjoying his own voice. He did not permit thoughts to appear freely and for the most part his associations, though primitive, were similar to intellectualized ideas. He was aided in his resistance to free associate by the analyst's lack of consistent interpretive effort to point out the patient's evasion and mockery of the analytic task. The regression which did occur did not seem to be due primarily to anxiety associated with the emergence of primary process material but rather to the loosening of ego boundaries encouraged by the total analytic situation. The patient viewed the analyst as a narcissistic extension of himself, and developed the fantasy of being protected by the omnipotent and omniscient analyst, so that he felt an increased freedom in his outside life to divest himself of his already meager sense of responsibility about his actions and behavior. It was only when the analyst began confronting him with his disorganized and chaotic life outside of the treatment that the patient began to experience anxiety, and he ultimately disrupted the treatment when the analyst proposed they shift to face-to-face psychotherapy.

Another instance of controlled associations preventing regression occurred in the case of a paranoid man who was in analysis under duress. The ego weakness of the *Suspended Student* was only partly suspected during the treatment process, and it was not until the follow-up period (and even beyond) that his inability to cope with ordinary life responsibilities became apparent. In the initial work-up of this patient there was no suggestion of a psychotic potential, although his presenting symptom of dissociative reaction was dramatic enough to raise this kind of diagnostic question. At the outset of his analysis he was too uneasy to assume the supine position and was permitted to sit up for the first two months. He was given to impulsive behavior like reckless driving, and occasionally showed evidences of paranoid distortions. The analysis *appeared* to proceed satisfactorily over a four-year period with what seemed to be an improvement rather than a deterioration in his controls. After the patient terminated treatment, however, and was graduated from professional school and began to assume a full share of adult responsibility, his life situation deteriorated seriously. One explanation for why an uncontrolled ego regression was not apparent during the treatment process itself was that this patient was in treatment under duress and hence did not give himself fully to a passive, free-associative posture. His compliance with the procedure was more apparent than real, and he seems to have gone through the motions of treatment without ever being genuinely involved in it except to the extent he feared being unmasked and harmed.

Another example of gratification within the analysis preventing regressive trends was the case of the *Historian,* who regarded analytic treatment as an end in itself. He adopted the view that his analysis was the central organizing core of his life, and he readily gave up relationships and gratification outside of treatment in favor of the expected gratification from the analyst. For four years his analysis was essentially stalemated in an insoluble transference neurosis while he was awaiting a magical process of change. During this period there were no overtly psychotic developments except perhaps for the rigidity of his anaclitic attachment to the analyst. When the analyst finally gave up attempting to interpret the patient's largely syntonic longing for nurturant protection from the analyst in favor of focusing upon the patient's rage and envy toward the father-analyst as this expressed itself in the masochistic-submissive transference, there ensued a psychotic regression during which the patient had delusional convictions about the analyst prohibiting him from having relationships with women, exercising control over all women, even including the patient's mother. When this psychotic transference showed no sign of reversing itself, the analyst shifted to supportive psychotherapy. Thus, as long as the analytic situation was gratifying, at least in fantasy, the patient experienced no incentive to alter his life or his treatment. At the same time he did not show any signs of regressive behavior except insofar as his entire attitude toward the treatment was regressive. The only exception was that the uncovering by interpretation of the inevitable frustration of his oral fantasies led to explosive rages and overtly paranoid developments. But for the most part, such regressive developments were absent.

In summary, then, an uncontrolled ego regression or a decompensation of defenses during analysis in patients with weak egos is likely to occur in those patients who do not struggle against the free-association process and give themselves over to it, and where the analyst actively interprets the patient's underlying resistances and fantasies when these are essentially gratifying. Such regression does not occur where the patient, consciously or unconsciously, controls his associations or otherwise maintains a stable, gratifying treatment situation in which analytic work is suspended.

SUMMARY

1. The major transference assumption was, expectedly, neither disconfirmed nor weakened. But certain predictive

errors pointed up the necessity to revise the assumption as originally stated by the Prediction Study team. First, it became clear that the introduction of supportive parameters in expressive treatments will reduce transference manifestations, particularly negative views of the therapist. Second, the more supportive the treatment mode, the greater is the tendency of the transference to conform to the actual personality attributes of the therapist.

2. Alloplastic resistances, particularly the use of alcohol to cope with anxiety, proved stubbornly resistant to treatment efforts, especially in analysis. However, we observed that a patient with a guiding fantasy of being cared for by a benevolent parent and who is unable to tolerate negative affects may experience even the analytic situation as quite supportive.

3. The expected development of a conscious sense of guilt in patients who have wrought real destructiveness upon significant figures in their life will not occur in patients who are highly narcissistic.

4. An uncontrolled ego regression in patients with weak egos occurred clearly in those patients who did not struggle against the free-association process and gave themselves over to it, and where the analyst actively pursued and interpreted the patient's underlying resistances and fantasies when these were essentially gratifying. Uncontrolled regression did not occur where the patient consciously or unconsciously controlled his associations and in those instances where the patient was able to establish a stable, gratifying situation where no analytic work was done.

CHAPTER 5

INDICATIONS AND CONTRAINDICATIONS FOR PSYCHOANALYSIS

The predictions concerning the overall outcome of psycho-analysis were based upon one major assumption: "To the extent that patients have good ego strength to effect psychological change in themselves they are able in expressive psychotherapies to resolve their intrapsychic conflicts with a concomitant remission of symptoms as well as characterological changes." The subsidiary assumptions in this series consist of a further spelling out of the various aspects of ego weakness, ego defect, or ego limitation which would hinder or obstruct the optimal result of psychoanalysis. Excessive pregenital fixation, low anxiety tolerance, emphasis upon primitive defenses like projection or denial, and proneness to autistic distortions of thinking are the generally accepted signs which would either inhibit an optimal result or would contraindicate the use of this particular form of treatment.

Twenty-two patients in our study began psychoanalysis. Four of these were shifted to a more supportive modality after the therapist decided that analysis was too stressful for the patient. Using the write-ups of the Treatment Variables Group at termination and follow-up and Dr. Wallerstein's detailed case summaries, the Prediction Study Group assessed the suitability of the remaining eighteen cases for analytic treatment. Six cases showed significant or marked improvement[1] associated with some degree of conflict resolution, and none of the researchers questioned the appropriateness of this treatment modality for them. There were three cases, however, which were less successful but who were still felt to be good analytic types. The less-than-hoped-for result was attributed to a number of factors including weakness of technique, such as a failure by the analyst to stick to analytic procedures because of strong resistances, and the presence of relatively immutable life circumstances. Ten cases, on the other hand, were regarded by the research teams as having been poorly selected for analytic treatment. Three cases fell into the questionable category.[2] (See Table 1)

Table 1

Suitability of Patients for Psychoanalysis

Analyzable	Unanalyzable	Questionable
Adoptive Mother	Script Writer	Prince
Snake Phobia Woman	Suspended Student	Movie Lady
Tantrum Woman	Alcoholic Heir	Heiress
Medical Specialist	Good Son	
Phobic Woman	Raconteur	
English Professor	Alcoholic Doctor	
Silent Woman	Editor	
Divorced Teacher	Historian	
Obese Woman	Travel Phobia Woman	
	Peter Pan	

1. These categorizations of change were made by Dr. Ann Appelbaum and the author. They rated each patient on a five-point scale of Absolute Global Change: worse, no change, slight improvement, significant improvement, and marked improvement.

2. These judgments were first made independently by Dr. Ann Appelbaum and the author; the final judgments were reached by consensus.

In this chapter we will discuss all of these twenty-two cases, but will focus on those patients who underwent analysis and, in the judgment of the research teams, should not have been offered this potent but stressful, regression-inducing modality. The unsuitable cases were all people with some kind of ego defect or deformation which either made it impossible for them to utilize psychoanalytic treatment or, in some cases, may have induced further regression. In elaborating upon the aspects of ego weakness in sufficient detail, we may hopefully contribute to improved selection of cases.

Lest it be thought that the ten unsuitable cases were incorrectly assessed by the research team, we should remind the reader that the actual clinical decisions were made independently of the initial research judgments and predictions. The Initial Study Group, in fact, explicitly forecast a treatment failure in one case (*Raconteur*) whose psychotic potential was clearly recognized. The researchers felt that the *Alcoholic Doctor* was not a good analytic prospect because of his strong passive, submissive, and masochistic makeup as well as his poor motivation. They were quite leery of the *Historian's* schizoid potential and narcissistic self-absorption, and believed that the *Alcoholic Heir's* low motivation and rigid denial of illness made his prognosis questionable. The researchers entertained the possibility of insoluble transference neuroses in at least two of the contraindicated cases (*Travel Phobia Woman, Editor*). In other words, the research team at the initial point vetoed psychoanalysis as the treatment of choice for two of the unsuitable patients and expressed serious misgivings about the outcomes in four of the other unsuitable ones. With a few exceptions, they were more sanguine about the outcome of the suitable group.

We shall now examine those patient variables, mainly factors related to ego strength, which had a bearing on the outcome of the analytic process.

PSYCHOTIC POTENTIAL: BORDERLINE PERSONALITIES

A clear contraindication for psychoanalysis is a proneness to psychotic thinking or a weakened ability to distinguish between fantasy and reality. A treatment which fosters regressive fantasies requires that the patient be able to recover sufficiently from the regressive aspects of the transference. A psychotic transference is one in which the patient has lost the capacity to reimpose reality upon his irrational transference reactions. The patient accepts his own views of the therapist, usually malevolent ones, as valid and factual rather than as products rooted in internalized infantile experiences.

Seven of the unsuitable patients showed this kind of psychotic reaction during (and in one case, after) the analysis.

The patient who was spotted by the research team prior to the beginning of treatment as definitely unsuited for psychoanalysis (*Raconteur*) was unable and unwilling in his analysis to control an outpouring of bizarre, chaotic, and primitive productions. He accepted his overidealized view of the godlike, messianic analyst without reservation or reality correction. While his life situation became increasingly disorganized, he seemed to revel in his fantasies of being indulged, protected, and nourished by the all-powerful and all-knowing analyst. When the analyst decided to switch the treatment to a less "prestigious" modality—twice-a-week psychotherapy—the patient terminated.

The *Editor*, severely alcoholic and actively homosexual, had the conviction that both his father and the analyst expected him to fail at anything he attempted, and he expressed the paranoid fear, bordering on a delusion, that his father would attempt to undermine any success he might achieve. He engaged in dangerous sadomasochistic homosexual adventures with the fantasy that he could emerge unscathed. His narcissistic omnipotence made it all but impossible for the analyst to confront him successfully with the dangers to which he exposed himself. He was never able to give up the conviction that the analyst was only interested in curing him of his homosexuality for his own narcissistic enhancement.

A third patient, the *Alcoholic Doctor*, started his analysis while hospitalized (as did the preceding two patients) because of addiction to drugs and alcohol. He was also overtly homosexual. Psychotic transference reactions were frequent during the treatment process. He experienced intense fears of the sadistic analyst-father and on one occasion got up from the couch to search for a knife which he was sure the analyst had concealed in the stand next to the chair. Murderous hostility toward the mother was constantly evoked by the analysis. For a period of time he had the psychotic idea that his mother was lodged in his stomach where she was producing gastric pains and nausea. He purchased a gun with the idea of shooting himself in the stomach to get rid of mother and pain once and for all. The tenuousness of his observing ego and the inability to distinguish transference fantasy from reality led to his once crawling over to the analyst to be petted.

A fourth patient, the *Alcoholic Heir*, began his brief abortive treatment in the hospital. Most of the treatment was spent in dealing with his episodes of drinking, severe marital discord, and his reluctance to accept rehospitalization. He struggled desperately against permitting himself to free asso- ciate with a rather clear indication that he could not tolerate the intense and primitive aggression which threatened to emerge. He had to scoff at all transference interpretations. During the year-long period of the analysis, malignant paranoid pathology emerged: the hospital staff was spreading malicious rumors about him, alienating other patients; once he rummaged through some attic trunks and found a "jeweled ice pick" which

he brought to his analyst for safekeeping, fearful that his wife
had intended to use it on him. On another occasion he asked the
analyst for permission to hire a detective agency to investigate
whether his wife had purchased a gun to use against him. At
times he voiced grandiose megalomanic ideas about his great
talents and skills as a financier and business entrepreneur.

The next patient (*Historian*) was in analysis for several
years before his psychotic reactions made it necessary for the
analyst to switch to supportive psychotherapy. In the initial
phase of the analysis he revealed paranoid fears of being
attacked which led to his always carrying weapons in his car.
He had the bizarre conviction that he could tell how sincere
people were by the shape of their fingers and gums. He settled
into an ego-syntonic passivity in his life and in his analysis and
accepted it as the appropriate course of action which would lead
ultimately to all of his wished-for passive gratifications. He
gave up his adult social and sexual life and substituted for it the
passive gratifications he received in his fantasies within the.
analysis. Later in the analysis, as the analyst began to attack
his passive defenses more vigorously, the regressive psychotic
potential became even more apparent. On one occasion, following a brief, casual contact between the analyst and the patient's
mother (arranged upon the insistence of the patient), the patient
angrily accused the analyst of attempting to seduce his mother
and elaborated this idea into the delusional belief that the
analyst was actually carrying on an affair with his mother.

Another unsuitable case by virtue of the psychotic potential
was a young man (*Suspended Student*) who entered treatment
under duress: While a medical student he had performed two
unauthorized pelvic examinations, presumably during a dissociative state. His need to be "certified" as having successfully
undergone treatment before being readmitted to medical school
probably helped to conceal his pathological thinking which did
not emerge as clearly during the treatment process as it did

afterward. In his work as a hospital aide he was fired for an act of blatant insubordination, and in his analysis he revealed an angry paranoid misinterpretation of what had happened. Later, when he applied for an externship appointment at a local hospital and was turned down, he had the paranoid suspicion that his analyst had contacted the hospital and had arranged the rejection. After having been readmitted to medical school, he pressed for termination of the treatment. It was during the follow-up period, however, that his paranoid ideation and behavior came into full view. He strenuously resisted the many contacts by the research team to be interviewed and tested, always professing willingness but deferring the appointment presumably because of time pressure. Gradually, however, with the responsibilities of private medical practice, his life became increasingly disorganized and filled with feelings of persecution, ultimately forcing him to give up his practice, his marriage, his few relationships, and finally his life by suicide.

The final case was *Peter Pan*, who started her analysis at the age of nineteen because of alternating anorexia and bulimia and kleptomania, particularly of food. She attempted to keep her weight at the magic number of one hundred in order to look like a prepubescent, asexual girl. She was a day hospital patient for the first eighteen months of her analysis, and she first started in treatment face-to-face with the objective of bringing her stealing under control. Prior to treatment there were no clear indications of a psychotic potential. During her analysis, however, she did develop the fantasy of moving into the analyst's home and living with him either as his wife or daughter. She was keenly disappointed that this arrangement was not possible and was never able to appreciate its transference implications. The analyst spent most of his therapeutic effort keeping a rather turbulent treatment situation under control. Because of the patient's frequent interruptions, absences, suicidal threats, and other forms of acting out, the analyst found it difficult to use a consistent interpretive approach with her. There were insistent, peremptory, and primitive oral demands whose frustration the patient could not tolerate, and which led to frequent acting out. During the height of the regressive sweep she wet the couch and did not discuss it until the analyst called it to her attention. Her analyst made a number of departures from the usual role of neutrality: frequent phone calls, many appointment changes, and numerous other deviations. These contained elements of support and gratification to the patient which tended to ward off further regression and may have kept the patient from manifesting her latent psychotic thinking during the analysis. Some years after treatment ended (actually disrupted by the patient), she began to decompensate in the face of a failing marriage attributable to her husband's refusal to continue meeting her inordinate demands. At this time she was described as showing more openly bizarre ideation concerning food, weight, and eating.

One of the suitable analytic cases, the *English Professor*, showed a good analytic result despite evidence of a borderline personality organization. The research team did not question the appropriateness of the treatment modality nor did they suggest that supportive or supportive-expressive psychotherapy would have accomplished the same result. The patient came to treatment mainly because of anxiety and phobias particularly connected with lecturing to large-size groups. He had made a number of efforts at psychotherapy prior to the present one and had shown some improvement over his previous state. There was a definite paranoid coloring to his earlier psychological test picture, but these signs had largely disappeared in the testing prior to the beginning of analysis. During the course of the analysis his phobic symptoms were seen less as a reaction to phallic conflicts and more as a defense against threats to organismic integrity: he suffered from the primitive fear of losing his sense of self, of being swallowed up by others, of being fused with them. Furthermore, he never gave up a depersonalized attitude toward his own productions; he never accepted his free associations as really being his own thoughts and he clung to the idea that they somehow belonged to the analyst once he uttered them, i.e., the "analyst's baby" for *him* to do something with. Despite these handicaps to analysis, the patient made substantial progress in overcoming many of his anxieties, inhibitions, and generalized passivity, although he never became entirely free of his phobias.

In this last case, the only one with borderline features in which analysis seemed to be indicated, the research team pointed to a number of assets which seemed to compensate for this man's obvious ego weakness. In addition to his very superior intelligence, professional talents, and capacity for hard work, he was able to withstand large quantities of anxiety. He was doggedly perseverant in struggling against his phobias while at the same time he made some adjustments to their limitations upon him. His borderline condition undoubtedly prevented a more definitive working through of the conflicts underlying his anxieties, but it did not prevent him from a moderate degree of conflict resolution which made for considerable improvement in his life situation.

Of the seven cases with a psychotic potential falling into the unsuitable category, only one (*Raconteur*) was clearly recognized by the predictors as unsuitable for analysis for that reason. One other (*Historian*) was suspected of "schizoid potential and narcissistic self-absorption." A few of the others were considered dubious risks, but not because of their proneness to regressive modes of thinking: the *Alcoholic Doctor*, because of his passive submissive masochistic makeup; the *Alcoholic Heir* for similar reasons, but also because of his rigid denial of illness in the face of severe alcoholism; the *Editor* because he was also passive and masochistic and was expected to show a negative therapeutic reaction; and *Peter Pan*, a somewhat doubtful prospect, because of her low anxiety tolerance. In other words, the predictors recognized either the presence or the possibility of thought disorder in two cases and expressed reservations about the outcome in the other five, but for other reasons than their thought pathology.[3]

ORAL AND NARCISSISTIC FIXATION

All of the cases discussed in the preceding section showed predominant oral fixations. Their symptoms were mainly addiction to drugs and alcohol, and, in one instance, incipient anorexia. Were there instances of strong oral fixations *without* psychotic potential in our study, and how did these cases fare in analysis?

Narcissistically Defended Patients

Three patients were significantly limited in their response to analysis by strong narcissistic fixations which made it necessary for them to strongly resist the uncovering of unpleasant aspects of themselves. Although never described explicitly as a borderline personality with psychotic potential, the *Script Writer* was not entirely free of such features. From the very beginning of her analysis (with a female analyst), this severely alcoholic woman who wrote TV and radio scripts was dominated by the expectation that the feared and hated mother-

3. The presence of a psychotic potential was difficult to recognize simply on the basis of the initial psychiatric examination. Had the psychological test results been given greater weight by the clinical teams and the predictors, at least some of these errors could have been avoided. A detailed discussion of this point may be found in Dr. Stephen A. Appelbaum's forthcoming monograph on the project's psychological test findings.

analyst would attack and criticize her, unmask her many deceptions, conscious and unconscious. But she rigidly denied these transference reactions, taking the explicit attitude that if the analyst ever began to resemble her real mother, she would quit the analysis. The research team agreed in retrospect that she not only lacked the ability to tolerate the anxiety generated by the analytic process, but her narcissistic needs for approval and ego-enhancement prevented her from engaging in the honest, searching introspection necessary for analytic work. She terminated analysis after only eight months.

The *Obese Woman* was an analytic case whose progress was hampered by oral-narcissistic features. The severity of her character pathology was underestimated partly because of the inadequacy of the initial work-up. After treatment was under way she revealed a sadomasochistic sexual perversion as well as tendencies toward kleptomania. She had an overriding narcissistic orientation toward life and the analysis, which took the form of expecting immediate gratification with little or no effort on her part. She promptly warded off anxiety, depression, and guilt by immediately discharging instinctual tensions in action (eating, shoplifting, perversions, etc.). Although symptomatically somewhat improved after analysis, her major oral conflicts were largely untouched, partly because her needs for gratification, support, and easy solutions predominated over her ability to tolerate the discomfort of uncovering her oral rage at the ungiving preoedipal mother. The research team also emphasized a major flaw in the conduct of this analysis: the analyst had a serious countertransference problem in avoiding negative transference, consistently interpreting it as a defense against erotic wishes. The researchers concluded that the patient was probably analyzable but the combination of her ego weaknesses and a clear-cut deficiency in technique produced a limited outcome: some improvement in her social adaptation but no substantial conflict resolution.

The third analytic case whose narcissism prevented a more thoroughgoing result was the *Prince*, a man who sought treatment because of strong feelings of discomfort and inhibition with women which prevented him from sustaining a satisfactory heterosexual relationship. During the course of a four-year analysis he came to understand better the ways in which he contributed to his difficulties with others and was better able to control his maladaptive tendencies. But he failed to uncover and resolve either his phallic or his oral conflicts within the transference mainly because of the intensity of his narcissistic fixation. He saw the analyst as a captive audience whom he could regale with impressive tales of his achievements. He expected the analyst to admire, applaud, and envy him. These intense needs to avoid narcissistic injury and threats to a shaky self-esteem prevented him from exposing the negative and uncomplimentary sides of himself and led him to avoid affective involvement with the analyst. The patient seemed to derive some nonanalytic benefits from his therapeutic experience (improved techniques of adjustment, identification with the analyst's equable interest in another person), but he lacked sufficient capacity to expose himself to narcissistic injury to undergo analytic treatment. Although this patient's narcissism was recognized at the outset by the predictors (who originally had expected an excellent analytic result), they believed that his narcissism was secondary to his phallic-oedipal conflicts; their conclusion in retrospect was that his narcissism was the major organizing factor in his personality organization.

Passive-Dependent Patients

The three patients discussed above showed a predominant narcissistic orientation which essentially prevented them from exposing their weaknesses and undesirable features to another person, or even to themselves. A companion group consisted of those patients with similarly strong oral fixations but who were more passive and submissive, who waited expectantly for, or actively sought, oral gratification but who did not explicitly have to defend themselves against narcissistic threats.

The *Good Son* came for treatment because of a generally inhibited and constricted existence and an inability to find gratification in his professional, social, or sexual life. Because of his presumed anal fixations, his need to rigidly isolate his affects, and his obsessional and intellectualizing defense, the predictors expected only a partial resolution of his conflicts. Actually, even less than this was accomplished in the course of a four-year analysis because of the fixity of his oral wishes. He expected the analyst to magically change him into a heroic superman without any effort on his part, and he essentially waited for the change to occur. This expectation was expressed in a totally helpless, dependent, compliant transference which hardened into an "insoluble" transference neurosis and did not respond to the analyst's interpretive efforts. Linked to this fantasy of external nurturance and succor was a weak motivation for personal change and development. The research team concluded at termination that the patient might have achieved a better therapeutic result had he been offered a supportive-expressive modality in which the therapist had greater opportunity to offer the patient more gratification of his wished-for counsel and guidance.

Another patient for whom psychoanalysis turned out to have been contraindicated largely on the basis of intense oral fixations was the *Travel Phobia Woman*. She was hospitalized initially for drug addiction and had a long-standing history of phobias and withdrawal into an isolated and constricted existence. Psychoanalysis beginning in the hospital was recommended by both the clinical and research teams as the only modality which could resolve her chronic neurotic conflicts, even though her strong oral fixations, her low anxiety tolerance and alloplastic tendencies were expected to make the outcome a limited one at best. The possibility of an insoluable dependent transference neurosis was entertained by the predictors as a distinct possibility. Though given a reasonable try, analysis was never possible with this woman. She was unable to free associate and assiduously avoided and denied the presence of transference reactions. She would never accept the idea that any of her emotional states were in any way related to feelings about the analyst. She rigidly adhered to the view that he was a strong, good, and helping figure who bountifully gave her his time and interest and she in turn made him "gifts" of improved functioning. Her very limited psychological-mindedness was compounded by the probable presence of a mild organic brain syndrome. But mainly she had an intense need to cling to a supportive and fatherly figure who would nurture and protect her, and she was too threatened by instinctual impulses which might arise to cut off the flow of these valued oral supplies. Eventually her treatment became explicitly supportive.

A young patient (*Phobic Woman*) whom the predictors believed to be an oral-infantile person with a potential for an insoluable transference neurosis had phobias that made it necessary for someone, usually her husband, to be near her most of the day. She was unremitting in her demands upon her parents, who themselves seemed to be willing partners in an infantilizing process. In the course of the analysis, however, her demanding and dependent stance was seen as a defense against a primary phallic-oedipal conflict. The patient was able to achieve a partial resolution of her phallic competitive problems and the secondary demandingness was diminished.

A case discussed earlier (*English Professor*) under the section on psychotic potential was strongly and primarily fixated at the oral level and achieved some degree of resolution

of these problems. He had entered analysis with the unconscious fantasy of finding the "golden apple," the all-giving, all-
nurturing, protective mother. Although he clung to this fantasy
during most of his analysis, he began to give it up during the
termination process. The termination was not initiated by
mutual decision but was imposed by the analyst because it
became apparent that the patient had settled onto a plateau and
was prepared for an interminable treatment. Was there evidence in this case of a resolution of the patient's oral conflicts?
He seemed to respond less to the interpretation of unrealistic
transference wishes than to the analyst's action of setting the
termination date, which convinced him that he could not be the
infantile, dependent child forever.

In a number of cases the predictors expected there would be
partial conflict resolution because underlying oral conflicts
would not be substantially modified, and they were largely
correct in these expectations. They expected the *Prince's*
narcissism to come under better control but not to be fully
exposed and worked through and this took place. The predictors forecast that the *Divorced Teacher's* dependency would
persist even though her phallic problems would be resolved and
this was essentially correct. Although unaware of the organic
pathology, they were concerned about the *Travel Phobia
Woman's* capacity to overcome her intense dependency, and
entertained the possibility of insoluble transference neurosis;
this actually occurred but was based also upon the unanticipated presence of organic pathology. The limited outcome
expected for the *Good Son* was based upon pregenital fixations;
the result of analysis was even more curtailed than expected,
partly because the intensity of the oral fixation was not
recognized at first. The predictors anticipated some alteration of
impulse-defense configurations rather than a thoroughgoing
resolution of conflict in the case of the *English Professor*, and
they were largely correct, except that it was not only due to the

oral fixation but to a borderline ego weakness which they had overlooked. They expected limited conflict resolution in the *Movie Lady* based on pregenital fixations, but unfortunately there was an insufficient test of this prediction because the analyst shifted to a supportive treatment (too quickly in the opinion of the research team), and the patient had not been exposed to a fair trial of analysis.

There were two patients with strong oral fixations who were expected to show substantial resolution of conflict. The *Obese Woman* showed some resolution of her phallic oedipal problems but practically no relief from the pressure of oral aggressive conflicts. The research team in this case attributed the lack of resolution of oral conflicts mainly to the therapist's failure to deal adequately with them. His difficulty in doing so stemmed partly from the narcissistic character of this patient. There was only one case (*Tantrum Woman*) in which predominating oral conflicts were at least partly worked through after a rather long and stubborn treatment. A clinging, dependent, and demanding woman, she was able to resolve to some extent her highly charged, ambivalent relationship with the pregenital mother.

One may conclude from this discussion that the predominance of oral conflicts, particularly when associated with alloplastic symptoms or strong passive features or intense narcissistic needs, frequently contraindicates psychoanalysis. Although some patients with predominant oral fixations were capable of being analyzed, the resolution of their oral conflicts was never more than partial.

PHALLIC CONFLICTS

The predictors assumed that patients with predominantly phallic conflicts should be able to achieve full or partial conflict resolution, in contrast to those whose conflicts were predominantly at an oral level and, in general, they were correct. This assumption was based upon considerations of both the nature of the patient's impulse life as well as the ego and defensive structure associated with phallic conflicts. First, it was assumed that the earlier the level of psychosexual fixation, the more fixed, rigid, and unyielding the libidinal position. Thus, the phrase "stickiness of libido" was used by the predictors in a number of cases with pregenital fixations but not in those with phallic conflicts. The patient who has experienced marked oral deprivation (or overindulgence) in the first year or two of life is rarely able in analysis to renounce these infantile strivings in favor of more mature gratification. On the other hand, patients who must retreat from adult sexuality and appropriate sexual roles because of conflicted relationships within the oedipal triangle are usually able to find the rewards of adult genitality more gratifying than their more inhibited orientation. With regard to defenses, pregenital conflicts are usually accompanied by the more primitive defenses of denial and projection which typically work against the possibility of conflict resolution. The ego structures that support reality testing and capacity to tolerate anxiety are usually weaker among infantile patients than in those with predominantly phallic problems.

In four of the six patients who showed the best analytic results, phallic conflicts either predominated or existed co-equally with the oral ones. The two other successful analytic cases were predominantly orally fixated and have been discussed in the preceding section.

Not all of the predominantly phallic individuals were successfully analyzed. Four of them failed to achieve conflict resolution leading to a more gratifying life. One of these (*Divorced Teacher*) was actually able to reach a fair degree of resolution of the problem which had contributed to marital discord prior to treatment. In identification with her mother, she had been unconsciously attempting to drive her husband away. The analytic resolution of her phallic problems led her to become a softer, more receptive and more loving person. Unfortunately the deterioration of her marriage prior to treatment led to divorce and loss of custody of her children. She was never able to come to terms with the tragedy of her life and she remained depressed. Another female patient (*Silent Woman*) was caught in a struggle between masculine, competitive strivings as opposed to a feminine, little-girl, ineffectual role. Neither was very satisfactory and during her relatively brief analytic course (she disrupted her treatment suddenly after one year marked by long stubborn silences) a serious transference-countertransference bind occurred in which she perceived the analyst-father as hostile, cold, and critical. Apparently the analyst's reaction to her provocation came close enough to her transference fears to inhibit any movement toward resolution.

The other two cases deserve special attention because they were both deemed to be unanalyzable by their analysts as a result of presumed borderline qualities, and treatment was switched to a more supportive psychotherapy. In both cases the therapist gave up his role of analytic neutrality and anonymity, gave direct counseling, revealed facts about his personal life, and attempted to make a corrective emotional experience available to the patient. Both patients were seen initially as having major phallic-oedipal problems and were thought to be suitable for analytic treatment. With regard to one of them (*Movie Lady*), the research team concluded that the intensity of the patient's competitive and hostile depreciation of the analyst led the latter into a countertransference reaction which made him view the patient's unreasonableness and inflexibility as evidence of a psychotic potential. After a six-month effort at analysis the patient was shifted to a more explicitly supportive approach. In terms of overt adaptive behavior (symptoms of anxiety and phobias reduced, marital relationship improved, and more gratification in all life activities), she did not achieve these improvements through anything approaching conflict resolution. The research team agreed that despite a difficult and stormy course the patient was potentially analyzable.

Similar considerations, although perhaps somewhat more equivocal, were brought to bear with regard to the *Heiress*. Prior to starting treatment, she showed both phallic and oral problems but with some suggestions of regressive, schizoid symptoms which took the form of withdrawal from others and a tendency toward depersonalization in which she felt like a mechanically driven puppet. Prior to the beginning of treatment she had been subject to "turbulent periods" which were triggered by intense rage: for long periods she would sit rigidly in a chair, trembling, fists clenched, seemingly out of contact. She explained these episodes as a need to withdraw in order to organize her thoughts and bring herself under control. Originally these periods lasted for a few hours, but later they went on for longer times. Apparently, there was no actual loss of reality contact, although she described feeling unattached to people and saw them as mechanical and unreal. The patient would drink heavily during these periods of painful confusion.

The analyst was impressed by her presumed borderline qualities, her rigid and blocked affects, and her seeming incapacity to free associate. The research team at termination did not agree with this formulation. Rather than characterize the patient as "borderline," they saw her as a hysterical character with strong masochistic trends. The researchers pointed to the fact that psychotic distortions of reality did not appear during her long treatment period nor were they reported in the psychological testing. They argued that the core conflict appeared to be around the phallic-oedipal constellation with strong erotization of the transference, which was more hysterical than borderline. Furthermore, the particular form of the transference was more hysterical and controlling than it was schizoid: the patient would call the analyst over the phone and pour out feelings of love, but on the next day she would claim she had forgotten the episode and resume her aloof and distant attitude toward him. The research team agreed that the patient was capable of being analyzed by means of classic analytic techniques. In altering his technique, the analyst, as in the preceding case, was acceding to the subtly controlling and competitive pressures of the patient who was attempting to remove him from his pedestal of analytic neutrality.

Most diagnostic errors were made mainly in the opposite direction, i.e., initially overestimating ego strength, with the result that several patients were recommended for analysis (both by the clinical and the research team) who did not have the requisite ego resources. One common diagnostic error was in overestimating the patient's analyzability on the basis of a presumably prominent phallic conflict. For example, one patient (*Alcoholic Heir*) was described as a case of "success neurosis" because his alcoholic and phobic symptoms grew more severe as he started to replace his father as the head of a large business organization. But a number of obvious ego weaknesses were being underplayed, notably his extremely low tolerance for anxiety which prevented him, when his emotional disturbance became prominent, from going to work without being bolstered by alcohol, and later he was unable to go to his office except on weekends, when no one was present. Similarly, an alcoholic woman (*Script Writer*) was seen as highly competitive with men and depreciating of a feminine-maternal role, but because her conflicts were not entirely "oral," she was considered a favorable risk for analysis. Furthermore, the predictors believed that her successful work as a radio broadcaster and programer indicated an active stance which boded well for analysis. They overemphasized these assets and underplayed her narcissistic and neglectful attitude toward her children. Both of these cases demonstrated an extreme degree of denial as well as externalization which took the form of blaming others for their current difficulties, particularly the drinking.

The data confirm the assumption that patients with predominantly phallic fixations are more amenable to analytic treatment than are patients who show predominant pregenital conflicts. Male analysts may encounter a countertransference tendency to regard the efforts of female analysands to compete with, defeat, and dethrone the analyst as evidence of more pathology than actually exists. On the other hand, the presence of prominent phallic competitive components may at times be seen as indicating a greater ego strength than actually exists.

MASOCHISM

Like the orally fixated patient, the masochistic person may be expected to use his treatment as an attempt to gratify his neurotic needs, in this instance, for suffering. Such patients are likely to develop insoluble transference reactions based upon unwillingness to give up the neurotic suffering in their lives as well as the discomfort associated with the analytic process itself (mainly the drain on time and money), so that a cure of painful symptoms or character traits becomes difficult. Furthermore, these patients also tend to show a "negative therapeutic reaction" in which signs of progress are typically followed by a retreat to the illness.

There were three analytic patients who were seen initially as predominantly masochistic and six others who were initially described as having strong masochistic features. Of the three cases judged predominantly masochistic, the prediction concerning a limited outcome for one (*Movie Lady*) could not be tested because the treatment had been switched to a supportive psychotherapy after about six months of analysis; as mentioned earlier, the analyst decided the patient was too sick—possibly psychotic—for analysis. The two other patients (*Alcoholic*

Doctor, Editor) were both expected to show limited improvement, with the strong possibility of an insoluble transference neurosis based not only upon prominent masochism but also upon marked pregenital fixations, strongly ingrained passivity, and oral yearnings. These two patients showed other features of ego weakness which would have made them poor candidates for analysis: they were highly alloplastic, homosexuals of long standing, and severely alcoholic. As if these symptoms were not severe enough, they also were in the group of patients who ultimately showed a potential for regressive sweeps of psychotic thinking (not recognized at first). With this superabundance of psychopathology, it would be hard to ferret out the interfering role of masochism. However, with regard to the *Editor*, the research team was able to recognize a definite negative therapeutic reaction in which every success and bit of progress was followed immediately by a drunken binge or a homosexual adventure. In the case of the *Alcoholic Doctor*, masochism seemed less influential than the thought disorder, which was in turn more prominent in him than it was in the case of the *Editor*.

Two other patients were initially seen as likely to be handicapped somewhat by their masochism. They were quite similar in showing strong passive dependent and submissive personalities with prominent streaks of masochism. One of these (*Historian*) was suspected of a latent thought disorder and became blatantly paranoid and psychotic in the course of the treatment with the result that he was shifted to supportive psychotherapy. With regard to the other man (*English Professor*), he made considerable gains in his analysis despite the presence of strong dependency and masochism. The latter tended to push him toward an interminable treatment which the analyst interrupted after six years by setting a termination date. It was clear that any limitation in what was achieved was based upon certain borderline features in the patient (the fear of loss of ego boundaries), and not upon the masochistic trends.

In summary, then, masochistic factors in themselves were never crucial determinants in producing an untoward outcome although, combined with other ego weaknesses, self-destructive tendencies could contribute to a negative outcome.

ANXIETY TOLERANCE

One aspect of ego strength generally agreed upon as necessary for psychoanalysis is the capacity to tolerate the experience of anxiety without resorting to either autoplastic or alloplastic devices which would disrupt the patient's life or his treatment or both.[4] Practically all of the thirteen cases for whom analysis was regarded by the research team as contraindicated or questionable showed a low tolerance for anxiety prior to the beginning of treatment. Six were addicted to either drugs or alcohol. Three others showed other disruptive symptoms: the *Historian* experienced borderline psychotic thinking (carrying weapons in his car to protect himself against attack); *Peter Pan* had been in difficulty with the authorities because of kleptomania; the *Suspended Student* showed low anxiety tolerance in his periodic indulgence in alcoholic binges, reckless drunken driving, assaultiveness, and promiscuity.

Two patients in this group did not manifest low anxiety tolerance in the form of disruptive symptoms. Rather, they exhibited a rigidity of narcissistic defenses and a rigidity of oral passive yearnings, a "stickiness" of oral libido, which prevented both of them from moving past their initial transference stance into an unfolding of a full transference neurosis. The *Prince* was intent on narcissistic self-aggrandizement and produced material designed to elicit admiration and applause of

4. Siegal and Rosen (1962) redefined the concept of anxiety tolerance in a paper based on their psychological test studies of project patients.

his analyst. The *Good Son* started and finished his analysis with the attitude that the analyst would be frustrating and critical, and he angrily and silently waited for the analyst to prove otherwise. Neither seemed to be able to give up these defensive positions sufficiently to expose themselves to the anxiety of a different kind of object relationship; this kind of frozen defensive organization suggested a special form of low anxiety tolerance.

Among the cases suitable for analysis, there were only two patients with questionable anxiety tolerance. One case, the *Obese Woman*, had a need to act in the face of impulse pressure: she engaged in a sadomasochistic sexual perversion with her husband, had episodes of kleptomania, and was a compulsive eater. Despite these suggestions of ego weakness and her strong oral-narcissistic features, the posttreatment researchers believed that a proper handling of the oral aggression toward the preoedipal mother would have resulted in a better outcome. The only other case of *possible* weakness of anxiety tolerance was the *Medical Specialist*, who presented symptoms of addiction to drugs and alcohol. His use of barbiturates started following an automobile accident which necessitated a number of painful surgical procedures. Over the subsequent years he resorted to the drug to help tide him over emotional pressures, but would characteristically cure himself of his addiction by "holing up" in a hotel for several days. He was not a chronic alcoholic; in fact, except for occasional alcoholic binges, he maintained a high level of professional activity until the time of his hospitalization. The Initial Study Group believed that while his anxiety tolerance was not high, it was "adequate" for analysis starting in the hospital because his symptoms were episodic and self-limiting. His preferred mode of handling anxiety was to engage in compulsive hard work, and it was only when this defense failed that he sought drugs and alcohol. His ability to carry through a regimen of solitary withdrawal bespoke a capacity to summon up high levels of anxiety tolerance. The excellent analytic result in this case with good conflict and symptom resolution and characterological modification tended to support this view of the patient's potentially good anxiety tolerance.

The other cases where psychoanalysis was indicated were described initially as showing *high* anxiety tolerance. Even the *English Professor*, who was seen in retrospect as having borderline features related to vulnerability of ego boundaries, was described both initially and after treatment as a person of high anxiety tolerance. Though phobic in the presence of large groups he consistently exposed himself to anxiety-laden situations in an attempt to overcome his emotional handicap.

An interesting refinement in the anxiety tolerance assessment was required for a patient who revealed a generally good capacity to tolerate anxiety but was hampered in dealing with specific conflict areas. The *Adoptive Mother* obtained a good analytic result insofar as she was able to achieve a partial resolution of conflicts concerning dependence and aggression with concomitant modification of a rigid superego. She had sought treatment because of inability to assume a feminine, maternal role (she had to return an adopted child to the agency after a couple of weeks) based upon a marked hostile identification with her mother. Although she was able to become more accepting of her femininity, she was not able in the analysis to deal with the roots of this problem, i.e., her conflict-ridden anger toward the preoedipal mother. This patient could tolerate uncovering her aggression toward men, and could even face her aggressive impulses toward children; but she could not deal with the aggression toward mother-figures, as suggested on the psychological tests and particularly on the TAT, where she linked the experience of aggression toward mother with being insane or being a psychopathic killer. When this material threatened to emerge in the analysis she began to avail herself of rationalizations, ready at hand, to terminate the analysis.

A second case showing a similar specific limitation to

tolerate a particular conflictual constellation was that of the *Snake Phobia Woman*, whose major conflicts around sexual identity, depreciation of femininity, and phallic competitiveness produced uncontrolled temper outbursts toward her two children. While substantial treatment achievements were realized during the two-and-a-half-year analysis—the symptomatic distress was much alleviated, and the marital relationship was somewhat improved with a partial resolution of the underlying phallic-oedipal conflicts—the transference neurosis was never brought to a full successful analytic resolution. At the point of termination there were persistent unresolved strong transference fixations, a conglomerate of dependent needs, erotic incestuous fantasying, and some unresolved anger at the disappointing analyst. The patient had terminated prematurely because of a significant disruptive and avoidant pattern associated with fright at facing the intensity of her positive erotic longings and the extent of her childhood frustration and reactive anger. She was satisfied with feeling considerably better, and glad to "quit while she was ahead." There were compelling external factors which also contributed to the premature termination but intrapsychically, despite a good overall ego structure, the patient was unable to tolerate the frustration of intense erotic feelings.

Thus, low anxiety tolerance generally contraindicates psychoanalysis. In our study addictive symptoms such as alcoholism and drug addiction were usually associated with nonanalyzability, although there was one notable exception, the *Medical Specialist*, a patient whose addictive symptoms tended to be episodic and more painful to himself than to others. Disorders of impulse expression such as kleptomania, perversion, promiscuity, etc., also do not bode well for analysis although, as in the case of addiction, the context of these symptoms and their qualitative nature must be considered. The cases for whom psychoanalysis was deemed indicated were generally in retrospect those described both initially and at termination as showing high anxiety tolerance. In fact, the *English Professor* had to cope with an ego defect of a borderline nature, his high anxiety tolerance enabled him to achieve a fairly successful outcome. There were two instances of good overall anxiety tolerance, but with inability to tolerate certain specific conflicts and aspects of the transference, in which the outcome of analysis was limited.

MOTIVATION

Related to anxiety tolerance is the capacity to view one's life difficulties in terms of internal, rather than external, problems; this is a first step in developing a motivational push to change one's habitual mode of relating oneself to others. Psychoanalysis in particular among the therapeutic modalities requires a willingness and capacity to withstand considerable frustration of one's wishes. It also demands of the patient considerable initiative in coming to grips with his problems insofar as he is faced with a situation of minimal external cues and structuring. Weak or questionable motivation is often regarded as a sufficient indication for face-to-face treatment. Conversely, the predictors occasionally considered high motivation as a factor counterbalancing ego defects which otherwise would be disqualifying.

As one might expect, the patients with the lowest initial motivation showed the poorest outcome. Two of the alcoholic patients (*Script Writer, Alcoholic Heir*) came to treatment only under considerable external pressure. They denied the seriousness of their drinking, and stayed in treatment less than a year. The *Alcoholic Doctor* came to treatment largely as an act of compliance to the wishes of his wife and parents, who were quite concerned by the steady downhill trend of his life. His own sense of participation in this decision was minimal. Contrary to the above three patients, the fourth (*Suspended Student*) was viewed initially as possessing good "cultivatable" motivation despite low insight into his three or four amnesic episodes, which he essentially viewed as "foreign bodies," unrelated to other aspects of his personality. Even more significant, but unfortunately only in retrospect, was the fact that the patient was required by the dean of his professional school to become involved in psychiatric treatment before his suspension for unethical behavior would be lifted. The combination of entering treatment under duress and a strong paranoid potential (not recognized at first) was a distinct deterrent to his effort to use treatment for personal change. He began to withdraw from treatment shortly after being reinstated by the school authorities.

Another group of patients were *ostensibly* motivated, but their desire for change was less strong than their guiding fantasy of finding nurturance and protection under the wing of a messianic figure.[5] The *Editor* struggled for years to get his family to finance his psychiatric treatment. The sacrifices made by the *Historian* in time and money with the conscious motivation of attempting to improve his relationships with women was actually part of an unconscious effort to find gratification in the treatment process itself and to withdraw from other relationships except perhaps those concerned with his work. The *Good Son* seemed initially to have the desire to change his inhibited, anhedonic, and solitary existence into one with more freedom and pleasure. But his underlying orientation of waiting for the superman therapist to make him into a new and more effective person ultimately transcended his own

5. Dr. Ann Appelbaum has written a paper (1972) on varying degrees and kinds of motivation based on the project's patients.

capacity and wish to pursue this goal with a sustained inner push. The predictors believed that the *Travel Phobia Woman*, although a definite candidate for an insoluble transference neurosis on the basis of intense oral fixation, would begin to develop anxiety as well as a sufficient motivation for change when deprived of the drugs to which she had become habituated and when frustrated by the analyst's interpretations instead of the hoped-for gratification and support. Actually, she was able to derive considerable gratification from the analytic process by clinging to her anaclitic fantasy of the all-giving analyst. She avoided free association and consistently attempted to present herself in a favorable light by making "gifts" to her analyst of her various adaptive achievements.

It was also possible for other patients to convert the analytic situation into one of support and gratification. The *Raconteur* was singled out by the predictors as likely to decompensate further under the regressive pressures of the analytic process because of his weak hold on reality. But as mentioned in Chapter 4, he appeared to derive considerable gratification from indulging himself in reminiscences, reveries, and memories of early childhood with very little focus on his current relationships and problems, either within the analysis or in his outside life. These productions were geared to the megalomanic fantasy that the all-powerful analyst, a narcissistic extension of his own exalted self-concept, would ultimately rescue him. A similar process, although on a less primitive and psychotic level, occurred in the case of the *Prince* whose "free associations" focused upon those exploits which gained him favor and applause in the eyes of the analyst.

The predictors expected that most of the patients starting with either low or limited motivation would eventually develop sufficient motivation to engage in the difficult and arduous task of analysis. With regard to the two alcoholic, poorly motivated patients (*Alcoholic Heir, Script Writer*), the researchers initially believed that a sufficiently long period of hospitalization would provide the necessary external control over their drinking and, at the same time, would provide them with an opportunity to develop a stable therapeutic alliance with the analyst. Unfortunately, the assumption that hospitalization could supply the necessary support and control for building sufficient motivation was never tested since both patients insisted on leaving the hospital shortly after beginning analytic treatment and disrupted the analysis shortly thereafter.

One important facet of the desire for change is the patient's life circumstances. The predictors assumed that the presence of "neurotic life circumstances" (relatively immutable factors working against an alteration of the patient's behavior) inhibited motivation, and hence intrapsychic change. In the few instances where this proposition was tested, it tended to be strengthened. The *Divorced Teacher* started treatment during a tenuous marriage, and the predictors forecasted that should a divorce occur, there would be a limitation in the treatment result because of the difficult life situation into which she would be thrust. Actually, the patient was divorced by her husband during the course of treatment and, despite the expected conflict resolution, particularly around her phallic oedipal conflicts, she was unable to establish a gratifying new life for herself. At the end of treatment she was a divorced woman in her late thirties who had lost custody of two children, left with a small child, and with little likelihood of remarriage. Her inability to find reality gratification of her dependency needs led her to cling to her analyst as a source of comfort rather than attempt to achieve some resolution and diminution of these transference wishes. Some time after termination she still clung to the nurturing analyst as the sole source of her dependent gratifications.

Motivation for change is also affected by the degree to which a symptom or behavior pattern is ego-syntonic. The predictors were generally quite accurate in anticipating the kinds of treatment problems likely to emerge as a result of high ego-syntonicity in certain areas. In two instances, however, in which they correctly assessed the fixity and rigidity of oral strivings, their forecast of extent of change and how the change would come about went awry. In the case of the *Phobic Woman* they correctly expected that her ego-syntonic expectation of indefinite nurturance would constitute a major problem in the treatment, and this problem was felt not to be amenable to significant change by analytic methods. She was viewed as an infantile, demanding person whose phobia for being left alone had blocked her husband's career while at the same time making it necessary for her well-to-do parents to become her chief source of financial support. The patient's capacity to bend the environment according to her own neurotic wishes was viewed by the predictors as evidence for viewing her as an intensely oral-demanding person. But this assessment apparently did not take into account the willingness of her family to be burdened and abused in this way. Even though the patient had strong ego-syntonic expectations of nurturance, the treatment revealed that she was equally intent on competitively controlling and downgrading the male figures in her environment. Thus, the predictors' anticipation that analytic interpretation of her ego-syntonic oral expectations would not make any substantial difference was not quite correct: she was able to give up a good deal of her oral demandingness, partly on the basis of such wishes becoming more ego-dystonic and partly because of a transference wish to please the analyst by displaying mature patterns of behavior.

A slight error in the opposite direction occurred with regard to the *Tantrum Woman* who used her temper displays to manipulate the environment into complying with her infantile expectations. While ego-syntonic at the outset of treatment, her outbursts were predicted to yield to analytic interpretation. Her ego assets were adjudged sufficiently high (including a high general motivation for change) to predict that she would eventually give up her tantrums by means of interpretation alone. The analyst discovered, however, that even though he developed a good understanding of the patient's unmanageable "affect storms," interpretations had little or no impact upon her. There were repeated episodes of torrential affective outpourings which obliterated all of the patient's reasoning processes and essentially prevented her from hearing the analyst. The analyst finally began to intervene more firmly and insistently—in effect telling the patient to cut out the shouting. After the introduction of this parameter, the analyst was able to work out the various meanings of the affect storms, including the patient's effort to defend against the erotization of the transference and her effort to get the analyst to force her into a submissive role. A similar parameter was used for the *English Professor*, who was content to remain indefinitely on a plateau of no change or improvement; the analyst interrupted the patient's fantasy of external nurturance by imposing a termination date. The predictors had expected him to attempt to make his treatment interminable.

In summary, patients with the poorest motivation (outright denial of illness, acceptance of treatment under external duress) fare badly in analysis and tend to have brief courses of treatment. On the other hand, patients who come to treatment with high motivation do not necessarily show a good response, particularly those with a strong unconscious motivation to find unending succorance. Neurotic life circumstances tend to inhibit intrapsychic change, partly because the environment discourages such change and partly because the patient seeks gratification in the treatment relationship rather than analytic understanding. Ego-syntonicity of behavior patterns tends to deter change, and, in some instances, may require the introduction of special parameters in order to induce movement.

SUMMARY

1. Twenty-two patients in this study began psychoanalysis; four were shifted to one of the other therapeutic modalities after the therapist decided that analysis was too stressful for the patient. Based upon the findings of the various research teams, the Prediction Study Group made retrospective judgments about the suitability of each case for analysis and decided that nine had been suitable cases for analysis, ten unsuitable, and three fell into the questionable category. The research team at the initial point had predicted an unsuccessful outcome for two cases and had expressed considerable doubt about the prospects for four others. All six were ultimately placed in the unsuitable category.

2. Borderline personality organizations with a potential for psychotic reactions emerged clearly in five cases during analysis, and in one instance afterward. This group of patients tended to react with delusional thinking, either within the transference or in their life situations. One patient who was described as showing borderline features associated with a primitive conflict concerning the loss of ego boundaries was successfully treated; psychotic ideation did not develop and he was found to possess some notable ego strengths.

3. All of the patients in the borderline category showed predominant oral fixations. In addition, there were seven nonborderline individuals whose conflicts were predominantly at the oral level. Three eventually fell into the suitable category, three into the unsuitable group, and one was considered questionable for analysis. We found that the predominance of oral conflicts—particularly when associated with alloplastic symptoms, strong passive features, or intense narcissistic needs—frequently contraindicates psychoanalysis. Although

some patients with predominant oral fixations were capable of being analyzed, the resolution of their oral conflicts was never more than partial.

4. In contrast, all eight patients with predominant phallic conflicts were judged to be analyzable, even though only four were successfully analyzed. Patients with predominantly phallic fixations are more amenable to analytic treatment than are those who show predominantly pregenital conflicts, and phallic conflicts as opposed to oral ones show a greater readiness to being resolved.

5. Three analytic patients were described as predominantly masochistic while six others were initially described as showing strong masochistic features. These masochistic factors were not in themselves crucial determinants of outcome, but when combined with other ego weaknesses, contributed to the failure of psychoanalysis to bring about significant improvement.

6. The capacity to tolerate the experience of anxiety without resorting to either autoplastic or alloplastic devices which would disrupt the patient's life or his treatment distinguished well between the suitable and unsuitable cases. Most of the "contraindicated" and questionable cases showed definitely low tolerance for anxiety prior to the beginning of treatment. Two did not show disruptive symptoms, but revealed extreme rigidity in their defensive organization. Conversely, only two of the indicated cases revealed low or questionable anxiety tolerance and one of these initially revealed a high potential for developing this capacity. Low anxiety tolerance was mainly associated with symptoms of impulse disorders such as alcoholism, drug addiction, kleptomania, perversion, and promiscuity.

7. The four patients with weak initial motivation (outright denial of illness, acceptance of treatment under external duress) fared badly in analysis and tended to interrupt early in the course of treatment. On the other hand, there were four other cases who came to treatment with ostensibly high motivation

who also did not show a good response and fell into the unsuitable category. They revealed a strong unconscious motivation to find unending protection and succorance in the analysis.

CHAPTER 6

CONFLICT RESOLUTION AND BEHAVIORAL CHANGE

Basic to the expressive aspects of psychotherapy, and particularly to psychoanalysis, is a group of assumptions describing the effects of conflict resolution. The supportive aspects of psychotherapy may produce personality change through a variety of mechanisms such as corrective emotional experience, need gratification, and introjection of the therapist's values. But the expressive-uncovering method involves a laying bare of the patient's unconscous conflicts, demonstrating them to him mainly in the transference relationship, and inducing change in those aspects of personality which had formerly been used in the service of defending against the anxiety associated with these conflicts. Thus, where passive and masochistic character defenses are used to deal with the anxiety and guilt associated with the patient's oedipal strivings, associated in his mind with the expression of sexual impulses, the uncovering and working through of his irrational fears permits him to assume a more active stance toward life problems and to become less self-defeating.

113

Theoretically, the successful resolution of conflict in the expressive psychotherapies should result in the following effects:

1. There should be at least a proportional change in the patient's character, symptoms, and life-style. We observe here the conception of *proportionality* between conflict resolution and personality change. Conflict resolution, not an all-or-none affair, actually ranges along a continuum from zero to an ideal, never-attained complete and full resolution. Pfeffer (1959), in fact, presents evidence that successful psychoanalytic treatment produces a "bleaching" effect upon the person's conflicts, to a greater or lesser extent, and that these conflicts continue to lie dormant and may be temporarily reactivated when external pressures and stresses become sufficiently intense. Nonexpressive aspects of the treatment contribute to personality change, and therefore one might expect that the psychological changes resulting from an uncovering mode of treatment would in many instances be greater than those associated with conflict resolution alone. One would expect a cumulative effect in which the changes due to conflict resolution could be supplemented by changes induced by the supportive aspects of treatment.

2. A most important corollary of this proportionality hypothesis is what we may refer to as the *necessity* hypothesis: conflict resolution is necessary in order to achieve change in those symptoms, character traits, and life-styles which are rooted in lifelong deeply repressed conflict. Thus, patients may be able to achieve a number of useful and adaptive changes by means of the supportive aspects. They may be able to alter self-defeating and narcissistic behaviors; they may enhance their self-esteem and thus achieve a more effective use of their talents and abilities; and they may perceive more accurately the impact of their behavior upon other people. But behaviors which are mainly conflict-determined may be altered only by ferreting out and resolving such conflict. Examples of these behaviors will be discussed later in the form of specific predictions.

3. A third major effect assumed to be associated with conflict resolution is that of *stability* of change. Changes associated with the supportive aspects of treatment are considered more vulnerable to relapse than are those stemming from conflict resolution. Symptoms resolved by expressive-uncovering methods are generally considered unlikely to reappear except transitorily and in attenuated form. In contrast, changes based upon supportive measures are usually considered less enduring and more likely to reappear under adverse conditions.

A methodological question which must be borne in mind throughout this discussion is the danger of circularity whenever one deals with the examination of the concomitants of conflict resolution. Conflict resolution is an intrapsychic variable which must be assessed by evidence which is independent of the psychological changes which are ordinarily *assumed* to result from it. If changes in symptoms, character traits, and life-style are used to gauge the extent of conflict resolution, then obviously one cannot legitimately test the assumption that character resolution produces at least a proportional change in these aspects of personality. One must take special care that the assessment of conflict resolution is based upon factors independent of these personality changes, including interview data reflecting transference resolution, treatment notes demonstrating the uncovering and working through of conflict, and psychological test changes.

THE ASSUMPTION OF PROPORTIONALITY

"To the extent that a resolution of unconscious conflict occurs via the acquisition of insight, there is at least a proportional change in symptoms, character traits, and character structure." This assumption expresses a basic explanatory idea underlying psychoanalytic treatment. The dichotomy between supportive and expressive approaches is expressed in this hypothesis which clearly states that the treatment objective is behavioral change, *not* simply by means of transference cure, gratification of infantile wishes, and corrective emotional experience—but rather by means of a modification or alteration of the underlying conflict producing the behavior. Psychoanalysis is assumed to be the optimum method for achieving conflict resolution, even though the ideal of full or complete conflict resolution is never attained, only approached. Residuals of old conflicts always remain dormant, ready to be mobilized by sufficiently intense conflict triggers, even if only in a muted form and for a brief period.

The proposition is stated in the form of minimum proportionality; i.e., change will be *at least* proportional to the degree of conflict resolution. Behind this is the reasoning that no expressive psychotherapy, not even analysis, is devoid of supportive elements and supportive-type mechanisms. Thus, a symptom change may be explained partly on the basis of conflict resolution but may be augmented as well by certain supportive dynamisms.

Our research population contained eight cases where some degree of significant conflict resolution occurred. For the purpose of assessing the proportionality hypothesis, a vignette of each of these cases will be examined with regard to the two elements of interest: (1) nature and degree of conflict resolution and (2) its relation to symptom and behavioral change. Ideally, this hypothesis should be treated in quantitative form but these two variables were not rated numerically. Hence we can only discuss the proposition in terms of rough approximations. The cases will be discussed in a descending order of degree of conflict resolution.

MEDICAL SPECIALIST

The *Medical Specialist* at the age of forty-one was brought
for psychiatric hospitalization because of violent temper
outbursts, superimposed upon a long-standing drug addiction and episodic alcoholism. A hardworking, compulsive
individual, he was mainly conflicted over phallic competitive strivings and had decompensated into oral addictive
symptoms. Following an analysis of seven years' duration,
he was judged by the research team to have substantially
resolved his core oedipal conflicts. He had achieved a
transference resolution concerning guilt over competitiveness with the father-analyst. The associated character
change was that he no longer found it necessary to
alternate between the extremes of passive submission and
rebelliousness against the perceived castrated position.
Also, he worked out a pattern of first evading and then
betraying the cold, threatening mother. His drug and
alcohol symptoms, used both to express and to defend
against these painful conflicts, disappeared entirely. He
was able to remove himself from a highly neurotic and
conflict-laden first marriage and entered into a more
gratifying second one. At follow-up the patient consolidated
his treatment gains, and showed a capacity to deal with a
variety of new stresses, and a distinct increase in his ability
to tolerate anxiety without having to act impulsively. Thus,
the high degree of conflict resolution correlates with
character and symptom change.

TANTRUM WOMAN

The *Tantrum Woman*, twenty-four years old and recently

widowed, came for psychiatric treatment suffering from a depressive and regressive reaction to the traumatic death of her husband, superimposed upon conflicted and unhappy relationships, especially with her mother. The patient's core conflict centered around her hostile-dependent tie to a mother who was perceived as smothering and overprotective as well as ungiving and frustrating. Added to these oral conflicts were phallic-hysterical difficulties manifested by a generalized inhibition. The patient's analysis occurred in two parts, the first treatment lasting almost five years; two years later (in the course of her research follow-up interviews) she decided to resume the analysis which lasted another four years. In the interim she had remarried and was experiencing an exacerbation of incompletely resolved difficulties with her new husband. The main thrust of the analytic work in the first phase consisted of working through her penis envy and competitiveness with males, as well as the oedipal yearning for the analyst-father and rivalry with mother. Relatively untouched was the dependence upon, and homosexual submission to, the controlling, preoedipal mother. Also incompletely worked out was the close hostile identification with this negative mother imago in the patient's own life and marriage. At termination of the first treatment, and for most of the two-year follow-up period, there was evidence of very substantial progress and change in the subsidence of her symptoms, the effective management of her life, and the pursuit of her educational and career goals. There was evidence, however, of continuing anxiety, excessive attachment to her ex-analyst, and difficulty in finding new and gratifying relationships, particularly with men. Shortly after her second marriage, her major presenting symptom of anxiety attacks returned. In the reanalysis, work centered upon the dependent and oral-aggressive, destructive relationship to the analyst and mother, and the hostile identification with the "dirty, punitive argumentative" mother. The patient was able to achieve a more stable and less tension-ridden marriage although some tensions and unresolved problems persisted. The husband was to the patient still too much of a reenactment of the passive, ineffectual father who would not contol her acting up. She still clung to some extent to the idealized analyst, reflecting some residues of unresolved oedipal and preoedipal conflicts. Again we may say there was an approximately proportional relationship between our two variables: hostile dependency to the mother introject as well as phallic problems were partly resolved, and symptomatic manifestations of these problems were reduced.

PHOBIC WOMAN

The *Phobic Woman* came for treatment at the age of twenty-three with severe anxiety and crippling phobias of many years' duration, for which she had been in psychotherapy intermittently since the age of fifteen. Just prior to treatment, her anxiety had reached the point where she would not permit her husband to be out of her sight. The research team at termination believed that her symptoms were largely based on penis envy and fear of oedipal sexual temptations and dangers expressed in pervasive prostitution fantasies and that these fantasies had contributed significantly to her fear of being alone. After five years of analysis the patient's major conflicts were partly resolved. Fuller resolution of her oedipal-phallic problems was not attained because the patient assumed a childlike, compliant stance toward the analyst, attempting to please him with mature behavior both within and outside of the analysis. These compliant efforts resulted in a toning down of oedipal fantasies within the transference. Nor was her orality resolved to any great degree analytically, because the analyst did not consistently interpret the basic stance of the patient (a good compliant girl who pleases her father and thus is taken care of and protected by him). Also relatively untouched was the hostile identification with mother and its attendant feelings of maternal deprivation. At termination the patient had been able to achieve a number of very significant gains which were largely maintained during the follow-up period. She was leading an active and productive life, no longer crippled by phobic symptoms. There were occasional blowups of neurotic anxiety, with periodic recourse to tranquilizing drugs but she had been able to liberate herself from her excessive dependency upon her husband and her parents. The partial working through of the neurotic conflict around her inhibited sexual and competitive aggressive feelings toward her husband and toward men in general undoubtedly contributed to the patient's ability to liberate her husband from the enslavement which she had imposed upon him. In addition to her castrating wishes, the patient was unconsciously striving to prevent him from becoming too much like her successful father by attempting to keep him tied tightly to her. But equally, if not more important, was the encouragement and support and dedication of the analyst which prompted this patient to become a more independent and mature person and to assume more responsible adult roles. She did this largely to gratify him and in so doing found gratification in her achievements. Thus, the substantial behavioral change was based partly on conflict resolution but also resulted in large measure from a "transference cure."

SNAKE PHOBIA WOMAN

The *Snake Phobia Woman*, twenty-eight years old and married, sought psychiatric treatment because of temper outbursts, increasing in tempo and intensity, directed at her children. She feared that her episodic loss of control presaged losing her mind. Her analysis lasted for two and a half years and was colored by the special circumstance of a "weekend marriage" in which she would be living away from home during the week in order to be close to the analyst, and only return home for the weekend. In reviewing the analytic process, the research team at termination stated that the patient found it difficult to face transference fantasies explicitly, both negative and positive, but particularly the latter. The analyst felt unable to elicit and analyze the full scope of her positive transference longings and the patient terminated treatment as a defense against her strong erotic transference feelings. In the course of the treatment the patient had become more aware of her intense envy of men, based largely upon hostility and competition toward her twin brother; her marital difficulties and sexual inhibitions, related to guilt over incestuous longings and anger over their frustration, were partly resolved. The patient's core conflicts around sexual identity and her need to depreciate men as weak, unreliable, and disappointing, were reduced in intensity, though not fully resolved. Her conflict with her mother and the identification with her in the effort to solve her dilemmas, to be the capable phallic woman who would eventually dominate the man, was even less worked with analytically. These partial resolutions were reflected in the patient's partial symptomatic improvement. A major presenting problem, temper outbursts at the children, was largely abated since her son no longer represented her hated twin brother and her daughter no longer her own deprived self. Other symptoms like hostile upsurges, acute depressive experiences, asthmatic attacks, and her snake phobias were markedly decreased. She continued to find her relationship with her husband frustrating and at times painful, but her marital distress was now less neurotically determined and more directly related to provocation by him. The symptom and behavioral changes she was able to achieve seemed to be proportional to the extent of conflict resolution.

ADOPTIVE MOTHER

The *Adoptive Mother*, a twenty-eight-year-old married woman, sought psychiatric treatment because of her inability to be a proper mother, culminating in returning an adopted child to the adoption agency after four months of mounting distress. In the course of her three-year analysis the patient achieved certain partial resolutions of conflict. She became more aware and better able to tolerate oral passive strivings and her wish to be mothered as a counterpart of the expressed desire to be a mother. Aggressive and hostile impulses were also more in awareness and allowed somewhat more direct expression without concomitantly arousing depression and guilt. But her core problem concerning feminine sexuality, penis envy, aggressive competitiveness with men and a need to dominate them, though somewhat more conscious, was not substantially changed. Her inability to achieve full acceptance of her femininity was linked to the continued repression of her hostile identification with the negative mother image. When the analysis was beginning to uncover this area of conflict, the patient began to plan for termination. During the follow-up period the patient was able to undertake successfully the adoption of a child, though not without considerable stress and anxiety for which she sought religious counseling and, occasionally, she relied upon sedative drugs. She had achieved a somewhat more stable and affectionate relationship with her husband, though a somewhat restricted sexual life persisted. Her greater conscious tolerance for her dependency had made it possible for her to become a mother capable of gratifying a dependent child without experiencing intolerable jealousy and antagonism. Her greater tolerance for hostile aggressive impulses made it easier for her to tolerate the child. But the underlying conflicts relating to the disturbing symptom were never really worked out: her underlying hatred for the rejecting and frustrating mother which prevented acceptance of a feminine-maternal role. Thus, the fact that she could go through with the adoption only with considerable emotional strain was evidence that this alleviation of symptoms was occurring in conjunction with only a partial resolution of conflict.

DIVORCED TEACHER

The *Divorced Teacher*, a thirty-year-old woman, married eight years, was referred for analysis because of deterioration in her marriage, marked by six years of bitter quarreling in which the patient felt constantly driven to question the love and fidelity of her husband. Her marital strife was a neurotic reenactment of her phallic competitive problems with men, as well as her identification with a domineering, nagging mother who tended to drive off the depreciated father. She experienced a deep-seated sense of frustrated oral dependency with concomitant oral demandingness. The analysis was conducted under the unusual circumstance of the analysand being separated by hundreds of miles from her husband and children. This condition not only complicated the analytic work but contributed in part to the husband suing for divorce and ultimately winning custody of the children. In the course of the five-year-long analysis the patient did indeed work out her phallic oedipal conflicts, including her feelings of disappointment in men, the angry provocations of her husband, and her revengeful castrative competitiveness with men. Never explicitly worked through, however, was the more primitive, oral dependent and homosexually tinged attachment to the mother. At the end of the analysis the initially presenting symptoms were abated, although the patient was no longer involved in a conflict-ridden marriage. She felt herself to be more feminine and better able to relate herself to men, but she continued to feel quite guilty over the way she had broken up her marriage. In her actual life she was depressively withdrawn and avoided the opportunity to meet men. There continued to be a depressive, guilt-ridden cast to her life. Strong dependency feelings toward the analyst were still in evidence after termination. Thus, the resolution and abatement of the phallic conflict, while apparently contributing to subjective feelings of enhanced femininity and acceptance of men, did not seem to be sufficient to permit her to actively seek out new relationships with men to replace the one she had lost. Could her persisting withdrawal, depression, and guilt be understood in terms of her unresolved oral dependency and oral demandingness? Could it be understood in terms of the shadow cast on her life by the loss of her children and her guilt associated with her role in this? Thus, despite the resolution of phallic oedipal problems the patient did not seem to be able to use her newfound freedom from conflict to apply it in bettering her life. Here we have an instance of a possible refutation of the proportionality hypothesis. Despite an apparent resolution of the patient's core problems associated with relationships to men, there was not a concomitant change in her behavior. Unless other factors prevented the emergence of her potential for new behavior, we have a disconfirming case.

ENGLISH PROFESSOR

The *English Professor*, a thirty-five-year-old single man, sought psychoanalytic treatment because of anxiety attacks, "fear reactions" which gripped him in almost every social and professional situation. He was seen as a compliant, inhibited, conscientious individual with a notable capacity for perseverance and hard work and with prominent oral and phallic problems. The patient underwent a six-year-long analysis, brought to an end only after the analyst unilaterally set a termination date in view of the impasse which had been reached. Despite an extensive range of insights into the meaning of his symptoms which helped him achieve partial mastery and control, the patient's underlying difficulties turned out to be of a borderline nature (the struggle against the loss of identity, loss of self, being swallowed up and fused), and this central ego weakness could only be partly overcome. As for intrapsychic change, the patient seemed to have achieved some capacity to give up his inordinate and persistent dependency needs and to recognize that such wishes could never be fulfilled. He learned there was no "golden apple" as a reward for his persistent efforts. His more mature behavior resulting from this recognition and acceptance resulted in enhanced self-esteem. In consonance with these internal changes was the fact that the patient's phobias and anxiety (in speaking before large classes, for example) were abated to some degree. He was able to take greater responsibility in directing his life and in his commitment to a woman. But the underlying primitive fears of fusion and loss of identity prevented him from achieving freedom from sexual inhibition and full freedom to commit himself to a close and intimate relationship.

PHOBIC GIRL

The *Phobic Girl*, a twenty-one-year-old obese young woman, was referred for psychiatric hospitalization and then psychotherapy with the chief presenting symptoms of a regressed, infantile, dependent life and chief presenting complaints of crippling phobias, including intense fears of being away from home, of the dark, of small enclosed spaces from which she could not readily escape. Her core neurotic conflict consisted mainly of inordinate oral demandingness and regression to infantile dependency in interaction with the parents' aggressive efforts to exploit her as but a narcissistic extension of their own ungratified neurotic strivings. Secondarily, there was a shadowy superimposed oedipal conflict. The patient was in a supportive-expressive psychotherapy for a period of seven years, the only patient in this group who was not treated by psychoanalysis. Although the patient achieved a more mature and more responsible attitude toward herself and others, the basis of this change was characterized by the termination research team as mainly a "transference cure": she had improved her controls and modified her behavior in more socially acceptable ways as a way of pleasing the therapist and expressing her gratitude for his interest. But the researchers observed that the patient had also shown a significant shift and *advance* in her core conflicts. She was less concerned and preoccupied with problems of oral dependent pressures and of rage over oral frustration, and much more concerned with oedipal issues involving feminine role questions and feelings about equaling and possibly surpassing her mother's achievements as a wife and parent. These intrapsychic changes were consonant with a much improved life situation involving a successful and stable marriage, a considerable abatement of her masochistic behaviors, and a considerable decrease in the number and intensity of phobias. Her obesity, however, was essentially unaltered. These changes seemed to be based largely on the patient's efforts to please her therapist and were reinforced by a heightened self-esteem when she accomplished these gains. Conflict resolution was minor at best but seemed to make some contribution to these changes.

In summary, there was a trend in the data which confirmed the proposition that changes in symptoms, character traits, and life-style are *at least* proportional to the extent of conflict resolution. We did not have quantitative ratings available on these two variables and therefore could not examine the proposition with greater precision. But there was unquestionably a trend toward more behavioral change as a consequence of greater conflict resolution and vice versa. Insofar as certain conflicts remained untouched, symptoms and anxieties tended to persist. The *Snake Phobia Woman* left treatment before she had dealt adequately with her erotic attachment to the analyst-father, although her competitiveness with men had indeed been a major piece of analytic work. Her relationship with her children improved, reflecting an abatement of competition with her siblings, but her marital relationship was only partly better. The *Phobic Woman's* underlying dependency was never worked through and her continuing anxiety reflected this unresolved problem. On the other hand, her incapacitating phobias and need to cripple her husband's professional growth significantly abated partly as a result of the partial resolution of phallic conflicts. The *Medical Specialist*, in contrast, was dealing with a primary phallic problem which he had resolved thoroughly with resulting improvement of symptoms and behavior.

The hypothesis of proportionality, of course, does not call for an exactly proportional relationship between conflict resolution and behavioral change. In response to supportive interventions, we know that there are changes which make great differences in people's lives. Frequently these supportively based changes are even more significant than the changes occurring due to conflict resolution. Perhaps the *Phobic Woman* is the best example of this: a "transference cure" was a major factor in change while conflict resolution was relatively limited.

But the reverse condition, i.e., less behavioral change than conflict resolution, should not occur according to the proportionality hypothesis. The only instance of such an occurrence was that of the *Divorced Teacher* who had achieved a considerable modification intrapsychically in her need to depreciate men but was unable to establish a gratifying relationship with a man at the conclusion of treatment. Reality factors, like her age and having a small child, may have been contributing factors. But even more significant was a sense of guilt and self-depreciation, a feeling that she had "nothing to offer" a man, which prevented her from actively trying to form such a relationship. These feelings were apparently based upon the actual suffering she had inflicted upon her ex-husband and children, and were related to her loss of custody of the children. These life experiences seemed to have left a strong enough impression to handicap her future relationships with men, despite the resolution of her conflicts.

THE ASSUMPTION OF NECESSITY

According to the assumption of necessity, "Symptoms, character traits, and life-style rooted in lifelong, deeply repressed intrapsychic conflict are significantly altered only on the basis of a full working through of conflict." In other words, conflict resolution is a *necessary* condition for certain kinds of change. The form of this proposition makes it relatively easy to disprove in the sense that it is a general, rather than a correlational, proposition. Thus, one clear instance of a significant and stable change occurring in a patient without conflict resolution would be sufficient to refute the assumption in question. Note that the assumption of proportionality, discussed in the previous section, was essentially a correlational proposition and in a strict sense required quantitative ratings for validation.

We have available fifteen instances in which the necessity assumption was tested, and *in almost 50 percent of the cases the proposition was negated.* Even though the assumption was clearly invalidated, it will be instructive to review the several instances of where change was not expected by the predictors unless conflict resolution occurred and where such change did in fact occur without essential modification of the related intrapsychic conflict.

First, there was the *Adoptive Mother* whose presenting symptom was her inability to adopt a child. The dynamic formulation involved a marked conflict over femininity based upon a deeply repressed hatred for mother; these impulses were triggered by the patient's attempts to assume a more feminine role, particularly when she tried to become a mother, which aroused intolerable anxiety. The predictors stated unequivocally that the patient would not be able to carry through an adoption (her first unsuccessful attempt made her decide to seek treatment) unless she was able to resolve the basic underlying conflict with mother. They stated further that other aspects of feminine life, including warm affectionate relationships with her husband and sexual responsiveness, would also not be attained unless the patient resolved these conflicts. The predictors were, in fact, proven wrong by the outcome of the analysis. The patient achieved a number of gains in her analysis, including an increased ability to tolerate her own aggressive feelings and a better acceptance of her dependency strivings. But she terminated analysis just at the time her core conflict (hostile identification with mother) was beginning to surface. The research team felt that despite her good overall ego strength she lacked the ability to tolerate the anxieties associated with this particular problem. With regard to her relationship with her husband, she was able to become somewhat warmer and closer to him although her sexual inhibitions were not substantially changed. Adoption of another child was accompanied by considerable stress and involved reliance on tranquilizing drugs, religious counseling, and casework help from the adoption agency.

A somewhat similar incident occurred in the case of the

Snake Phobia Woman who came to treatment mainly because of rage attacks toward her children. In addition, she experienced considerable marital conflict and was disturbed by a snake phobia. These symptoms were viewed as a reflection of her hostile competitive attitudes toward men and her poorly resolved oedipal attachment. The predictors expected that her major symptoms would not be altered unless her intrapsychic conflicts were analyzed and resolved. The research team at termination believed that considerable analytic work was accomplished but that the patient fell short of a thoroughgoing resolution of oedipal problems, particularly an inability to deal adequately with the sexual aspects of the transference to the analyst-father. Yet the patient was able to achieve significant changes in her major symptoms including an improved relationship with her children, a diminution of her phobia, and better ability to cope with her marriage. The partial resolution of conflict was bolstered by certain supportive aspects, and permitted this patient to achieve the desired changes.

An even clearer instance of disconfirmation of the necessity assumption occurred in the case of the *Phobic Girl* who came to treatment because of her infantile dependency, lifelong obesity, severe phobias, and sexual promiscuity. The predictors stated that unless she could modify her deeply rooted oral conflicts she would not be able to marry successfully nor would she be able to overcome her phobias. Neither of these predictions was correct, inasmuch as the patient actually made a fairly good and stable marriage despite the continuing presence of underlying oral conflicts. The underlying dynamic basis for these changes was not conflict resolution. Rather, there was a large element of "transference cure" in which the dependent child made changes in a desired direction in order to please the parent-therapist. The gratification of dependency needs in the therapeutic situation permitted more mature patterns to develop in her other relationships: she was able to make a satisfying marriage. Thus important and unexpected behavioral changes occurred despite the relatively small degree of conflict resolution.

There were at least two cases in which the research team agreed that *no* conflict resolution had taken place but where significant behavioral change had indeed occurred. One analysis (that of the *Prince*), which was considered a failure in terms of the analytic goal of resolving a regressive transference neurosis, nevertheless helped the patient to achieve a marked change in his life. An unmarried professional man in his early thirties, he came for treatment because of his inability to establish a sustained relationship with a woman. He enjoyed being pursued by women and feared committing himself to a single relationship largely because it would interfere with his narcissistic gratifications. He had an intense need for admiration and applause from others, and this characteristic proved to be the major stumbling block to the analytic work: he was unable to face painful or embarrassing aspects of himself and the uncovering process was therefore severely curtailed. The predictors believed that his basically derogatory attitudes toward women could be changed only by uncovering and resolving his conflict vis-à-vis a seductive, controlling mother introject. Such a resolution did not take place, but the patient was able to marry and establish a stable relationship with his wife, despite the presence of tensions and dissatisfactions on both sides. The dynamic basis for such a change was mainly identification with the interested and dedicated analyst who became a model for the patient in his dealings with others.

A second instance of significant symptom change without conflict resolution was the case of the *Playboy*, a twenty-seven-year-old professional man who sought treament because of a long-standing history of recurrent depression interspersed with manic periods and decompensations into paranoid thinking. He did poorly in his work because of a strong tendency to shirk unpleasant or difficult tasks. His core problems centered around intense feelings of primitive oral deprivation and reactive oral rage, all set within a borderline ego functioning. Since the patient did not possess the necessary ego strength for psychoanalysis, the predictors expected little resolution of his oral conflicts to occur, and therefore predicted that his major symptom of periodic manic and depressive attacks might be somewhat attenuated but would persist as a problem for the patient. Actually, the prediction was incorrect; both at the termination point and at follow-up the patient reported that his cyclical mood swings were a thing of the past. The patient had undergone a four-year course of supportive psychotherapy in which interpretation, probing, and uncovering were carefully avoided by the therapist. The very significant gains seemed to be built upon two major factors: the therapist in a fatherly and benevolent way helped the patient achieve gratification and enhanced self-esteem from discharging his professional responsibilities more adequately, and from building a more secure and stable marriage. Also significant was the introjection of a warmly supportive therapist which served to sustain the pervasive denial and repression of fantasies of loneliness and bleakness.

In summary, there is clear evidence that significant changes in symptoms, character traits, and life-style are capable of occurring without the uncovering and resolution of intrapsychic conflict. In the above review of cases we have observed that help with peripheral areas of conflict may contribute substantially to a patient's capacity to deal with symptoms which are primarily determined by central conflicts that remain untouched. The best example of such a situation was the *Adoptive Mother* whose inability to adopt a child was clearly based upon hostile identification with a maternal introject. Although this problem was never uncovered or resolved, the patient's greater tolerance for her own hostility as well as her increased ability to accept her dependency strivings permitted her to use a number of helping resources and agencies to find external supports sufficient to enable her to adopt a child. Another dynamic basis for change is frequently referred to as "borrowing the ego strength" of the therapist. It appears to be largely a function of an internalization or identification process in which a gratifying relationship gets substituted for an underlying fantasy or introject of a depriving figure. This appeared to be the therapeutic dynamism in the case of the *Playboy*.

THE ASSUMPTION OF STABILITY

The third cardinal assumption regarding conflict resolution was that stable change associated with psychotherapy can be achieved only when the patient's intrapsychic conflicts are resolved. Stability of change has to be assessed from two standpoints: one requirement is that the change be maintained over a given period of time, and in the case of this study we have available only a two-year follow-up period. A second facet is that the change should be relatively independent of situational pressures. The relevant assumption is that "patients treated by expressive psychotherapies with subsequent manifest relief of symptoms and shifting behavioral patterns based upon conflict resolution maintain these improvements even under the impact of external stress." The converse of this proposition is that patients who achieve change primarily via supportive measures will not be able to maintain these changes in the face of external stress and adverse situational pressure.

We propose to scrutinize this proposition by examining the stability of the successful psychoanalytic cases. Six of the psychoanalytic cases can be judged as successful in that significant change occurred in conjunction with some degree of resolution of intrapsychic conflicts. How did these patients fare over the two-year follow-up period? Four of them were able to maintain and consolidate their gains during this period. They had in some way taken on further life responsibilities in the form of marriage and children without significantly increased symptoms. The *Adoptive Mother*, for example, whose inability to adopt a child had precipitated her entering treatment, adopted another child; despite her anxiety she seemed to carry it off without any substantial recurrence of the previous decompensation. The *English Professor*'s major problem was an inability to commit himself to a permanent relationship with a woman, and during the follow-up period he was able to marry and have a child with no recurrence of symptoms. Both the *Medical Specialist* and the *Snake Phobia Woman* similarly took on increased commitments and responsibilities and maintained the gains.

Two patients, however, showed some degree of regression in the face of life pressures. The *Phobic Woman* maintained her major gains in that incapacitating phobias did not recur, but her anxiety increased sufficiently in the face of substantially increased new responsibilities, making it necessary for her to resort to tranquilizing drugs. During the follow-up period she had to deal with her competitive feelings toward an increasingly successful husband, and with the responsibilities of mothering a growing young family. She apparently had mastered her phallic competitive conflicts sufficiently to better accept a feminine role and to permit these life changes to take place, but the conflict resolution had not been thorough enough for her to master such changes with equanimity. The *Tantrum Woman* showed a similar pattern in response to substantially increased life pressures. During the follow-up period the patient, a young widow, had married a widower with two teenage children. Her ability to find and establish this new relationship was to some extent a reflection of her relative freedom from phallic conflicts. But the persistence of a strong, unresolved need to find a good mother, and her failure in her analysis to rid herself of a hostile mother introject, made the new role of wife and mother excessively stressful for her. At the end of the follow-up period she decided to reenter analysis for a second course of treatment.

The above data is *suggestive* evidence in favor of the assumption of stability insofar as the recurrence of symptoms seemed to depend upon incomplete conflict resolution. Insofar as internal problems had been dealt with and resolved in the analysis, additional life pressures did not bring about a recurrence of previous symptoms.

A more complete answer to the question of whether or not the assumption of stability is valid, however, rests on evidence from the successful supportive cases. Where changes were brought about as a result of ego strengthening not based upon uncovering or insight or conflict resolution, do the improvements prove less stable? We shall address this issue in Chapter 10 where we examine the stability of supportively induced changes.

SUMMARY

Three major assumptions concerning expressive psychotherapy and psychoanalysis were discussed: proportionality, necessity, and stability.

1. The assumption of proportionality holds that changes in symptoms, character traits, and life-style are at least proportional to the extent of conflict resolution. Although this proposition is clearly quantitative, the relevant variables were not measured and hence could not be tested with precision.

However, seven of the eight cases which showed some degree of conflict resolution tended to confirm this assumption. In one case there seemed to be certain overriding situational factors, both past and present, which prevented the patient from showing changes commensurate with her analytic accomplishments.

2. A significant finding was that the assumption of necessity was clearly invalidated. The relevant conception is that symptoms, character traits, and life-style rooted in lifelong, deeply repressed intrapsychic conflict, are significantly altered only on the basis of a full working through of conflict. Alteration in peripheral areas of conflict may contribute substantially to the patient's capacity to deal with symptoms which are primarily determined by central conflicts that remain untouched. A major "supportive" mechanism, internalization of the therapist's ego and superego attitudes, contributed to significant change without conflict resolution.

3. The stability assumption states that changes based upon conflict resolution permit the patient to maintain these improvements even under the impact of external stress. Four of the six successful psychoanalytic cases maintained and consolidated their gains despite assuming increased responsibilities during the follow-up period. The other two, with clearly incomplete conflict resolution, showed partial symptom return. There was suggestive evidence that changes based upon conflict resolution tended to persist despite external stress.

CHAPTER 7

ADJUNCTIVE SUPPORTS TO PSYCHOTHERAPY

One characteristic of our patient sample was the high frequency of hospitalization during some part of their treatment. Seventeen of the forty-two cases were hospitalized at some time during their treatment. The hospitalizations tended to last less than a year since one of the requirements for the sample was that psychotherapy be the primary modality of treatment. Because of the ready availability of hospital treatment in our setting, the predictors gave considerable thought to the optimal use of the hospital and other adjunctive supports to psychotherapy, such as the day hospital or a supervised family care program.

Three major assumptions were made regarding the need for hospitalization or other adjunctive supports. Most important was the belief that patients whose symptoms were destructive or self-destructive needed hospitalization to supply the necessary controls to such behavior in order to protect the patient as well as the treatment situation. Prominent in this group were the addictive patients, but other kinds of acting out (promiscuity, antisocial behavior, suicidal danger) were also included. A second assumption concerned patients whose symptoms were not destructive or self-destructive, but who were seen as unable to form a stable therapeutic alliance without the support and gratification of a hospital, at least in the early phases of the psychotherapy. And last, individuals for whom expressive psychotherapy was deemed desirable or necessary but whose ego strength was not sufficient to tolerate the stress of such treatment required hospitalization in order to make expressive treatment possible.

DESTRUCTIVE AND SELF-DESTRUCTIVE SYMPTOMS

Eleven patients in the study presented a significant problem with addiction to either drugs or alcohol or both. All were hospitalized at least in the early phases of their treatment. Four showed fairly favorable outcomes while seven showed unfavorable responses. A prominent differentiating feature between the two groups was the use of psychoanalysis. Psychoanalysis was offered to five of the seven unsuccessfully treated patients, while only one of the four successful cases underwent psychoanalysis. (One of the successful cases began psychoanalytic treatment, but it soon became apparent to the analyst that she was unsuited to the procedure and the treatment became explicitly supportive.) The five unsuccessfully treated addictive patients were unable to profit from analysis even when combined with hospital treatment. In two of these cases the research team thought hospitalization had been too brief, but in every case there was agreement by the research team in retrospect that these patients were not good candidates for analytic procedure. The predictors did not believe that psychoanalysis was the treatment of choice for two of the patients, and were not optimistic about the results for the others (see Chapter 5, on indications). There is strong suggestive evidence that the use of analysis for these impulse-ridden people, despite the support of the hospital, may have contributed to the unfavorable outcomes.

How may we account for the differences in outcome between the two successful and two unsuccessful outcomes in the nonanalytic cases? The answer is to be found in the respective capacities of the patients to form therapeutic alliances upon which to build gratifying and adaptive life adjustments. The *Fencer* had been addicted to barbiturates for a three-year period which finally culminated in a chronically drugged state. The addiction served to ward off a severe depression centering around feelings of intense inadequacy and worthlessness as a person and a woman. She was treated by psychotherapy two times a week for two years. For the first six months this was supported by concomitant hospitalization; the next six months by day hospital; and during the second year of her treatment the patient was a full outpatient. The patient's addicition, her homosexual tendencies, and her abrasive interpersonal relationships were considerably modified. She completed her higher education with honors and performed very successfully as a quasi-professional worker in a rehabilitation center for the handicapped. Finally, she was able to marry, albeit with another ex-addict who was also sexually conflicted. The research team judged these achievements to be based largely on a mutual liking and trust of patient and therapist within the context of a good therapeutic alliance. Hospitalization seemed to be a silent partner in helping to build this alliance. It gave the patient much-needed support and control while the therapeutic relationship was being cemented.

The *Covert Addict*, who improved under a combined regimen of hospitalization and psychotherapy, was a man in his early thirties when he started treatment. He was severely alcoholic, had a masochistic sexual perversion, and carried a diagnosis of "schizophrenic character." The patient actually showed very little improvement during the first long phase of his treatment. He was an inpatient for over two years, but the expected increase in reflectiveness and compulsivity did not develop during his hospitalization. The research team believed that the patient's masochistic propensities were reinforced by the hospital personnel because of their countertransference. In this initial phase his psychotherapy did not "take" because of a deep-seated sense of mistrust which made it necessary for him to maintain a safe distance from the therapist. After he left the hospital he continued a relatively high drug intake which he concealed from his therapist; this further contributed to his paranoid view of the therapeutic relationship. In fact, improvement occurred only after the termination of his first course of psychotherapy and the occurrence of a coronary occlusion which necessitated absolute abstinence from drugs. At this point, some two years after the end of the first phase of treatment, he developed a "counseling" relationship with his therapist and became more capable of using the help that the therapist had to offer. Perhaps the difference was that the patient was now faced with a threat to his life if he failed to use the therapist's help. He no longer forced the therapist into the role of destructive prosecutor who was trying to uncover "illegal" drug activity. Through a significant and fortuitous situational factor, the patient now relied upon and used the therapist's efforts to help.

A patient who clearly failed in treatment was the *Addicted Doctor*, a professional man in his thirties, who was irresponsible in his job, constantly in debt, had an unstable marriage, and was addicted to drugs. He suffered a severe impulse disorder and was given to lying. The therapist attempted to treat him as an outpatient until the downward spiral of his life necessitated hospitalization. Unfortunately, certain administrative complications prevented the therapist from continuing his treatment with the patient. The case provided an excellent example of the need for hospitalization in such cases in order to control drug intake and other kinds of self-destructive behavior; it was also important in gratifying his needs for nurturance and comfort as a prerequisite for the development of a therapeutic alliance in psychotherapy. So long as the therapist was experienced as the sole source of such nurturance, the inevitable frustration felt by the patient prevented the development of a therapeutic alliance.

The *Salesman* is of special interest because he was considered by the termination research team as relatively refractory to the best of therapeutic interventions. He was a forty-two-year-old salesman with symptoms of severe alcoholism, promiscuity, financial irresponsibility, and severe depression. These symptoms were embedded in a narcissistic and infantile character structure centering around oral longings, oral frustrations, and reactive oral rages. His achievements in life were minimal, and he was living a basically dependent existence. He was an outpatient for almost two years except for an interruption of some four months in the middle when he took flight in an effort to prove his independence. After the patient's second interruption of treatment and his subsequent failure to function independently, he returned for a ten-month period of hospitalization without psychotherapy and once again left treatment against medical advice. His subsequent course was a rapid deterioration in functioning terminating in his suicide.

Psychotherapy without concomitant hospitalization in this case was recognized in retrospect as a misjudgment of the patient's ego resources. Even though he was able to control his alcoholism, he had done so with the *quid pro quo* of being rewarded by the therapist with a symbiotically dependent relationship. The therapist's original overestimation of the patient's capacities had led to some disillusionment about the possible accomplishments with this patient. For his part, the patient sensed the impossibility of finding the oral-embracing infantile state which he had been seeking while stridently asserting his readiness to take on new responsibilities each step of the way. Although the psychotherapy was lacking in the explicit support which this primitively organized person needed, his psychiatric management during hospitalization largely focused around direct supports, limit-setting, and effective controls. Nevertheless, the patient's difficulty in accepting his own intense dependency needs, combined with his wife's antitreatment efforts, led him to break off his one hope for possible rehabilitation. Because of the failure of this effort at hospitalization, the research team doubted whether this patient could be treated at all. He was not only lacking in the usual ego resources (frustration tolerance, capacity for delay, reflectiveness), but he was beset by an intense conflict concerning dependency wishes. On the one hand there were deep-seated wishes for an infantile state of bliss; on the other he had constantly to assert his independence, his masculinity, and his potency. This pattern is not unlike that found in some recalcitrant schizophrenic patients who reject every contact presumably due to fears of losing the remnants of ego intactness through fusion with an object to whom they might become attached.

In addition to these addictive cases, there were six nonaddictive but self-destructive patients whom the predictors thought required hospitalization with psychotherapy. Four patients had relatively successful outcomes, while two were unsuccessful. In the successful category the behaviors were mainly characterized by promiscuity, irresponsible work

behavior, and suicidal depression. Each of these cases had at
least several months of hospitalization concomitant with psychotherapy which helped to bring the behavior under some
degree of control. In both of the unsuccessful cases the major
deterrent to a successful outcome was either no hospitalization
at all or a premature interruption of hospitalization with the
result that the psychotherapy was insufficient to keep the
patients' impulsive and reckless behavior from getting out of
hand. One patient (*Sociopath*) was not only involved in legal
difficulties, but he was consciously untruthful with the therapist, usually a pathognomonic sign for treatment failure.
Among the successful cases, the major work of treatment was
undoubtedly accomplished in the psychotherapy, but the
research team saw the initial period of hospitalization as
making a significant contribution to the progress of the
therapy.

FOSTERING A THERAPEUTIC ALLIANCE

For those patients with destructive and self-destructive
alloplastic symptoms and weak impulse controls, hospitalization was clearly needed in order to prevent a deleterious effect
upon their life situations as well as helping to preserve the
treatment situation itself. But beyond that, hospitalization is
useful and necessary for patients with limited resources to
permit the development of a therapeutic alliance. All psychotherapies, no matter how explicitly expressive, contain supportive and gratifying elements which contribute to the development of a positive and trusting relationship with the psychotherapist. These factors, combined with the patient's capacity
to appreciate the reality of the therapeutic relationship and his

ability to view parental figures as potentially helpful and need-gratifying, contribute to a bond of trust and hope between therapist and patient within which successful therapeutic work is done.

In general, the patients who were successfully treated with concomitant hospitalization were considered helped by a hospital treatment that facilitated a useful working relationship with their therapists. Those who fared poorly either did not get the needed hospitalization, received it for an insufficient period, or were treated with an expressive modality like psychoanalysis which they could not tolerate, even with hospitalization. But what about those cases who seemed to have received the correct dosage of both hospital treatment and therapy and who still failed to form the necessary alliance with the therapist?

In our study, two cases, which the research team judged to have sufficient concomitant hospitalization with their psychotherapy, failed to develop the expected therapeutic alliance. This was true in the first long phase of treatment of the *Covert Addict* (described in the preceding section), a thirty-three-year-old man who was given to perverse sexual practice, suffered from chronic alcoholism, and showed paranoid distortions of reality. He started psychotherapy six months after his hospitalization and continued as a full hospital patient for the next several months. He received therapy for approximately five years (three times weekly for the first three years), but at the patient's insistence the frequency was gradually decreased. Although he was able to control his alcoholism, he had substituted high doses of tranquilizing drugs, and toward the end of his therapy he was frequently drug intoxicated. During this time he was rehospitalized for brief periods for the purpose of withdrawing him from drugs. During the five-year period of active treatment, the therapy was strongly colored by a cat-and-mouse game relating to the patient's refusal to give up his use of drugs. The patient sought out prescriptions from a number of town physicians and had them filled by a variety of pharmacists. He attempted to conceal and minimize these activities from the therapist. He took a paranoid stance concerning the therapist's attempt to stop his drug intake: he believed the therapist was trying to deprive him of pleasure and comfort. The therapist felt he was constantly forced into the role of detective-prosecutor, trying to detect evidence of the patient's subterfuges. When it became clear to the therapist that he was unable to influence the patient in controlling his addiction, he terminated this first phase of treatment.

Although a series of fortuitous circumstances, described earlier, contributed to a more favorable ultimate outcome to this treatment, the first period unquestionably failed in its major objectives. Rather than a growing attitude of trust, the patient became increasingly suspicious and withdrawn from the therapist. How to understand this? Certain characteristics of the patient's pathology undoubtedly contributed to the difficulty in achieving the desired therapeutic relationship. Mainly, an underlying, chronic, serious paranoid potential made him suspect the therapist's motives. His addictive propensities combined with a basic mistrust to produce lying, evasiveness, and withholding—serious barriers to the growth of a relationship. Although the patient was initially willing to accept a dependency role in the hospital, after discharge he resisted giving up his facade of independence and accepting rehospitalizations when needed, even though he invariably returned to drugs when discharged from the hospital. One could justifiably ask why some level of hospital control (day hospital or daily visits with a hospital doctor) was not used during most of his therapy. Also, how much of a transference-countertransference bind developed, fed by both the patient's secretiveness and the therapist's propensity to demonstrate that he could not be fooled?

The second instance of concomitant hospitalization and psychotherapy which did not reach the desired result was the *Grandson*, hospitalized at the age of seventeen by his wealthy grandfather and guardian. He had engaged in a couple of episodes of bizarre exhibitionistic behavior set against a background of chronic unhappiness, isolation, and poor school adjustment of seven to eight years' duration. The patient did not start formal psychotherapy until almost a year of hospital treatment. When he began psychotherapy he moved into the day hospital, lived in a foster home, and attended a local high school. During the two-year-long, two-to-three-times-a-week psychotherapy, he was rehospitalized on a few occasions during crisis periods. The first year of psychotherapy was characterized by a long period of cautious aloofness, but afterward his fear and mistrust gave way to a greater closeness and confiding within the therapy. He was impressed with the therapist's real concern for him when he made an emergency request to be seen in the midst of a growing panic state. He showed a greater willingness in the therapy to talk about his real inner concerns and fears. Unfortunately, however, this closeness only persisted during the period of one of the patient's rehospitalizations. When he was released he gradually withdrew into bland denial and isolation in the treatment, and an intensification of an alloplastic life-style outside the treatment. He finally manipulated his guardian to force a termination of treatment.

How may we explain this premature interruption? The termination research team agreed that this impulse-ridden boy needed more structure during his life outside the hospital than he had been receiving. They also believed, however, that the close positive relationship that had developed during the middle phase of treatment began to pose new and deeper threats to the patient which were not worked with actively enough within the psychotherapy. The growing relationship posed a severe threat of ultimate rejection which had been his fate in the past and also aroused impulses toward homosexual submission. Neither were sufficiently dealt with. The patient's fear and distrust of the therapist's power to exploit him and his guilt about his own unexpressed negative feelings pushed him into a further need for distance and for termination. One of the researchers wrote, "If the therapist had been able to deal more inclusively with the total transference expression, with more interpretive attention to just these negative and erotized positive elements, the patient's constantly tenuous treatment motivation with the repetitively allowed wish to quit might have been overcome." Thus, even though more use of the hospital structure might have been helpful, the decisive element seems to have been a failure to deal actively with intensified transference fears.

In summary, both of these cases of psychotherapy coupled with hospital support failed primarily as a result of impairment of the therapist's skill by countertransference elements—in one case a countertransference dominated by the need of the therapist to prove his ability not to be taken in, in the other case by the therapist's failure to deal with the negative transference.

An interesting sidelight to both of these cases was, despite their lack of change during the treatment period itself, they both showed some improvement when they were seen at the follow-up point. These changes seemed to be based on certain developments in their life situations. The *Grandson* had come into a sizable inheritance and was beginning to establish himself as a member of the business community. He had married and had found some degree of stability and narcissistic gratification in his new family. He was no longer in the midst of the adolescent *sturm und drang* which had created so much havoc for him and his environment. The *Covert Addict*, on the other hand, experienced a serious life-threatening illness which forced him to abstain from drugs and created a necessary, face-saving dependence on his internist and then a return to his therapist for further treatment. In both instances, however, there may have been a common thread of latent positive feelings toward the therapist which contributed to the improvement at follow-up. The factor was explicit in the patient who returned for a second phase of treatment. The *Grandson* began to find supporting figures in his environment, possibly aided by the beginning experience of trust he had developed within the psychotherapy.

ENHANCED EXPRESSIVENESS OF TREATMENT

In addition to controlling destructive symptoms and contributing to a therapeutic alliance, the hospital was seen by the predictors as making it possible for some patients to be treated more expressively in their psychotherapy than would otherwise be possible. The rationale of this assumption was that the strain upon defenses involved in the uncovering techniques of expressive psychotherapy could be better tolerated by patients when the hospital structure compensated for their ego defects. It could supply help to the patient for disturbing affects which might get aroused, it could bolster his self-esteem through his contacts with hospital personnel, and could prevent excessive and destructive acting out stimulated by the uncovering process. To what extent did we find evidence that patients who were hospitalized for some portion of their treatment were able to be treated in a more expressive way than would have otherwise been possible?

Hospitalization as an Adjunct to
Psychoanalysis

Hospitalization was used in a relatively large number of our analytic cases. In most settings psychoanalysis is conducted

without concurrent hospitalization, but the percentage of hospitalized cases in our research population was 45 percent, quite
high for two main reasons. First, more than 30 percent of the
patients treated in psychotherapy and psychoanalysis at the
Menninger Foundation are drawn from the psychiatric community and for reasons of confidentiality these patients were
excluded from our research population with the result that the
research sample consisted largely of our more severely ill
patients. Second, the ready availability of psychoanalysis for
our hospital patients tends to facilitate referrals for psychoanalytic treatment. Many of the patients in our population would
more than likely not have been recommended for analysis had
hospitalization not been available to provide the support they
clearly needed.

Among the analytic cases there were nine patients whom
the predictors believed required some hospitalization during at
least the beginning phases of treatment in order to achieve
treatment goals. They were all hospitalized but the termination
team considered seven of them as having been nonanalyzable,
whether hospitalized or not. In general, these were the patients
whose anxiety tolerance was minimal and in the ordinary stress
of living, not to speak of the stress of the analytic process, they
found it necessary to resort to self-destructive behaviors,
mainly alcoholism.

The other two patients in this group derived good results
from analytic treatment despite having been ill enough at the
beginning to require hospitalization. The *Medical Specialist*
was hospitalized for the first year and a half of his analytic
treatment because of his tendencies toward alcoholism and drug
addiction. As mentioned earlier, these symptoms differed from
those of the other alcoholic patients in that he resorted to
occasional binges and did not use alcohol on a chronic basis.
Also, by means of immense exertion of will, he was capable on

several occasions of withdrawing himself from addiction to barbiturates. The hospitalization was useful insofar as it permitted a therapeutic alliance to be developed and consolidated, and this provided some protection against harmful acting out which would have threatened the treatment situation.

The second patient (*Phobic Woman*), believed by the predictors to require a fairly extensive period of hospitalization while being analyzed, was originally thought to be an infantile, demanding person mainly fixated at an oral aggressive level. But as mentioned earlier, she demonstrated considerably more strength and a higher level of personality development than was originally recognized by the treatment team. The helpless dependent state which made it necessary for others, mainly her husband, to be constantly in her company because of her phobias was less evidence of infantilism than it was a defense against oedipal sexual temptations and dangers, a defensive use of the oral position against the genital. She was able to move out of the hospital after only a few months and became a full outpatient in less than a year with no deleterious effect to the analysis, contrary to the expectations of the prediction team. Hospitalization was useful as a way of interrupting her pathological dependency upon her husband but was not needed to control her manipulative behavior or to gratify her presumed intense oral needs.

Thus, the majority of cases seen by the predictors as analyzable, provided they began their analysis in the hospital, actually proved to be incapable of tolerating analysis. Four of these cases were of the so-called "heroic" variety where the chances of success were considered low, but the predictors felt nothing short of analysis could produce the necessary change. It is instructive that every one of these "heroic" cases failed in treatment and at termination were considered nonanalyzable. One must seriously question the validity of the "heroic" indication. On the other hand, there was at least one instance of a patient who required hospitalization for a substantial period of his analysis, but whose treatment was ultimately quite successful.

Hospitalization for Greater Expressiveness in Psychotherapy

The predictors expected that hospitalization would permit greater expressiveness than would otherwise be possible for eight psychotherapy cases. In two cases we were unable to test the predictions because the period of hospitalization was substantially shorter than called for. The *Dancer* left the hospital prematurely and her psychotherapy, which nevertheless was continued for over a year as a compromise measure, proved unfruitful in helping her to control her impulse-ridden, unorganized life. The *Thespian* was forced by economic circumstances to cut short her hospitalization, but was able to use her psychotherapy to effect a more stable life albeit handicapped by a somewhat anhedonic homosexual pattern. Her therapy involved a mutual implicit agreement between patient and therapist not to delve into anything unpleasant. The termination research team believed that a more expressive approach, in which the patient's tendency to act out her negative transference in terms of her lesbianism were more vigorously interpreted, might have produced a more satisfactory outcome.

Among the other six cases, all of whom underwent the expected period of hospitalization, four received psychotherapy which lacked any significant expressive elements, but each for different reasons. The *Bohemian* needed considerable help in extricating herself from an unsuitable marriage and to bolster her self-esteem by finding constructive and creative outlets in work and recreation. The therapist chose to emphasize supportive measures, despite her hospitalization, and the patient flourished under this regimen, achieving an excellent treatment result. The *Grandson*, on the other hand, did not make much progress in his two years of psychotherapy and interrupted his treatment. The termination research group believed that the premature termination could have been prevented had the therapist taken a more active interpretive stance vis-à-vis the patient's fear of positive, sexually colored transference wishes and fears. The other two cases (*Covert Addict* and *Salesman*) were not deemed suitable by the termination research team for a more expressive approach despite hospitalization. They lacked the ego qualities associated with basic trust as well as the capacity to tolerate dependency wishes to be able to profit from the stress of an uncovering treatment.

None of these four cases demonstrate that hospitalization facilitates expressiveness, but neither do they disconfirm this conception. It is clear that in some instances, as in the last two cases, a patient may be incapable of attempting to uncover unconscious conflict despite the support of a hospital.

The final two cases were hospitalized for some part of their treatment and underwent some expressive-uncovering experiences. Neither case (*Phobic Girl, Fencer*), however, was primarily expressive in the sense that there was a major focus on the transference. There is no clear evidence that hospitalization facilitated the use of expressive techniques in either case. The termination research team believed that the hospital served an important role in helping the *Fencer* give up her drug habituation and the *Phobic Girl* check some of her self-defeating patterns. But its role in contributing to a more expressive treatment was not clearly demonstrated.

Thus, the proposition regarding the enhanced expressiveness of treatment being made possible by adjunctive supports was invalidated for certain types of patients, i.e., those who lack the ego resources necessary for the stress of an uncovering experience. For those who have this capacity but who have ego defects which require adjunctive supports, hospitalization may have enhanced this potential, but the evidence is not clear on this point.

SUMMARY

1. Hospitalization is a necessary, but not a sufficient, condition for a favorable treatment outcome with patients whose symptoms are destructive to the environment or to themselves—in particular those addicted to alcohol or drugs.

2. The destructive and self-destructive patients in this sample who did not show a favorable outcome fell into three main categories: (a) those who did not get any hospitalization and were treated solely as outpatients; (b) those who did not receive sufficient hospitalization to permit them to develop a strong therapeutic alliance; (c) patients treated with psychoanalysis who were not able to profit from this procedure.

3. The one patient in this sample of addictive individuals with weak ego resources who seemed to have been offered adequate treatment opportunities but who failed nevertheless was a person with a weak ego and a prominent, intense bipolar conflict concerning dependency. He craved nurture and comfort, but with equal intensity he needed to stridently assert his independence and masculinity, a combination which made for a most difficult, if not impossible, treatment course.

4. Patients who experience marked mistrust, fear, and excessive frustration in close relationships require a period of concomitant hospitalization in order to develop a therapeutic alliance within which a favorable treatment experience may occur. But even with hospitalization, the therapist's countertransference reactions or technical errors with these mistrustful

people contribute to their failure to establish a favorable working alliance.

5. The assumption that concomitant hospitalization makes it possible for the therapist to conduct a more expressive psychotherapy than would be possible otherwise does not hold up for those patients who seem to lack the ego capacities necessary for an uncovering process. Patients who find it difficult to establish a therapeutic alliance even in optimal circumstances or who cling to a massive constriction and inhibition against intrapsychic exploration do not become capable of an expressive approach. For patients who have the capacity to work expressively, hospitalization may have enhanced this potential but the evidence is not conclusive on this point.

CHAPTER 8

THE THERAPEUTIC ALLIANCE

The therapeutic alliance is a necessary, but by no means sufficient, condition for the success of the therapeutic process in psychoanalysis. It provides the framework within which the main work of the treatment, the development and analysis of a regressive transference neurosis, occurs. To the extent that a psychotherapy is supportive, the therapeutic alliance, with its various by-products, becomes both an end in itself and the major vehicle of the treatment. Thus, in a primarily supportive treatment the alliance is not only necessary, but often sufficient, for therapeutic change to occur.

Without offering an extended discussion of this concept, the following working definition of a therapeutic alliance was used by the research project: "Both patient and psychotherapist consistently know, believe, or feel .... at some level of consciousness .... that their primary goal in working together is to help the patient. The cognitive-affective attitudes which constitute this belief create the therapeutic alliance (Zetzel) or the working alliance (Greenson). Various vicissitudes of their relationship or personalities (principally transference and countertransference) may temporarily or permanently obscure, interfere with, or dissolve this alliance. We see this as essentially the same as Freud's conceptualization of the 'mild positive transference' necessary to the continuing progress of the analytic treatment." (See Appendix 3, Glossary of Terms)

Our earlier discussion on indications for analysis demonstrated that patients with significant ego defects and ego weakness were unable to profit from the analytic procedure. Another way of conceptualizing this finding, at least for some of these patients, would be that they were unable to establish and maintain the necessary therapeutic alliance within which to carry on the frustrating and regression-inducing process. Whereas the capacity for forming a therapeutic alliance tended to be assumed for the analytic cases, the psychotherapy cases—especially those requiring supportive treatment—were often glaringly lacking in this capacity. Hence the predictors dwelt at some length on the processes whereby a therapeutic alliance would develop and the research team at termination and follow-up also focused upon these developments and their vicissitudes.[1] In this chapter we shall be examining two major sets of propositions, one concerning the characteristics of the treatment and the other concerning the characteristics of the patient, which presumably foster or interfere with the necessary alliance between patient and therapist.

1. The concept of therapeutic alliance was only starting to be introduced into the literature in the mid-1950s, around the time that the predictions were being written, although the importance of a prevailing positive relationship was used by the predictors. Hence there were very few predictive assumptions written which directly used this concept. Many more were written as postdictive assumptions after the concept had gained currency in analytic thinking.

NEED GRATIFICATION

A major assumption of the study was that sufficient need gratification must occur in the treatment if a therapeutic alliance is to develop. Need gratification, of course, must vary in degree and in kind, depending upon the patient, his impulses, his controls, his tendencies to distort reality, his frustration tolerance, his capacity to tolerate closeness, etc. There are obvious limits to the amount of gratification which can be supplied by the therapist within the structure of the therapy and, for this reason, adjunctive treatment like hospitalization may be necessary. Furthermore, excessive gratification may not only contribute to undesirable dependency but may also diminish the patient's self-esteem.

The predictors did not view need gratification solely in terms of its contribution to the therapeutic relationship. They also made a number of assumptions regarding its other more immediate effects: establishing a satisfying dependency relationship, finding a gratifying human contact, experiencing tension reduction through a cathartic verbal expression of feelings—all contributing to a reduction of anxiety and the opportunity to replace pathological defenses and behaviors with more adaptive ones. This kind of anxiety reduction and strengthening of defenses unquestionably has a value of its own but it also contributes to a growing therapeutic alliance which in turn may lead to other more stable therapeutic changes (see Chapters 9 and 10). In this section we shall focus upon the need gratification assumption and its corollaries as it related to the development of a therapeutic alliance.

The predictors believed that certain patients required the therapist (or other persons in the treatment situation) to "perform parental functions" for them for a therapeutic alliance to develop. The parental functions included gratification of dependency needs, bolstering of impulse control, clarifying reality, and direct advice-giving. Five patients were singled out by the predictors as requiring this kind of treatment regimen as a basic ingredient of the treatment process.

The *Grandson*, a seventeen-year-old boy who had never enjoyed a stable family life, was seen as needing a family care home as an adjunct to his psychotherapy in order to help him internalize his therapist and his family care parents as stable, interested figures. This development did not occur because the patient interrupted treatment prematurely in reaction to a deepening transference involvement which was not actively interpreted. However, it was significant that in the posttreatment phase the patient used his ex-family care parents as parent surrogates and as benign, supporting figures. The *Bohemian*, a forty-one-year-old woman who suffered a psychotic depression in reaction to the strains of an incompatible marriage, was also viewed as requiring support and guidance to help her see that her attempted compromise solution of her marital predicament was impossible. This was indeed what happened and the patient, with the therapist's guidance, was able to establish a more viable and gratifying life adjustment. A third patient for whom such active interventions were deemed necessary was the *Sociopath*, a man with a severe weakness of impulse control. The therapist's attempts to restrain him in his antisocial behavior were unsuccessful because the adjunctive controls of the hospital, which the predictors had felt would be necessary, were not available. A similar development in another poorly controlled patient (*Addicted Doctor*) occurred in connection with the predictors' expectation that the patient would follow the therapist's advice on giving up his drug intake and engaging in more constructive leisure time activities. Again, the patient's impulse control and self-destructive propensities did not permit such interventions to be effective without the supporting control of the hospital. An anticipated development which did occur was the predictors' expectation that *Peter Pan's* petty thievery of food would come under rapid control in the analytic situation when the therapist would firmly prohibit such behavior. The symptom rapidly disappeared and the therapeutic alliance was thereby strengthened.

Postdictively there were two instances of the therapist performing parental functions which led to an enhanced therapeutic alliance. They were both cases which were started in analysis but after a period of time were switched to psychotherapy because of the patient's inability to tolerate the regressive features of an analytic procedure. With the *Heiress*, the analyst was impressed with the patient's borderline qualities, her rigidly blocked affects, her seeming incapacity for free association, and her intellectualized reactions to his interpretive efforts. He therefore introduced a number of treatment parameters, like entering into her real life decisions, and allowing her more knowledge of himself and his life than is usual in most psychotherapies. His effort was to give the patient a corrective emotional experience with a benevolent and genuinely interested father-figure who did not abandon her. Another treatment switch from analysis to psychotherapy occurred in the case of the *Historian*, a thirty-one-year-old college teacher, who began to show a psychotic regression in the course of his analysis when the analyst shifted his interpretive focus from the patient's libidinal elements (craving for nurturance and dependency) to an interpretation of his rage and envy toward the father for prohibiting him from exercising his adult prerogatives. As a result of the patient's severe regression, the therapist shifted to a supportive psychotherapy in which he offered fatherly advice, made suggestions as to how the patient could best cope with day-to-day difficulties, and actively encouraged him to overcome his inhibitions about moving forward in his profession and achieving an advanced degree. The patient blossomed under this kindly protection and felt considerable appreciation for the help he was receiving.

Thus, in both the predictive and postdictive instances, we see evidence of parental functions being performed by the therapist for patients who lack the capacity to regulate their own lives properly, contributing greatly to the development of the therapeutic alliance. The major instances of failure in this technique occurred with patients who suffered from severe impulse disorders and did not get the needed additional controls of a hospital environment.

Related to the "parental function" assumption is a special hypothesis particularly applicable to young, psychologically immature patients. The predictors believed that these patients required the provision of suitable identification figures in the treatment situation as a necessary part of the change process. Two of the youngest patients in the study, both seventeen years old, were singled out by the predictors as requiring this kind of identification process for a successful treatment outcome. Even though both patients terminated treatment prematurely, the *Grandson* had begun to show evidence of identification with his therapist in reaction to conscious efforts by the therapist to present himself as an identification figure. For example, the therapist did reveal facts about his life and interests and on one occasion invited the patient to a medical school lecture he was giving. In reaction to this approach the patient began considering medicine as a career and in other more superficial ways began to emulate the therapist (his brand of cigarettes, the same style haircut, etc.). The *Prep School Boy* was in treatment for only a year and did not show evidence of beginning identifications.

Postdictively it was observed that in at least four young

patients an identification process with the therapist's values was a significant factor in establishing a therapeutic relationship. The major vehicles of the treatment in the cases were primarily supportive, and in all of them the research team believed that some degree of identification with the therapist had occurred. The analytic case (*Peter Pan*), a nineteen-year-old girl who suffered from anorexia, was unable to utilize the interpretive efforts of the analyst because of her borderline qualities. Her disturbed behavior frequently made it necessary for the analyst to abandon his neutrality and intervene actively in her life. Not only did he interdict her petty stealing of food but on frequent occasions she would present herself in his office soaking wet after walking in the rain, and he provided her with a blanket. On two occasions she made suicidal threats that seemed serious enough to warrant brief hospitalization. The positive relationship between patient and therapist tended to be strengthened by his interventions and the termination research team inferred that some identification with the therapist's caretaking function had occurred.

In the other three cases the therapists likewise placed a heavy emphasis upon reinforcing less pathological, more adaptive behaviors, which encouraged both a therapeutic alliance and an identification with their therapist's values. The *Passive Student*, a twenty-three-year-old graduate student, was attempting to liberate himself from his excessive dependence upon his parents and was encouraged in these efforts by his therapist. Similarly, the *Rebel Coed*, a twenty-year-old college student, found herself constantly embroiled in provocative and rebellious behavior against authority figures. Her therapist assumed a benign, avuncular role in helping her to tone down her maladaptive, belligerent stance.

The fourth case, the *Phobic Girl*, a twenty-one-year-old college girl, is perhaps the best example of the use of direct suggestion and advice. Her chief presenting symptoms were a regressed, infantile, and dependent life and a number of crippling phobias including a fear of being away from home, of the dark, and of small enclosed spaces. The therapist made many concrete suggestions concerning this patient's living arrangements, schooling, her interactions with her parents, and boyfriends. He pointed out how her provocative, demanding, and masochistic behaviors led to self-defeating consequences and how more socially attuned behaviors could win the gratification she was ostensibly seeking. He made a deliberate effort to foster and "ride" on the positive transference elements and, in general, refrained from confronting the patient with even the most conscious and obvious aspects of negative transference feelings. He attempted to clarify how the patient's experiences of things done to her were very often situations brought about by her own provocative behaviors. The climate of the therapy was friendly and positive, one of mutual acceptance in which the therapist served as a teacher, educating the patient to reality, to the consequences of her attitudes and her behaviors, rather than serving as analytic interpreter uncovering and resolving unconscious conflicts. Within this solidified therapeutic alliance the patient gradually identified herself with the more healthy attitudes and behaviors fostered by the therapist.

Thus, the younger and psychologically less mature patients in this study, with less crystallized identities, responded to the active interventions of their therapists with a tendency to solidify an identity around the therapist's values. It would seem that an important psychological need for such persons is to find a gratifying and protective parental figure in the therapy situation which they had not been able to find in their childhood and adolescence and in this way complete the normal maturational sequences toward adult life.

CAPACITY TO PERCEIVE A GOOD OBJECT

The other side of the dyad, the patient, brings certain characteristics to the treatment that are often decisive in fostering or preventing the development of a therapeutic alliance. As indicated earlier, the predictors were not as explicit in using this concept as were the research teams which evaluated the treatment at termination and follow-up. Hence, the predictive assumptions (which we shall examine first) were less complete and less explicit about therapeutic alliance than were the postdictive assumptions written to explain various treatment developments.

Predictive Assumptions

One group of statements referred to the relatively long period of time which would be necessary in a supportive relationship before the patient would be able to "achieve partial freedom from destructive symptoms," or be able to "tolerate a clear picture of his ego operations without being overwhelmed by anxiety and guilt." These were patients with limited ego strength, low anxiety tolerance, and poor psychological-mindedness. Nine patients were specifically chosen by the predictors as likely to require a long period of relationship-building before being able to experience significant therapeutic gains. Six of them were never able to establish a working relationship; in fact, all terminated treatment prematurely and, in most instances, they were not in treatment for more than a year or two. Their common characteristic was weak impulse control and all, with the possible exception of one, were judged by the research team to have had insufficient hospitalization concomitant with their psychotherapy.

Positive Therapeutic Relationships. More interesting for our purposes, however, were the predictive errors in the three other cases where positive relationships developed more quickly than expected. The *Bohemian*, a woman in her early forties, was hospitalized because of severe depression. She had been living more or less separated from her husband for a number of years prior to receiving his ultimatum that she return. When she complied, her downward course was swift and dramatic, and hospitalization was necessary. She began psychotherapy six months after being hospitalized.

The predictors expected her psychotherapy course would be long and difficult and the transference would be burdened by "suspicion and doubt." They believed that the hospital doctor would absorb much of these negative feelings but, especially following termination of the adjunctive treatment, that there would be stormy battles with the therapist which conceivably could result in a disruption of the treatment. These pessimistic predictions were based upon an expected recapitulation of her severe pathology and her primitive, exploitative object relationships. She had shown poor impulse control, low anxiety tolerance, the lack of good object relationships in her life, a need to depreciate men, as well as a view of herself as a talented superior person who had never been adequately appreciated. Contrary to these expectations, the prevailing transference was friendly and positive and became increasingly so as the treatment progressed. The main explanation for this outcome appeared to be the therapist's explicitly supportive stance in contrast to the predictors' expectation that the therapist would be conducting at least a partly expressive psychotherapy. He was a constant, kindly counselor who entered actively into an advice-giving role in relation to her myriad life difficulties and who encouraged her gently into gratifying vocational and avocational interests. He consistently underplayed interpretation of the negative components of the transference which were mildly acted out. The researchers at termination and follow-up believed that the patient's ability to form a stronger therapeutic alliance than had been anticipated was due to the therapist's active and benevolent interest, and not to an underestimation of her ego resources. But one may seriously question whether the unexpectedly high emphasis on support in the treatment is a sufficient explanation for the unexpectedly friendly atmosphere in the treatment. One could at least entertain the possibility that the predictors were unduly influenced by the acute, agitated depressive picture which disposed them to underestimate her capacity for using a helping figure. Thus, despite her history of having to maintain a split between good and bad objects in her life and her very strong narcissistic propensities, she was able to establish and solidify a positive relationship with her therapist which enabled her to make a number of significant life changes: she dissolved an ungratifying marriage and found a new one (during the follow-up period) which more adequately suited her needs and within which she was able to return libidinal interests and supplies.

A second case in which the predictors underestimated the patient's capacity to form a positive relationship was that of *Playboy*, a young professional man who was given to severe cyclic disturbances, a tendency to shirk unpleasant responsibilities, and marked marital difficulties with promiscuity. He was diagnosed as a schizo-affective disorder in a narcissistic character organization. The predictors expected that with predominantly supportive psychotherapy with concomitant hospitalization in the initial phases, the patient would respond to a therapist's friendly, understanding interest by becoming better able to deal with internal and external pressures. But they predicted a stormy course for the psychotherapy on the basis of his history of depressive episodes with a paranoid coloring since the age of thirteen; these had twice necessitated hospitalization with electroshock therapy. They expected it would be difficult for the therapist to keep himself in focus as a helpful and optimistic figure, particularly when he would have to confront the patient with reality aspects of his maladaptive narcissistic behavior. They believed that his magical expectations of what the therapist would be able to do for him, and their inevitable frustration, would result in outbursts of rage or marked depressive swings. Rehospitalization at various times was considered a distinct possibility.

The patient's treatment course was considerably smoother than anticipated. He underwent a four-year period of explicitly supportive psychotherapy in which his growing attachment to the therapist was reflected in a succession of adaptive life achievements. He consistently viewed the therapist as a benevolent and powerful father whom he liked from the start and in whom he had the fullest confidence. In a follow-up interview the patient described his feelings unabashedly as "I was almost willing to say I loved him." Although the patient's underlying narcissistic character structure was basically unchanged (his lack of empathy for his wife and his clients), his overt behaviors were drastically altered. Not only did his mood swings rapidly disappear but he was able to modulate his demandingness, particularly toward his wife. The therapist benignly accepted the patient's fear of fully confiding in him, particularly with regard to his sexual behavior, and attempted quite successfully to consolidate and use the patient's positive dependent attachment to him.

Even more than in the previous case, this patient's capacity to develop, maintain, and build upon a positive relationship with a parent figure was underestimated by the predictors at the outset. Without diminishing the considerable skill which the therapist carried out in his treatment plan, we may infer in retrospect that the patient brought to the treatment an internalized image of a reliable and giving parent upon which to build in his treatment experience. The positive aspects of the relationship were emphasized while the negative transferences were not explored. (Yet we have seen other cases where this kind of "gentlemen's agreement" between patient and therapist worked to the disadvantage of the treatment. The *Grandson*, for example, began to develop feelings of closeness to his therapist but the therapist's failure to interpret the submissive and homosexual implications of this intimacy resulted in a premature termination. The *Thespian*'s unchallenged and uninterpreted tendency to confine all positive feelings toward the therapist while acting out her negative, depreciating transference feelings via homosexuality resulted in a better organized, but definitely handicapped, life adjustment.) Thus the *Playboy*'s capacity to perceive and internalize a good object combined with his therapist's skillful ministration to his emotional needs led to a better result with this patient than had been expected. The case points up, however, the difficulty both in assessing a patient's potential for utilizing a good object and his being able to maintain repression of the ever-present bad object.

Returning to the *Thespian*, she was the third patient whom the predictors mistakenly expected to experience a long and difficult period before establishing a useful therapeutic alliance. She was a nineteen-year-old girl who was hospitalized after showing disorganized and turbulent behavior in college. She had been involved in excessive drinking, heterosexual and homosexual promiscuity, and other grossly disturbed behaviors. Like the other two patients she was diagnosed before and after treatment as a narcissistic character disorder. The predictors observed that her relationships were characterized by an "as if" quality, confabulation, and hypersensitivity to criticism. They expected her to be distrustful of the therapist's interest in her, and anticipated that she would be excessively demanding and jealous of the therapist's other patients. Since the patient was given to histrionic performances and role-playing, the therapist would have considerable trouble in distinguishing reality from fantasy in her life. Thus they believed that significant changes in symptoms would appear only after a long period of testing the relationship. She would tend to withdraw from whatever she perceived as criticism.

The patient was in a primarily supportive psychotherapy for four years during which the expected burdened relationship did not actually develop. Because of financial limitations the patient was discharged from the hospital sooner than was desirable, and the first several months of outpatient therapy were marked by drinking, promiscuity, and a generally chaotic existence. But she responded fairly quickly to the therapist's regimen of firm direction and advice and settled into a friendly, positive relationship which predominated throughout the treatment. The transference attitude throughout was that of respectful friendliness to an interested and nonjudgmental benevolent parent. Her self-destructive behavior gradually ceased; she began to work regularly and avoided her previous pattern of hurtful, sadomasochistic relationships. Despite all of these adaptive achievements there was one major flaw which had developed in her life: she had settled into a stable homosexual existence, becoming involved with one homosexual partner for a fairly long period before moving on to another liaison. The research team thought she could have been helped by more intensive therapy to move on from the homosexual phase to the development of more mature heterosexuality.

The psychotherapy of the *Thespian* was marked by an almost exclusive attention to the patient's day-to-day reality experiences with little or no exploration of fantasy, dreams, or interpretation of transference. (Note the similarity to the therapy of the previous two patients.) Despite some sporadic effort on the therapist's part to uncover such material (at one time he encouraged her to use the couch for a number of sessions), the patient seemed to be unable to work expressively. In the opinion of the research team, however, both therapist and patient had unconsciously colluded to maintain a "gentlemen's agreement" of polite friendliness. The termination team thought that the patient's homosexual behavior was the acting out of the negative side of the transference expressing her contemptuous attitude toward the therapist and men in general, and at the same time avoiding awareness of the frustrations in therapy by finding infantile gratifications outside treatment. Perhaps a more vigorous and interpretive stance with regard to the hostile and erotized aspects of the transference might have broken through this displacement of the transference.

In each of these three cases the expected suspicion, oral rage, narcissistic defensiveness, and aloofness in the therapeutic relationship did not materialize. The therapists, by design or not, permitted the therapy to ride along on a friendly, positive relationship with no concerted effort to interpret the anger, frustration, and sexual longings of the transference. The first two cases were resoundingly successful, while the marked improvement in the third case was mortgaged to a pathological (homosexual) life pattern. These cases illustrate that at least in some instances a long-term supportive psychotherapy which excludes the negative transference may contribute to considerable therapeutic gains. But an unanswered question persists. How is it possible to differentiate in advance between those supportive therapies which can be expected to ride smoothly and successfully on the positive transference from those cases where, despite the therapists' efforts, the patients are unable either to repress or split off the negative transference elements?

The differentiation would seem to be based upon a favorable balance of the internalized good and bad parental images, bolstered by some capacity to maintain the bad internalized object relationship in repression. Such a constellation seemed to exist in the first two of these three cases where a mainly supportive approach was successfuly used; in the third instance, the split-off negative transference solidified a grossly pathological development.

The Effect of Passive Dependency. Another predictive assumption which was at least partly tested was one which stated that "patients with limited ego strength, poor impulse control, and poor anxiety tolerance, *but* who are passive and dependent, respond positively to the appropriately controlling aspects of supportive psychotherapy by engaging in more adaptive behavior." This proposition was predictively applied to three patients and seemed to be confirmed by one, disconfirmed by another, and partly disconfirmed by the third.

The *Playboy's* relationship with his therapist has been discussed at length and it is quite likely that his ego-syntonic passive dependent character structure contributed substantially to his ability to form a strong and enduring therapeutic alliance. The *Covert Addict* was similarly disposed, but he experienced considerably more difficulty in establishing a workable alliance (although eventually he did). The deterring factor in this patient, diagnosed as a schizophrenic character, was his strong paranoid potential manifested by a strong sense of mistrust of the therapist's motives, expecting at any moment to be fleeced of his sizable inherited fortune. The *Addicted Doctor* never achieved a therapeutic alliance; the obvious defect in his treatment program was the failure to provide hospitalization soon enough when his self-destructiveness (drinking, gross irresponsibility in his job) was going out of control. The patient's passive dependency might ultimately have been an important contributing factor to a supportive psychotherapy, but it was not sufficient in itself to cement a therapeutic alliance.

Need for Distance. Another predictive assumption in the area of therapeutic relationships was formulated as follows: "Patients with markedly ambivalent object relations and fear of affect require that the therapist maintain distance until a firm therapeutic alliance is established, or else they institute distance devices of their own that prevent the achievement of therapeutic goals." This assumption was used for only one patient, the *Loner*. A thirty-five-year-old divorced man, he sought outpatient treatment because of loneliness, alienation, and isolation from others. He was a rigid, constricted, and suspicious individual who was diagnosed as a schizoid personality. Because of his paranoid hyperalertness, his extreme secretiveness, and his need to be in control of all relationships (to be the hunter rather than the hunted), the predictors forecast that a therapeutic alliance would be very slow in forming and would necessitate a slow nondemanding and nonintrusive approach by the therapist.

The prediction regarding the importance of maintaining distance with this patient was strongly confirmed. During a six-year period of psychotherapy which was still continuing (but artifically "cut off" for research purposes), the patient had made two changes of therapists at his request and was in the process of working with his third therapist for over two years. He resented the intrusiveness of the first two therapists: one tried to inquire into the details of his outside life; the other attempted to focus upon his interactions and resistances within the transference. Both were ultimately rejected. The third therapist has been able to maintain a relatively nonthreatening therapeutic relationship by tolerating the patient's need for distance. The patient continues to have relatively little to report or volunteer during his once-a-week, half-hour visits, and the therapist places little demand on him. When the therapist's mild inquiries exceed the patient's limits of tolerance, the patient begins to arch his eyebrows, which is a signal to desist. Within this limited relationship, the patient has been able to find some degree of gratification and to widen his sphere of social contacts, but one would be straining the concept of therapeutic alliance to subsume this relationship under it. The patient seems to have the conviction that the therapist has a benevolent, friendly interest in him and that he is useful as a kind of adviser and counselor. But his paranoid fears prevent him from disclosing most of the details of his external life and all of the details of his inner one. In part, he seems to fear that the disclosure of these secrets would render him unacceptable. But even more, he needs to be in control of the relationship, to set limits on it, and at all times to let the therapist know that he is the predator and not the prey.

In terms of object relations theory, the bad introject in this patient's inner world seems to predominate over the good, and the split or barrier separating the two is highly permeable, always threatened with incursions or contaminations of the good by the bad.

Another aspect of the therapeutic relationship is that though this patient was able to perceive the therapist as benevolent, he was not able to experience him as accepting of his instinctual drives. His silences, withholding, and minimum self-disclosure all suggested the conviction that the therapist would indeed *not* be able to accept his aggressive or libidinal strivings. One might even say that he struggled to keep himself unaware of what the therapist's attitude toward his drives might be, presumably because of the deep-seated conviction that they never would be found acceptable. Thus, in order to establish an optimal or maximal therapeutic alliance, one must not only have a realistic perception of the therapist's benevolent intentions but also a capacity to feel that the therapist accepts one's instinctual drives.

Postdictive Assumptions

There were a number of cases about whom no particular predictions were written concerning the expected vicissitudes of the therapeutic alliance but whose treatment faltered or failed because of a difficulty in establishing a sufficient alliance. Thus, a set of assumptions written after the treatment, postdictively, will be presented here.

Perhaps the primary deterrent to the development of the therapeutic alliance is the patient's paranoid potential: the patient whose reality testing is markedly impaired and who tends to develop a deep-seated mistrust of the therapist's intent and motives cannot develop a therapeutic alliance. We have already referred to a number of patients, in psychoanalysis as well as in psychotherapy, who manifested such reactions.

But there were a few patients, not particularly paranoid in their orientation, who nevertheless had difficulty in perceiving the therapist as friendly and benevolent. These were usually individuals who had strong expectations of being disappointed and frustrated in a close relationship and thus failed to develop a sense of closeness and mutual working together with the therapist. Two analytic patients unexpectedly displayed this reaction. The *Good Son* suffered from a marked sense of oral frustration and deprivation which was never fully uncovered and worked out. He was seeking oral supplies and sustenance but he was neither gratified in this wish nor was it sufficiently interpreted for him to overcome the feelings of disappointment which colored the analytic transference. The *Silent Woman* similarly never overcame her feelings of frustration and disappointment during a less-than-one-year analysis which the patient prematurely terminated. She assumed a phallic competitive stance from the outset and expected a critical and unaccepting response from the analyst. Another patient, the *Dancer*, was discharged from the hospital early in the course of psychotherapy because of certain external factors. From that point on she was never able to view the therapist as a need-gratifying object because her needs for external controls as well as for nurturance could not be gratified in the psychotherapy alone.

A related reaction, a depreciating attitude toward the helping figure, was found to be another severe deterrent to the treatment process. The *Hypochondriac* never really became engaged in treatment, in part because her intense denial of illness led her to insist upon being released from the hospital against medical advice. A complicating feature was her capacity to make the therapist feel insufficient and impotent: she not only externalized her difficulties but the target of the externalization tended to be the therapist; her unwavering message was not only that the therapist was the cause of her suffering but also that he was incapable of doing anything to alleviate it.

An interesting development which substantially contributed to the growth of a therapeutic alliance occurred in the case of a forty-seven-year-old patient, the *Claustrophobic Man*, who had developed anxiety attacks after undergoing presumably successful surgery for cancer of the larynx. The life-threatening illness had caused a regression to marked dependency on his wife and phobias about being left alone. He suffered from a loss of self-esteem and assumed a dependent stance toward the therapist while feeling ashamed of his need for help. During one of his therapy hours he experienced an anxiety attack and expected his therapist to intervene medically to relieve him of his tachycardia and palpitations. Instead, the therapist informed him that he would be able to manage these symptoms successfully by himself which he was then able to do. The incident was the beginning of increased feelings of autonomy and the resulting rise in his self-esteem based upon an enhanced sense of self-reliance contributed to a significant increase in the therapeutic alliance.

SUMMARY

1. A therapeutic alliance is characterized by the conviction on the part of both patient and psychotherapist that their primary goal in working together is to help the patient. It is a necessary part of all treatment, whether psychoanalysis or supportive psychotherapy, but in the latter it often becomes a major curative factor.

2. The development and consolidation of a therapeutic alliance is a function of certain gratifying elements in the treatment situation geared to the special individual needs of the patient which predispose him to view the therapist's efforts as helpful and constructive.

3. One component of a need-gratifying treatment is the performance by the therapist of some parental functions for those patients who are unable to manage certain life tasks. By reinforcing adaptive behaviors through bolstering controls, reality clarification, and sometimes direct advice-giving, a therapeutic alliance tends to be fostered. In our study the major exceptions were those instances where the patients were so lacking in impulse control that the therapists, without the adjunctive support of the hospital, could not prevent a disruption in both their lives and the treatment situation.

4. The assumption that patients who were psychologically immature and who lack a crystallized sense of identity require active supportive interventions by the therapist in order to form a therapeutic alliance was confirmed by the data. The therapists tended to reveal their personal values more readily to younger patients than to the older ones in order to foster identification with these values which, in turn, solidifies the therapeutic relationship.

5. In certain instances of supportive psychotherapy it was possible to establish a predominantly positive relationship with

the patient without significant negative transference reactions intruding upon the treatment situation or being displaced outside of it. We infer that such a situation is made possible by a predominantly good internalized parent-image coupled with a gratifying therapeutic situation.

6. The predictors' assumption was confirmed that passive-dependent traits, especially when they are ego-syntonic, contribute to the development of a therapeutic alliance, provided other negative factors (like a paranoid potential) do not interfere.

7. Patients with a need for distance may reap limited benefits from a psychotherapy in which the therapist cooperates in maintaining a respectful permissiveness and distance.

CHAPTER 9

EFFECTS OF SUPPORTIVE ASPECTS OF PSYCHOTHERAPY

Supportive psychotherapy involves a more complex set of operations and processes than does expressive treatment, which may be conceptualized with great simplicity: it involves the uncovering of unconscious impulse and defense configurations by encouraging regressive transference reactions. This exploratory, uncovering, insight-giving process leads to a diminution of infantile drives and to defenses that are less pathological, i.e., to structural change in the ego.

In contrast, the goal of supportive psychotherapy is to help the patient achieve more adaptive behaviors without uncovering unconscious conflicts. The patient is encouraged to develop more effective means of coping with internal and external pressures through a wide variety of mechanisms all ultimately dependent upon a predominantly positive, trusting relationship or therapeutic alliance. The main processes assumed to influence change in supportive psychotherapy are (1) a corrective emotional experience, (2) the patient's wish to please the therapist, (3) gratification by the therapist of some of the patient's emotional needs, and (4) introjection of the therapist's ego and superego attitudes. While certain cases might emphasize one of these factors more than the others, they usually operate together and reinforce each other.

When the treatment is mainly dependent on these supportive aspects or mechanisms, we describe it as supportive psychotherapy. Of course, all treatments, including psychoanalysis, contain supportive aspects even though the dominant curative factor is interpretation. In a few cases of analysis in this study, the supportive mechanisms unexpectedly loomed larger than the expressive ones.

Supportive psychotherapy was viewed by the predictors as less effective than expressive treatment in achieving thoroughgoing and stable therapeutic change. They saw it as necessary for those patients whose ego resources could not tolerate the strains and anxieties of undergoing a more probing, exploratory process. But they expected these patients to pay the price of such compromise via a limitation in the *degree* of change and a lesser *stability* of change in the face of life's vicissitudes.

Some of the assumption statements representing the thinking of the predictors convey the sense of limited outcome expected with supportive treatment:

> Patients in supportive psychotherapy with limited ego strength, low anxiety tolerance, and limited psychological-mindedness but with a strong motivation for change are unable to achieve major intrapsychic change but can achieve more socially acceptable modes of expression of unconscious conflict and therefore an improved life adjustment.

Supportive aspects of psychotherapy do not alter the infantile fantasies which underlie symptoms.

Supportive psychotherapy does not lead to the integration of infantile instinctual aims and objects into a mature personality organization.

Patients who achieve at most a minimal resolution of conflict in response to the supportive aspects of psychotherapy effect a more adaptive adjustment, but continue to show behavioral evidence of the unresolved core conflicts.

In this chapter, we will examine the findings in those cases which showed a positive response to predominantly supportive aspects of treatment. We shall assess the extent of change as well as the extent of limitation. In addition, we shall present findings concerning the changes in expressive treatments induced by supportive aspects. Stability of change in these cases will be discussed in Chapter 10.

SELECTION OF IMPROVED CASES

The Prediction Study team gave a 5-point absolute global change rating[1] to every patient in the study at termination and follow-up. Using the scale for the 24 patients in psychotherapy, judged at the termination point, 10 were deemed moderately

1. The 5-point ratings consisted of 1—worse, 2—no change, 3—slight improvement, 4—moderate improvement, and 5—marked improvement with conflict resolution. The ratings were first made independently by the two judges (the author and his co-worker, Dr. Ann Appelbaum), and then a consensus rating was decided upon. The scale is described in greater detail in a paper by the authors (1969).

improved (rating of 4), and 3 were described as slightly improved (rating of 3). Of the other 11 patients, 5 did not change and 6 got worse. Since we are interested in investigating both the changes that are possible and the limitation of such changes in supportive treatment, the discussion in this chapter will be confined to those patients who had (1) a clearly positive response at termination (rating of 4) and (2) a psychotherapy which was mainly supportive. We shall be mainly interested in assessing the accuracy of the predictors with regard to supportive treatment. The patients in psychotherapy who either did not improve or got worse have already been discussed under the headings of adjunctive supports and therapeutic alliance (Chapters 7 and 8).

There was one (*Heiress*) in the group of 10 patients receiving an absolute global change score of 4 whose treatment was clearly more expressive than supportive. She was the only person in the group of 24 psychotherapy patients whose treatment had the outer trappings of psychoanalysis for the entire 7 years of her treatment course (the couch and free association). She was in a classical analysis for the first 2 years; and, after a stalemate occurred, she was transferred to another analyst who first attempted a classical procedure but then introduced a number of parameters when he decided that she could not tolerate psychoanalysis. He interacted with her more freely, deliberately attempted to convey his warmth and friendliness, encouraged adaptive behaviors, and was more free in revealing himself as a real person. These nonanalytic parameters were maintained throughout the treatment and were not analyzed. At the same time the therapist attempted to use, wherever possible, interpretation of unconscious conflict mainly based on extratransferential material. There was agreement on all sides that this was an expressive psychotherapy and not an analysis.

Table 2

Absolute Global Change and Health-Sickness Rating Change on the Psychotherapy Cases

Patient	Global Change Termination	HSRS Residual Change at Termination [a]
Phobic Girl	4	73.5
Fencer	4	64.0
Obedient Husband	4	59.6
Playboy	4	74.0
Thespian	4	65.0
Involutional Woman	4	59.1
Historian	4	42.4
Travel Phobia Woman	4	66.2
Claustrophobic Man	4	73.2
Heiress	4	64.7
Bohemian	3	71.6
Passive Student	3	54.0
Prep School Boy	3	61.0
Movie Woman	2	61.2
Dancer	2	64.5
Loner	2	38.6
Grandson	2	37.1
Rebel Coed	2	57.0
Covert Addict	1	53.6
Salesman	1	44.5
Addicted Doctor	1	37.6
Hypochondriac	1	37.6
Sociopath	1	31.0
Spinster	1	28.9

[a] The residual change score is the difference between the initial and termination HSRS scores, corrected for the "law of initial values"—the tendency for low initial scores to increase more than do high initial ones. The units of change differ from the units of the scale itself.

Table 2 presents the absolute global change ratings and also the Health-Sickness Rating Scale (HSRS) residual change scores. The latter is based upon a 100-point anchored rating scale but, for statistical reasons, the units of change differ from the units of the scale itself (see footnote, Table 2). As mentioned earlier, the main criteria of the HSRS consist of personal autonomy, extent of disorganization, subjective discomfort, productivity, interpersonal relationships, and range of interests. The two scales for the entire 42 cases were highly correlated ($r = .91$) and inspection of the table reveals few individual discrepancies of any magnitude. The major discrepancy for our purposes is the *Bohemian*, whom we called only slightly improved (rating of 3) but whose HSRS residual change score was 71.6, the highest score for 13 patients with global change scores less than 4. We are therefore adding her to our group of moderately changed patients, bringing the group (after the deletion of the *Heiress*) back to an *N* of 10.

SUMMARIES OF TREATMENT TECHNIQUES AND PATIENT CHANGES

Ten cases will be presented, with an eye toward examining the hypothesis that supportive treatment is not capable of producing extensive change. The vignettes for each case will include (1) the main technique used by the therapist, (2) the predicted changes given a particular modality, and (3) the actual changes which occurred.

The cases have been grouped into two categories: those whom the predictors expected to get supportive treatment, and those they expected to get an expressive or at least somewhat expressive approach. The question in each instance is whether the cases expected to get supportive treatment reached or exceeded the predicted goals; and similarly, how did the actual developments with supportive measures compare to predicted outcome, where the predictions were made for a more expressive treatment? If expectations for expressive treatment were actually reached under a regimen of supportive treatment, one would be forced to question the assumption that supportive techniques are, per se, less effective than expressive techniques.

Predictions Based on Supportive
Psychotherapy

Four cases in this group of improved patients were expected to have a predominantly supportive treatment. In three instances the actual outcomes exceeded the predictors' expectations. A summary of each treatment follows:

BOHEMIAN

The *Bohemian*, forty-one years of age, entered the hospital with a marked agitated depression precipitated by her husband's insistence that she return to their home and live with him and their child. She had been living the life of a Bohemian artist for a number of years prior to receiving this ultimatum. Upon her return home her downward course was swift and dramatic; hospitalization was essential. She began psychotherapy a few months after hospitalization.

The predictors expected that with supportive psychotherapy she would be able to achieve a somewhat improved life situation without any appreciable intrapsychic change. They predicted she would be able to resolve the dilemma of an impossible marital situation in favor of giving it up, which she indeed did. But they believed her weak ego resources, her depressive potential, and her marked narcissism would prevent her from achieving more than a limited outcome. They forecast an asexual outcome in which the patient would settle for some gratifying, artistic, and intellectual pursuits with a few female friends. A new and better marriage was not seen as a possibility. Contrary to this prediction, the patient at termination had not only reestablished sublimatory gratification in work (as an art teacher), but had also become involved in a stable romantic relationship. There was a distinct rise in self-esteem.

Treatment consisted largely of skillful counseling about the complex life circumstances she had to untangle. At all times the patient felt the final decision was hers, and could take pride in having worked things out for herself. She usually rejected interpretive efforts to link the present with the past and to call transference reactions to her attention, although she was able to recall and accept her childhood hatred of her mother's demandingness, and to recognize how she now treated herself with the same uncompromising strictness she had so resented as a child. The therapist respected her rejection of transference interpretations and used the uninterpreted positive transference as a vehicle of the treatment, allowing the negative aspects of the transference to be deflected upon the hospital doctor.[2]

PLAYBOY

The *Playboy*, a twenty-seven-year-old professional man, applied for treatment because of periods of depression since his boyhood and an inability to apply himself in his work since finishing professional school. He was admitted to the hospital with a diagnosis of manic-depressive

2. This treatment paragraph and a few others in this section were written by Dr. Ann Appelbaum and are taken from a paper by Appelbaum and Horwitz (1969; unpublished).

disorder in a narcissistic personality. The Initial Study team expected the regressive course of his illness characterized by excessive drinking and promiscuity would be stopped, that the cyclic mood swings would become attenuated, but doubted his capacity to establish a satisfying heterosexual relationship.

All of the expected gains occurred in the course of four years of psychotherapy, but there were considerably more changes as well. The cyclic mood swings had practically disappeared. The patient married and, despite his narcissistic as well as sexually sadistic tendencies, was able to establish a fairly gratifying relationship with his wife, marred somewhat by the persistence of masturbation. Elements of borderline thinking still persisted but in a markedly attenuated form. He was able to assume a more responsible professional attitude toward his patients without constantly feeling the need to rid himself of these pressures. He had achieved a considerably enhanced self-esteem and was no longer painfully shy and awkward in social situations.

The therapist focused upon day-to-day problems, offering himself as a benevolent, helpful authority figure, never insisting that the patient discuss matters that were too upsetting for him. The climate of the transference was consistently friendly, and the therapist tactfully withdrew when the patient's warm feelings toward him began to make the young man uneasy. The therapist's major goal was to help the patient establish himself productively in his chosen field; to this end he manifested respect for the patient's professional responsibilities, even permitting the patient to give them precedence over scheduled therapy meetings. At the same time the patient implicitly was expected to respect the therapist's responsibilities, so that the therapist would reschedule hours only during the regular working day, and charged the patient for appointments missed without notice.

OBEDIENT HUSBAND

The *Obedient Husband*, a thirty-eight-year-old businessman, sought treatment because of feelings of inadequacy, depression, and a tendency to drink excessively. He was dominated by his wife, an emotionally disturbed woman who started her own psychiatric treatment in the hospital. In view of his initial weak motivation, the Initial Study team agreed that his psychotherapy would be a "holding action" which would permit him to reestablish a more satisfactory neurotic equilibrium with his wife. But these minimal expectations were certainly exceeded, even though supportive treatment twice a week lasted for only eighteen months. The patient was able to become more assertive both at home and on the job, he was able to modulate his excessively dependent and pathological interaction with his wife, his depression was greatly reduced, and he was able to give up his drinking. His new assertiveness in his work and marriage was achieved through compliance with the pressure of his therapist; it resulted in a considerable enhancement of the patient's self-esteem.

The first step forward in this patient's treatment occurred when the therapist recommended, after a few months, that he stop his drinking. The patient's success in this attempt encouraged him to assert control over other aspects of his life to which he had hitherto submitted as his lot. When strong feelings of love and fear toward the therapist threatened to emerge into awareness, he asserted his newfound "manliness" by insisting upon termination. The therapist did not attempt to interpret the unconscious sources of his wish to end the treatment, just as she had refrained from interpreting the transference implications of some of his hostile behavior toward other women during the treatment.

THESPIAN

The *Thespian* was hospitalized at the age of nineteen because of serious behavior disturbances at college, such as excessive drinking, promiscuity, histrionic behavior, and lying. She was diagnosed as an infantile and narcissistic personality with borderline "as-if" features. Deep-seated oral conflicts were evident as well as contemptuous attitudes toward men. After a hospitalization cut short by economic necessity, she began outpatient psychotherapy which continued for more than four years.

The predictors believed she would be helped to stabilize her life, give up the play-acting and histrionics which characterized her relationships, and be able to control her more self-destructive behavior. They were reluctant to forecast the direction her sexual adjustment would take and tended toward predicting an "asexual" outcome.

The first phase of treatment was characterized by hetero-sexual and homosexual promiscuity with a strong self-destructive coloring, drinking sprees, wild parties, and a generally chaotic life. Gradually these misbehaviors were brought under control and the patient settled into a more stable existence. She found regular employment as a salesgirl and more stable social and sexual outlets, although she moved steadily toward the life of a confirmed homosexual. When the treatment ended, she felt pleased with the arrest of the downward, regressive course her life had been taking. She had given up her interest in dramatics and was planning to continue earning her living as a secretary, as she had begun to do during treatment.

The therapist first tried to work interpretively with her, but her chaotic life made this impossible, especially without concomitant hospital treatment. At last, she and the therapist found a common basis upon which they could proceed with their task: they implicitly agreed to work toward a reasonably stable social and vocational adjustment, to accept her homosexuality, and try to help her live thus with dignity and satisfaction. Meanwhile, she maintained toward the therapist the demeanor of a good and polite little girl being counseled by a patient and kindly parent. Her hostility and sadomasochistic proclivities found expression outside the treatment in feuding with hospital personnel and in a gradually diminishing succession of tumultuous encounters with lovers and friends.

These four cases illustrate the minimal expectations associated with supportive treatment in which behavioral changes as well as symptom remissions are associated with direct suggestion, advice, and the wish to please the therapist. More was accomplished with the first three cases than was expected under a regimen of supportive treatment, yet all of the treatments were mainly supportive. The changes in the fourth case were not substantially different from what was expected.

Predictions Based on Expressive Aspects of Psychotherapy

The next four patients were expected to make significant gains in treatment provided they had either a primarily expressive psychotherapy or analysis. Although each of the treatments did have some expressive elements, they actually were more supportive than expressive in terms of *the therapist's consistent avoidance of transference interpretations.* Nevertheless, each patient was able to achieve behavioral and symptomatic changes comparable to those predicted with the expectation of a more expressive treatment.

PHOBIC GIRL

The *Phobic Girl*, a young woman of twenty-one, sought treatment because of lifelong obesity, severe phobias, and promiscuity. Under a regimen of expressive psychotherapy the predictors expected that her obesity would persist to some extent but that her phobias would be significantly modified as would her passive dependency, her severe narcissism, hostility, promiscuity, and impulse control. Unless the treatment were to evolve into an analysis, the predictors thought that close and satisfactory heterosexual relationships would be beyond this girl's capabilities and that marriage would be unlikely.

In a treatment which was much more supportive than had been anticipated the patient was able to achieve all of the predicted changes and more. In addition to diminished phobias and a generally better organized life, she was able to effect a fairly stable and gratifying marriage.

The therapist did not hesitate to offer advice when it seemed to be needed, told her that she had to modify her more self-destructive sexual behavior and, on a few occasions, met with her parents in order to help protect the therapy situation. The expressive aspects of the treatment consisted of clarifying for the patient her own contribution to the unpleasant experiences which were besetting her. This appeared to be crucial in helping her gradually behave in a more sensible manner. The therapist did not interpret the living out of hostile and erotic aspects of the transference in the patient's life, though he did intervene with direct prohibitions when necessary for her safety. Often he was able to show her how her current relationships with others were a repetition of earlier experiences. He fostered the positive aspects of the transference, using her trust for him to influence her behavior in the direction of greater independence and a more gratifying life. But an equally important determinant of change was the therapist's sustained benevolent interest in her and his ability to partially gratify some of her infantile needs, which contributed to a rise in the patient's self-esteem.

FENCER

The *Fencer*, a thirty-year-old unmarried woman, was hospitalized in connection with a severe barbiturate addiction of three years' standing. She suffered from feelings of intense inadequacy and worthlessness as a person, and particularly as a woman, and was angrily competitive with men for their presumed superior role. She had been involved in overt homosexual activity, and all of her relationships were impaired by arrogance and competitiveness. Most of her overt symptoms dropped away during the course of a two-year psychotherapy: the addiction, the homosexual tendencies, her aggressive hyperintellectualism, as well as her perennial feelings of frustration and inferiority. But the basis of these altered behaviors was the enhanced self-esteem, and the greater sense of being accepted and appreciated, and this was not what had been anticipated. The changes did not reflect any significant working through of conflict with concomitant insight as had been expected. Rather, the substantial life achievements which occurred, including a successful romance and marriage (albeit to a rather disturbed man), were based upon a variety of supportive mechanisms which the patient had experienced within a therapeutic alliance and a positive unanalyzed transference attachment. Many of her behavioral gains consisted of "living out" her underlying competitive conflicts in a more socially acceptable form.

The predictors had expected that expressive psychotherapy, offering a lesser degree of conflict resolution than analysis, would help her dampen some of her less agreeable traits and permit her to use her good intelligence in the service of more productive and gratifying work and achievement. Even these achievements, however, would presumably be based upon the patient's ability to at least partly resolve the phallic conflicts which lay at the basis of her difficulty—issues which were barely touched in the treatment.

Overtly negative feelings never entered the transference, being displaced onto the administrative hospital doctor. Similarly, she warded off erotic feelings by defensive flights into extratherapeutic encounters. The therapist made some sporadic efforts to interpret her masculine, competitive strivings, but when she protested, he backed off. At no time did he attempt to point out her efforts to assert her superiority over him. Rather he accepted the positive transference role of a kindly, protective, and interested father and permitted the treatment to ride on this alliance. In this sense, it became a mainly supportive treatment. This patient achieved as much behavioral change as had been predicted for her as the outcome of a more expressive psychotherapy; although conflict resolution had not occurred, she made significant gains in self-esteem and in her capacity to control her maladaptive tendencies.

INVOLUTIONAL WOMAN

The *Involutional Woman*, a fifty-four-year-old housewife, entered the hospital for treatment of depression and was referred for psychotherapy shortly thereafter. The wife of a lawyer, she had been valedictorian of her own law school class but had never practiced law. Throughout her life she had depreciated the role of housewife and mother, enviously depreciating her husband's competence in his professional activities. Reaction formation, frequent somatic illness, and a critical attitude toward her husband, which was barely kept under control, characterized her premorbid adjustment. In the course of a seven-year supportive treatment, the patient's depression abated, she became warmer and more accepting toward her husband and children, and she was able to find gratifying avocational outlets in community work. On the other hand, a severe somatic problem necessitated frequent medical attention which seemed to involve secondary gain.

Although the predictors did not expect the patient's problems of penis envy and phallic competitiveness to be uncovered and resolved, mainly because of her characterological rigidity, they did forecast that the expression and ventilation of angry feelings *within the transference* would gradually permit her to better accept her hostility. Actually, the outstanding characteristic of the two purely supportive treatments which she underwent (her first therapist left the city after two years of treatment) was the avoidance of negative feelings the patient had toward her therapists. Whenever these feelings threatened to arise, they were promptly deflected into a discussion of the relationship of the patient with her husband, a tactic which the therapist encouraged on her part. Both therapists behaved in a benevolent fatherly manner toward her, permitting some mild depreciatory acting out to occur without interpretation. Under this benign regimen, the patient not only overcame her depression and was better able to attain some limited gratification in work outside the home, but she was able to achieve a more mutually satisfying relationship with her husband—her competitiveness became modulated and disagreements between them could be discussed more openly. The patient had indeed been able to become more accepting of her angry critical feelings and was not obliged constantly to smother them. This result had been achieved primarily on the basis of the patient introjecting the therapist's more benign superego attitude toward hostile impulses.

CLAUSTROPHOBIC MAN

The *Claustrophobic Man*, a forty-seven-year-old successful businessman, came for outpatient psychiatric treatment as a result of phobic anxieties which started in the wake of a series of operations for cancer. He feared that he would die of a heart attack, alone and unattended in a crowded place among strangers. To guard against this possibility, he insisted that his wife never leave him unattended. The research team viewed his severe phobia and his regressive, clinging demandingness as reactive symptoms to the life-threatening cancer, a fear which the patient vehemently denied. The patient's core conflicts around oral dependent strivings which heretofore had been warded off by denial, reaction formation, and counterphobic mastery, were now being reactivated by the reality threat to his life.

The patient was successfully treated by a supportive psychotherapy of only forty-six hours strung out over a period of eighteen months. Gradually the intensity of his phobic symptoms diminished, his grip on his wife lessened, and his self-esteem was enhanced. He became relatively symptom-free and was delighted with the restoration to his premorbid level of functioning. The big insight he achieved was that the responsibility for his "nervousness" rested within him, that it could be "controlled," and that he would not die of it. The predictors had called for substantial shifts both behaviorally and intrapsychically, including insight into his denial and regressive reaction to the cancer which, in addition to the reality threat, had the meaning of castration and abandonment. Although extensive insights did not occur, he achieved substantially the kind of life changes which the predictors believed could occur only with successful uncovering of conflict.

The therapist constantly encouraged the patient in his efforts at counterphobic mastery over his anxiety attacks, insisting that he enter the phobic situations which he had avoided. The therapist interdicted all alcohol intake prior to appointments. The patient was impressed with the therapist's calm attitude and understanding as he related his paralyzing fears. A turning point in the treatment occurred when the patient began to experience an anxiety attack during a therapy hour. To the patient's consternation, but then relief and pride, the therapist calmly conveyed to the patient that he could control this reaction if he wanted to. A dependent, positive transference attachment was encouraged and maintained uninterpreted. In effect, the therapist had made an implicit promise that he would never abandon the patient, and in return the patient was willing to give up his symptoms; this was a transference cure.

All four of these cases were expected to make considerable change provided expressive psychotherapy, including an emphasis upon transference interpretation, helped the patient achieve at least a partial resolution of conflict. This treatment contingency was not fulfilled, the treatments were predominantly supportive, yet most of the expected symptom and behavioral changes occurred.

Predictions Based on Psychoanalysis

The final two cases which ultimately ended as successful psychotherapy cases had started in psychoanalysis and were switched to face-to-face supportive treatment after analysis had proved unworkable or unhelpful.

HISTORIAN

The *Historian*, a thirty-one-year-old college instructor, came for treatment because the problems which led to the breakup of his first marriage were now threatening a new budding relationship with a woman. He was beset by severe sexual inhibitions, a strongly passive-dependent orientation, and struggles over latent homosexual strivings. Diagnosed as a compulsive character neurosis, psychoanalysis was recommended, and a fairly complete resolution of his neurotic problems was expected. After a six-year analysis in which the patient clung tenaciously to a passive-dependent stance, his psychotic potential finally emerged in the form of a full-blown transference psychosis. The analyst altered his interpretive focus from the patient's wish for enduring nurture and gratification to a concentration upon the patient's rage and envy toward the analyst-father for his sexual prohibitions. In response, the patient developed delusional convictions that the analyst was indeed prohibiting him from having relationships with women and was exercising control over all the women he knew, even including the patient's mother. This psychotic transference development led the analyst to reverse his field and to institute an explicitly supportive psychotherapy. Once the treatment modality was shifted, the implicit understanding conveyed to the patient was that his need for indefinite nurture was indeed going to be gratified. The therapist offered fatherly advice, made suggestions as to how the patient could best cope with day-to-day difficulties, actively encouraged him to overcome his inhibitions about moving forward in his profession and achieving an advanced degree. The patient blossomed under this kindly protection and soon reestablished his prepsychotic transference position—he was docile, compliant, and appreciative toward the analyst. He went on to achieve his doctoral degree; his psychosomatic symptoms decreased, and his homosexual preoccupations lessened. Although his social isolation diminished, he was still unable to develop enduring relationships with women.

The optimism of the predictors, both diagnostically and prognostically, was reflected in their failure to diagnose his psychotic potential and their expectation of a highly successful analytic result. The actual result with supportive treatment was, of course, far short of the predicted changes.

TRAVEL PHOBIA WOMAN

The *Travel Phobia Woman*, a forty-one-year-old divorcee, was hospitalized in connection with prolonged addiction to drugs and alcohol, phobic withdrawal, and a generally chaotic and disorganized life. Despite the seriousness of her symptoms, psychoanalysis was recommended as the treatment of choice. The predictors were not sanguine about the probable outcome of the analysis because of the patient's strong oral fixations, but they felt that analysis was the only treatment which afforded a possibility for the patient to achieve a reasonably autonomous life, free of her constricting phobias and dependency. Shortly after beginning analysis, it became clear that the patient was unable to tolerate it. She was either unable or unwilling to free associate, and was particularly averse to expressing either hostile or erotic feelings about the analyst. Indeed, she seemed to be making a distinct effort to maintain an image of him as highly idealized and uncontaminated by her libidinal and aggressive strivings. The patient's first analyst died unexpectedly after six years, and her second analyst made an effort to reinstitute an analytic procedure but met with the same barriers experienced by the first. A complicating feature in this case was a mild but significant organic brain syndrome (definitely established by psychological testing during her second course of treatment) which made it difficult for the patient to generalize from the concrete instance to more general attitudes. This accounted for the severe limitation in her psychological-mindedness.

Both therapists played the role of the protecting, nurturing parent who would always be available to her. They were friendly counselors on whom she could lean and for whom she was willing to make a number of adaptive changes: abstinence from drugs and alcohol, and an effort to master her phobias. Though she became immeasurably better organized and more productive than in the years before the treatment, she did continue to live a rather lonely and constricted existence. Furthermore, her treatment was continuing with only slight reduction in frequency at the end of eight years, at which time an artificial cutoff point was made for research purposes. The predictors had considered the possibility that her analysis would bog down into an insoluble transference jam (based on her intense orality), which actually had occurred. But supportive treatment allowed her to make certain adaptive changes which approached, though fell short of, the changes predicted for a moderately successful analysis.

EXTENT OF SUPPORTIVE TECHNIQUES

To what extent were these ten cases treated by the use of supportive techniques, and to what extent did expressive measures play a role in their improvement? Unquestionably the major emphasis in most of the treatments, if not all, was on supportive measures. A few of the cases had some expressive aspects, and we propose to look more carefully at the issue of whether any of them should be labeled anything other than mainly supportive psychotherapy.

There were four cases which may categorically be called supportive psychotherapy from beginning to end in terms of the therapist's intentions, his goals, and his techniques. The therapist relied almost exclusively on encouraging more adaptive behavior through counseling, advice-giving, encouragement of constructive changes, and discouraging (or even interdicting) noxious behavior. Treatment did not attempt to elicit regressive transference reactions, either negative or positive. The therapeutic alliance, bolstered by positive transference feelings, was a major vehicle for influencing the patient in positive directions. There was no effort to uncover unconscious wishes either through the use of the transference or by means of extratransferential interpretation.

Thus, the *Playboy*'s therapist deliberately sidestepped the exploration of issues (like his sexual difficulties) which were potentially disturbing, while he emphasized the ways the patient was dealing with his professional and family responsibilities. At follow-up, the patient complained mildly that the therapist may have treated him too gingerly on certain matters like his sexual concerns. *The Obedient Husband*'s therapist used the patient's passive compliant propensities in the service of encouraging him to become more masculine and assertive. Without exploring his underlying submission to a powerful maternal introject, she used this transference propensity to help him become less of a pawn in his wife's hands with a resulting rise in self-esteem as he felt more successful as a man. The *Involutional Woman* was helped to use her talents and abilities vocationally and in community volunteer work while encouraged to soften her competitiveness and envy toward her husband. The obvious depreciating tendencies toward the therapist, largely acted out in her reliance on other helping figures beside the therapist, remained uninterpreted. And the *Claustrophobic Man*'s therapist neither interpreted the patient's denial of anxiety about his cancer, nor his dependency wishes on the therapist and wife, nor his underlying castration fears. He simply conveyed the attitude that the patient's anxiety attacks were not life-threatening and more under his control than he thought.

We may add the two "psychoanalytic" patients to this list if only their postanalytic treatment is considered. The *Travel Phobia Woman* was unable to use the method of free association. She did respond to the analyst's interest, and the shift of modality was a recognition of what the patient could and could not use. The *Historian* first remained on a plateau and then finally decompensated seriously in analysis. He began to make progress when the therapy became face-to-face and explicitly supportive.

The remaining four cases had varying elements of expressiveness. The therapist made sporadic efforts to interpret the *Bohemian's* competitiveness with him as well as her anger at him for not gratifying her intense oral needs. She displaced her transference competitiveness and anger onto her hospital doctor and acted out transference love in her romantic entanglements. But she dismissed the therapist's efforts to interpet these displacements and he eventually permitted her improvement to continue and consolidate without further transference interpretation or, for that matter, without any effort to produce insight into her competitive and narcissistic needs. Throughout the treatment she saw the therapist as a kindly, helpful father-figure and he exploited this positive transference in the service of encouraging adaptive change.

A similar situation prevailed in the case of the *Thespian*. A polite and friendly, though perhaps slightly distant, relationship prevailed throughout the treatment. An unspoken gentlemen's agreement was established in which the patient did not express aggressive or sexual feelings toward the therapist, and he refrained from attempting to uncover such feelings. The research team believed that the patient split the transference, allowing only mildly friendly feelings toward the therapist and expressing angry, provocative feelings in her homosexual encounters. The therapist made a few efforts to uncover some of her less accessible feelings, for a brief period even putting her on the couch and asking her to free associate, but these attempts were not fruitful and were quickly abandoned. Once again, we see a mainly supportive treatment with practically no uncovering or insight in transferential or extratransferential events.

Several of the researchers referred to the *Fencer's* treatment as expressive psychotherapy, but others questioned this. When the therapist attempted to explore the sources of the patient's extreme competitiveness with men, the patient could readily recall memories (mostly from adolescence) of the struggles with father and brother for recognition. But when he sought to probe more deeply into the sources of her envy and aggression, she characteristically engaged in a verbal fencing match in order to disprove his point. The therapist did not attempt to interpret the transference need to vanquish him at his own game. Even though some clarification of the more conscious connections between past and present occurred, there was practically no work on the transference feelings which found expression in her behavior outside the treatment hour. The patient preferred to ride through the treatment on an unanalyzed positive attachment, the liking and admiration for the new, more benevolent version of the previously rejecting father, and the therapist went along with this. One could say that there was a beginning effort in the direction of expressiveness in the uncovering of unconscious meanings of her behavior and the relationship between past and present; but the essential element, the interpretation of transference and resistance, did not occur. Hence we would not classify this treatment as mainly expressive.

The last case in this series, the *Phobic Girl*, probably had more expressive elements than any of the others but still fell short of involving a fully, or even mainly, expressive treatment. The therapist did considerable interpretive work on the daily manifestations of her masochism as it showed in her social and sexual encounters. He emphasized the ways in which her victimization resulted from her own behavior and provocation. But these insights, valuable as they were, were not related to genetic reconstruction or to transference reactions. The therapist carefully avoided dealing with hostile or sexual transference feelings, preferring to counsel, advise, guide, and protect her by relying on an unanalyzed positive transference. Once again, the expressive elements of the treatment were secondary to the supportive aspects because transference expression was neither encouraged nor interpreted.

Although the ten cases varied in the relative emphasis on supportive and expressive techniques, they all shared a common supportive core in that none of them had a primary emphasis on the interpretation of transference. The improvement that occurred was primarily attributable to the opportunity provided these patients to identify themselves with a benevolent object that gradually served to modify pathological aspects of ego and superego functioning.

EXTENT OF IMPROVEMENT AND LIMITATION

The Prediction Study provides us with a method of assessing whether a mainly supportive treatment produces the kind and degree of limited outcome assumed by our predictors and presumably by other analytic therapists as well. In some instances, the predictions of change were based on mainly supportive treatment; in others the predictions assumed important expressive components. The outcomes of these predictions offer an opportunity to assess the correctness of the assumption that supportive treatment makes possible certain adaptive changes but that its behavioral and intrapsychic effects are limited by comparison with those of treatments aimed at uncovering and resolving unconscious conflicts.

With regard to the four cases of expected supportive treatment, three of them reflect a clear underestimation of the patient's predicted gains. Each of the three was expected to experience a remission of his presenting symptoms but no significant behavioral changes. Neither the *Bohemian* nor the *Playboy* was thought to be capable of a satisfactory sustained heterosexual relationship without extensive uncovering, expressive work (which they were not thought capable of doing). The

Obedient Husband's gains were expected to hinge upon the vicissitudes of his wife's illness and her willingness to permit him to "appear" more assertive. In actual fact, the first two of these patients made satisfactory marriages and the third patient changed from lamb to lion in reaction to the therapist's suggestions and encouragement. The fourth patient, the *Thespian*, reached the expected improvements in achieving a more stable life with somewhat more genuine relationships, although the development of a homosexual way of life was not expected. The predictors thought she was more likely to withdraw from sexual attachments. Unlike the other three cases, no greater achievement occurred than anticipated.

The next four cases were expected to have psychotherapy with important expressive components. They all received a predominantly supportive treatment which brought them to the level predicted for a mainly expressive psychotherapy. The changes that occurred were rarely on the basis expected by the predictors. The *Phobic Girl* was not expected to establish a satisfying heterosexual relationship unless the therapy succeeded in uncovering and resolving her deep-seated oral conflicts. This resolution did not occur; yet she made a seemingly stable marriage before the end of treatment. The predictors thought the *Fencer* might be able to overcome her disturbed competitive relationships with men if her angry, envious feelings toward that sex could be expressed and dealt with interpretively. Therapy did not achieve this conflict-resolving goal, but the patient made great behavioral strides, including a marriage, albeit one with many problems. We have already shown that the *Claustrophobic Man* was relieved of most symptoms and freed his wife from the bondage of his dependency on her, without recognizing his regressive reaction to a life-threatening illness or gaining insight into his strong dependency needs. The *Involutional Woman* reached most of the goals set for her by the predictors. She did not deal with her hostile transference within the treatment but she was able to establish a closer, more open relationship with her husband with substantially less depression and inhibition. All of these patients—expected to be treated with significant expressive techniques but receiving supportive treatment instead—achieved outcomes equal to or exceeding those predicted for the more intensive treatment.

The final two cases had been started in analysis but were switched to an explicitly supportive modality. The *Historian's* predicted outcome was as erroneous as his initial evaluation. The grossly inaccurate initial assessment and prediction prevent any useful comparison with his response to supportive treatment. But the *Travel Phobia Woman* was more accurately assessed. The predictors thought she was likely to develop an insoluble transference neurosis because of the intensity of her dependency needs, and they predicted a most limited outcome. If she was able to avoid that hazard, they thought she would still emerge as a less than fully autonomous individual, but capable of functioning without ongoing therapeutic support. The actual response (at an artificial cutoff point) was midway between the two analytic results insofar as her functioning had indeed improved but she needed to cling to her therapist.

There appears to be clear evidence that supportive treatment tended to accomplish more than expected, and that it frequently reached the expectations associated with expressive treatment. Thus, in terms of the *extent* of change, supportive treatment has been underestimated by analytically oriented therapists as represented by our predictors.

But this conclusion does not mean that supportive treatment should be considered as effective as expressive psychotherapy. The stability of change issue has not yet been discussed (see Chapter 10) nor has an actual comparison been made between the two modalities on comparable patients. We have only compared *predictions* of one or the other with supportive treatment.

Actually, the data on these ten patients raises some questions, unfortunately unanswerable, regarding the possible limitations of a supportive approach even when we confine ourselves to the issue of extent of change. All of them were significantly improved but four of them revealed handicaps of some importance.

The two "refugees" from psychoanalysis had not really severed their connection with their therapists at the artificial cutoff point, and seemed to have developed an addiction to treatment. We know that these two patients were not suitable analytic cases, but this does not necessarily mean they were unable to tolerate an expressive, or partly expressive, approach. Is it possible that the dependency gratification of supportive treatment tended to foster the use of treatment as a crutch? Or, was the treatment approach a necessary measure and the continuing dependence a small price for the gains accomplished?

Similar questions may be raised about the sexual "compromises" reached by the *Fencer* and the *Thespian*. In a complex acting out of a number of transference wishes, the *Fencer* married a man with considerable pathology and instability. If the envious, competitive transference had been worked with, instead of sidestepped, would this patient have resolved her phallic conflicts sufficiently to have made a potentially more stable marriage? One might speculate that such conflict resolution was within her capacity and that it might well have improved her marital choice. The *Thespian* moved into a stable homosexual way of life during her treatment. The termination research team believed that the therapist's failure to work actively with her angry, contemptuous feelings toward men in the transference as well as her feelings of oral deprivation toward the therapist may have encouraged this less-than-desirable sexual orientation. The homosexuality represented an acting out of these phallic and oral conflicts which did not find direct expression in the transference because of a collusion by patient and therapist to maintain a "friendly and polite" relationship. If this formulation is correct, and the patient had been capable of working expressively, the sexual perversion might have been reversed.

SIGNIFICANT CHANGES IN EXPRESSIVE TREATMENTS BASED UPON SUPPORTIVE FACTORS

In a number of cases the predictors were quite explicit about the occurrence of conflict resolution as a necessary condition for certain behavioral or symptomatic changes to develop. Their assumption was captured by the following statement: "Symptoms, character traits, and life-style which are rooted in lifelong deeply repressed intrapsychic conflict are significantly altered only on the basis of a full working through of the conflict." This assumption was used 31 times for 17 cases; it could be tested only in some 50 percent of the instances, usually because of wrong initial patient assessments. But it has the dubious distinction of garnering the highest number of disconfirmations (disconfirmed seven times for six patients) in our total population of assumptions. Not only did the predictors underrate the potential influence of supportive treatment, but they made the converse error of overestimating the necessity for conflict resolution in order to achieve certain results. Thus, they made certain clear-cut predictions about failure to change (like the inability to marry, the inability to successfully adopt a child, the inability to achieve a compatible marital relationship, etc.) unless the patient was able to resolve the unconscious conflicts associated with these behavioral problems. The following vignettes describe these predictive errors, again illustrating the greater potency of supportive treatment than is generally attributed to it in the psychoanalytic theory of psychotherapy.

ADOPTIVE MOTHER

The *Adoptive Mother* had come to psychiatric treatment because of her inability to adopt a child successfully. She had made one brief abortive attempt to do so but had to return the child to the adoption agency after four months because of mounting distress and fear of harming the infant. The predictors believed that her incapacity to be a proper mother was based upon a hostile identification with her own mother. They forecasted that the patient would be able to adopt a child successfuly *only* if the deep-seated, repressed conflict with the dangerous and hated mother imago was uncovered and resolved. The prediction, however, was incorrect; the patient was indeed able to successfully complete the adoption of an infant even though her three-year-long analysis did not result in the resolution of this particular conflict. In fact, the patient quit analysis at the point where these painful feelings were beginning to emerge. The predictors were partially correct in that the patient was experiencing considerable discomfort with her mother role and had to rely upon considerable support both from her minister and her physician, who helped her to weather the attendant tensions.

In what way did the patient's analysis contribute to her ability to overcome her disabling symptom? First, the patient had overcome a number of more peripheral conflicts which may have contributed to the symptom. Hostile feelings could be more openly acknowledged and expressed, thus reducing markedly the Pollyannaish cast to her personality. "I used to think I was an angel. I know now that I'm not perfect." Her area of greatest insight was her awareness of her oral-receptive wishes. She said she had found out in analysis that she was "still a child" and for that reason was afraid to try to be a mother and raise a child. Thus, in regard to both aggression and dependency, there was diminished superego pressure and a greater capacity to accept these aspects of herself. Although these gains did not alter the pregenital conflicts interfering with the assumption of a maternal role, they undoubtedly contributed to making it possible for her to adopt a child successfully. As a result of the changes which did occur, she was able to think better of herself and to accept some of her shortcomings. Anger and resentment toward the child did not panic her so easily. Thus, the resolution of peripheral conflicts made it possible to overcome, at least in part, a symptom primarily rooted in a conflict that remained unresolved.

What evidently happened in this incomplete and not entirely successful analysis is that she profited from the expressive aspects of psychoanalysis by a partial resolution of conflicts concerning dependence and aggression with concomitant modification of the superego. But she also selected from the analytic situation some of its supportive aspects, and responded to them with a diminution of superego pressures due to introjection of the therapist's benign superego attitudes. Her self-esteem increased, not only as a result of changes in her superego, but also in response to feeling loved by the benevolent therapist to whom she transferred positive feelings based upon the good maternal introject.

PRINCE

In the case of the *Prince*, a thirty-four-year-old college professor, we have an even more striking instance of adaptive behavioral change occurring on the basis of supportive aspects of treatment, even though the predictors stated that such changes would be dependent upon a resolution of conflict. He came to treatment not only because of generalized feelings of insecurity but also because of an inability to maintain an intimate relationship with a woman for any length of time. The patient's difficulties with women, mainly manifested by Don Juan behavior, were seen by the Initial Study group as based upon a negative oedipal reaction. He preferred to be pursued by many women rather than to settle into a stable relationship with one. The overall character configuration was felt to be phallic-hysterical and his very evident narcissism was seen as secondary and protective to that.

The predictors expected that his fears of sexual inadequacy as well as his hypermasculine protest and his inability to become emotionally attached to one woman would eventually become modified by means of the uncovering and working through of his oedipal problem. In fact, they believed it was *only* through the resolution of this core oedipal conflict that the patient would be able to alter his characterological defects. But what was assumed by the predictors to be the patient's narcissistic defensiveness actually turned out to be a deeper and more pervasive narcissistic character structure which constituted an insurmountable barrier to the analytic process. The patient was intent on protecting his narcissistic integrity against injury, and instead of using the analysis to understand himself more fully, he attempted to elicit admiring appreciation from a captive, listening audience. As a result, the analysis never progressed to the uncovering of layered transference positions, much less their working through.

Despite the failure of the analytic process, the patient's presenting symptom of an inability to establish a satisfactory relationship with a woman showed considerable improvement. The basis for this change was not even remotely connected to the presumed oedipal problem nor even to an uncovering of the patient's oral-narcissistic conflicts which were obviously of great importance. Rather, the patient's major gains seemed to be based upon an identification with his analyst, who had patiently and perseveringly attempted to help him. During the patient's treatment he married and was able to find gratification in this new relationship as well as afford satisfaction to his wife. In the same way that the analyst had steadfastly and conscientiously attempted to listen and understand his needs, he was able, at least to some extent, to introject these same attitudes toward a significant person in his life, and to take pride in doing so. In addition, he was helped by the analysis to develop a greater degree of reflectiveness about the results of his actions and thus interpose some control over his more blatantly contemptuous and narcissistic attitudes toward others. Without ever getting to the roots of his narcissistic behavior, he was able to learn in his treatment how to limit the more destructive and self-destructive aspects of his narcissism.

HEIRESS

A third case of expressive treatment which unexpectedly ran on supportive parameters was the *Heiress*, a thirty-two-year-old mother of four children, who came to treatment because of marital discord, episodes of withdrawal, apparent disorganization, and increasing difficulty in carrying out her responsibilities as wife and mother. Diagnostic study revealed her presenting difficulties to be reflections of core neurotic conflicts at the phallic development level in intensely competitive, jealous, and destructively aggressive and derogatory relationships with men. Also she revealed strong oral-dependent yearnings, deprivations, and frustrations in relation to unreachably remote parent imagoes. Analysis was recommended and started, but the analyst gradually shifted to a supportive-expressive psychotherapy because of his belief after a trial period of analysis that he was dealing with a borderline personality structure who could not tolerate an analytic procedure.

The patient's conflicts were not dealt with analytically, but she was able to make considerable progress in becoming a more feminine, maternal, and giving person as seen mainly in her improved relationship with her children. The research team believed this result could only accrue from an uncovering analytic approach dealing with her problems of penis envy. This did not happen and the research team concluded that the positive changes occurred because of a corrective emotional experience: she had the neurotic expectation that she would be unloved, rejected, and abandoned by a father figure because she was only a woman, and when the analyst did not show this reaction, she felt increased gratification with her femininity. The research team also mentioned that she introjected the analyst's ego attitudes and hence was capable of becoming a more benevolent and giving person rather than someone in constant need of engaging in power struggles.

In each of these three cases psychoanalysis was attempted but a full analytic result was not attained. In each instance, the predictors stated that the significant presenting problem would not be altered without resolution of the underlying conflict producing the difficulty: a baby would not be adopted successfully without uncovering the hostile identification with mother, or a male patient would not be able to establish a stable relationship with a woman without resolving his core oedipal and narcissistic conflicts, and finally a woman would not achieve a satisfactory feminine and maternal relationship without the resolution of phallic, competitive conflicts. In each of these instances the core unconscious conflicts were *not* resolved for a variety of reasons, but the attached symptoms or behaviors were significantly altered by supportive aspects of treatment.

One might argue that the extent of the change would have been greater had the underlying conflicts also been dealt with, and there is some evidence in this direction. Second, one might question whether these "supportive" changes are as stable as they would have been had the basis of the change been a more thoroughgoing expressive procedure. It is this question which will be addressed in the next chapter.

SUMMARY

1. A major assumption regarding supportive psychotherapy is that the extent of change which is possible is *limited* when compared to expressive treatment both in intrapsychic shifts as well as in character and symptom change.

2. Ten of the psychotherapy patients showed significant improvement at termination and they were investigated from the standpoint of the "limitation" assumption of the supportive treatment.

3. Although some of these ten patients underwent treatment characterized by the use of certain expressive elements (interpretation of unconscious determinants of behavior, linking of past with present), none of them relied on the core technique of expressive treatment—the interpretation of transference. All treatments were therefore categorized as mainly supportive psychotherapy.

4. Four patients were expected to get a predominantly supportive treatment and three of the four showed outcomes which clearly exceeded the expectations of the predictors.

5. Four other patients were expected to be treated with significant expressive techniques, involving transference interpretations. Even though this contingency did not occur, the supportive treatment yielded results in each case which at least reached or exceeded the results expected from expressive treatment. Thus, seven patients exceeded the predictors' expectations, implicit or explicit, from supportive therapy.

6. Despite the better-than-expected results obtained from supportive treatment, there were certain limitations in the results (like treatment dependency and persistence of sexual conflicts) which might have been precluded by the use of a more intensive, interpretive approach if the patient could have tolerated it.

7. Another major assumption of the study was that symptoms and character traits rooted in deep-seated unconscious conflicts will be altered only when conflict-resolution occurs. This assumption was negated by disconfirmed predictions in six cases who had received either psychoanalysis or expressive psychotherapy. In each case the relevant core conflict was unresolved but the symptom or behavior was significantly modified by a variety of supportive measures.

CHAPTER 10

STABILITY OF CHANGE WITH SUPPORTIVE TREATMENT

We demonstrated in the last chapter that a predominantly supportive psychotherapy was often capable of producing greater changes than the predictors had expected. But the changes we described were those achieved and sustained up to the point of termination. They occurred in the context of an ongoing relationship with the therapist with all of the gratification and reinforcement which a continuing contact with a dependable and helpful figure might be expected to produce. To what extent were these changes contingent upon such continuing contact and to what extent were they vulnerable to the vicissitudes of life experiences? Or, on the positive side, did the posttherapy period lead to further consolidation of gains already achieved?

The psychoanalytic theory of psychotherapy as articulated and applied by the predictors in this study clearly distinguishes between the stability of therapeutic gain attributable to the expressive aspects of treatment and the stability accruing from supportive aspects. The patient treated successfully by an expressive approach who has been able to resolve his disturbing intrapsychic conflicts is considered to be more impervious and immune to life stress and conflict triggers. The supportively treated patient, on the other hand, whose ego-strengthening depended upon such factors as a wish to please the therapist (transference cure), corrective emotional experience, or identification with a new set of values and attitudes was not expected to weather the stresses of his future life as successfully. Such supportively based changes were considered less stable than the "structural" changes achieved through the uncovering processes of expressive treatments.

These views are expressed by a series of assumption statements such as: "Patients with limited ego-strength and long-standing symptoms require some long-term contacts with the therapist or therapist surrogate in order to maintain changes brought about by the supportive aspects of psychotherapy." "Patients who achieve at most a minimal resolution of conflict in a predominantly supportive psychotherapy effect a more adaptive adjustment, but are vulnerable to some continuing life difficulties consistent with the unresolved conflicts and may require further treatment after termination."

But the predictors were not prepared to be quite so sweeping about the instability of supportive treatment. They allowed that quantitative and qualitative differences, particularly in the identification process, will affect the stability of the change. Thus, one assumption stated, "To the extent that changes resulting from introjection of the therapist's ego and superego attributes are consolidated into identifications, the resulting improvement is stable." The project[1] defined identification as

---

[1] A special committee compiled a glossary of terms (see Appendix 3). The committee consisted of Drs. A. Appelbaum, L. Horwitz, O. Kernberg, I. Rosen, R. Siegel, H. Voth, and R. Wallerstein.

"a more differentiated form of introjection taking place at a time when perceptual and cognitive capacities of the psychic apparatus have increased to the point of reacting to the role aspects of interpersonal interaction. Role implies the presence of a socially recognized function that is exerted by the object or by both participants in their interaction . . . the affective coloring of the interaction is of a more differentiated, less intense and less diffuse quality than in the case of introjection."

In assessing stability of change in the present study, we are handicapped by the relatively brief two-year period of follow-up. Clinical experience indicates that continuing changes, for better or for worse, may be expected to occur over a somewhat longer period, perhaps for as much as a five-year span. With this shortcoming in mind, let us examine the available data regarding stability of change in our successful supportive cases.

OVERALL CHANGE SCORES

Before describing the qualitative changes observable in our improved patients during the follow-up period, we propose to present the two sets of ratings used in the last chapter as they bear on the stability issue. One is the absolute global change score using a five-point rating scale, the initial point as the base line, and made both at termination and follow-up. The other set of scores derives from the HSRS, the measure of behavioral adaptiveness and effectiveness ranging from 0 to 100, with ratings made by the research teams at initial, termination, and follow-up points. As in the previous chapter, we shall be presenting a residual change score, corrected for initial rating bias.

In the last chapter, on the effects of supportive psychotherapy, we presented quantitative and qualitative data on ten patients who showed significant improvement at termination. What do the quantitative data, presented in Table 3, indicate about these patients during the follow-up period?

Table 3

Stability of Change in Improved Psychotherapy Patients

Patient	Absolute Global Change [a]		H.S. Residual Change Scores [b]	
	Initial to Termination	Initial to Follow-up	Initial to Termination	Initial to Follow-up
Bohemian	3	4	71.6	77.3
Playboy	4	4	74.0	77.1
Obedient Husband	4	4	59.6	61.4
Thespian	4	4	65.0	65.1
Fencer	4	4	64.0	75.1
Phobic Girl	4	5	73.5 [c]	75.1
Involutional Woman	4	4	59.1 [c]	61.1
Historian	4	4	42.4 [c]	59.1
Travel Phobia Woman	4	4	66.2 [c]	72.4
Claustrophobic Man	4	3	73.2	66.6

(a) It will be recalled that a rating of 3 indicates slight change, 4 moderate change, and 5 marked change with conflict resolution.
(b)—The residual change score is the difference between the initial HSRS and those at termination and follow-up. However, they have been corrected for the "law of initial values"—the tendency for low initial scores to increase more than do high initial scores.
(c)—Artificial Termination (cut-off).

Assessing the stability of these ten patients, both the global change score and the HSRS residual change scores are consistent in showing that one patient (*Claustrophobic Man*) dropped in score from termination to follow-up. All of the others either maintained their level or showed some increase. The quantitative evidence, then, is that in nine out of ten cases of predominantly supportive treatment in patients who showed significant improvement, the gains were maintained. A crucial question, of course, is the extent to which these patients experienced continuing support from either the therapist or a therapist surrogate during the follow-up period.

STABLE CHANGE WITHOUT CONTINUING THERAPEUTIC CONTACT

Of the nine patients who maintained their therapeutic gain from termination to follow-up, there were at least five who did so without any significant continuing therapeutic contact. The following vignettes present both a description of the way they fared during this two-year follow-up period as well as a psychodynamic formulation of the kind of stability they seemed to attain.

BOHEMIAN

The *Bohemian* made an excellent recovery from an agitated depression during her three-year course of psychotherapy. She had been able to extricate herself from an imcompatible marriage and had been helped to recognize and come to terms with her inability to perform a maternal role toward her adopted son. During the follow-up period she not only consolidated her gains but continued to make further strides. She met and married a man who shared her intellectual and artistic interests, and they were both establishing a mutually gratifying life together. The research team at follow-up wondered how this narcissistic woman would tolerate the stresses of an approaching menopause and waning sexual attractiveness but there were no indications at that point of impending trouble. The consolidation of gain is reflected in the global change rise from 3 to 4, and a jump in HSRS residual change from 71.6 to 77.3

This excellent outcome appeared to be the result of effective therapeutic work combined with fortuitous external circumstances. The therapy was explicitly supportive: the therapist assumed a benign fatherly role, gave counsel about her life problems, and offered explanations for puzzling emotional reactions. ("Depression means that you're angry about something.") He rarely interpreted her mild acting out and permitted the therapy to ride on a moderately positive transference. Both at termination point and again at follow-up the patient reported having imaginary conversations with the therapist when she was feeling distressed, conversations which were soothing and stabilizing and clearly illustrate an internalization process.

The fortunate development of finding a compatible husband was probably attributable to her treatment, at least in the sense that she was helped to a better awareness of the kind of spouse she needed. Also, she seemed to have transferred the residual positive transference from the therapist onto the husband, which further increased their harmonious relationship. And finally, the gratifying marriage enhanced her sense of femininity and helped to stabilize an otherwise shaky and vulnerable ego. The only contact she had with her therapist during this time was a single consultation with him prior to deciding upon the marriage, actually a bid for his blessing for a decision already made.

PLAYBOY

The *Playboy*, a young professional man who came to treatment with serious cyclic disturbances and a marked difficulty in seriously assuming professional responsibilities, was also able to maintain and perhaps consolidate his termination result. He had spent the follow-up period as an army officer overseas and toward the end of this period his wife had their first child. He had performed well in his military duty, had practically no recurrences of his mood disturbance, and his relationship with his wife was mutually satisfactory. The patient's unresolved conflicts continued to give him some difficulty but they were not disruptive factors: the patient continued to masturbate occasionally and sexual relations with his wife were somewhat less frequent than usual; he was unduly jealous of his wife but was able to keep such feelings from getting out of hand; he had little incentive to keep up with developments in his field and improve his professional skills. His surprisingly bland reaction to the death of his therapist, which occurred while he was overseas, perhaps was consistent with his narcissistic character. He stated that it did not affect him very much because he had not expected to see the therapist again. He maintained similar scores at follow-up that he had had at termination—global change of 4, and HSRS change scores of 74.0 and 77.1.

Despite the persistence of significant pathology, the patient had been able to maintain his previous therapeutic gains and was continuing to function adequately in his work and family responsibilities. As in the previous case, the therapist had presented himself to the patient as a benign father-figure and, in this case in particular, as a model of the considerate male and conscientious professional. This model seemed to have been internalized by the patient.

The therapist had made clear the kind of behavior he believed best for the patient, and the patient wished very much to please this powerful and benevolent figure. The patient's marriage was also a source of support in that his wife seemed to understand and tolerate his shortcomings. The research team emphasized the importance of the internalized, warmly supportive, and closely interested therapist who served to sustain a pervasive denial and stern repression of the disturbing fantasies of loss, loneliness, and bleakness which had been so prominent at the initial point.

Although the evidence pointed in the direction of stabilized gain, the special circumstances of the patient's life during the follow-up period should be noted. He lived and worked within the sheltered orbit of the military service overseas with a nondemanding professional work setting, built-in hierarchical privileges, and frequent recreational and vacation opportunities. Also, the couple's recently born child was still too new in the family to accurately assess its impact upon him. How the patient would fare under the increased pressure of working in a civilian life that is generally more demanding would be a further test of the stability of therapeutic change.

OBEDIENT HUSBAND

The *Obedient Husband* was able to achieve a significant alteration in his overly compliant and unassertive attitude toward his disturbed, infantile, and demanding wife. He had given up drinking, which he had used as a retreat from her. He was able to set limits on his wife's excessive demands and took a more active role in the rearing of their ten-year-old son who also was in treatment. Concomitantly, he became a more effective and responsible worker on his job.

All of these changes occurred during a relatively brief (eighteen-month) period of a mainly supportive psychotherapy which was itself colored largely by compliance to the therapist's implicit recommendations. The female therapist, seen as a powerful but protective mother, had in effect challenged him to stand up to his wife. According to the therapist, "I just helped him into a pseudoactiveness. It was all unspoken ... I was a kind of countermagic for the patient with regard to his wife. He used my white magic against her black magic." As a result, the patient felt more manly, less depressed, and less chronically anxious.

To what extent was this clear-cut "transference cure" capable of being sustained without continuing therapeutic contact? In the course of the follow-up period the patient did return to see the therapist three times over a period of several weeks when he found himself in a crisis situation. He also saw a social worker in the same institution at weekly intervals during the follow-up period in connection with his son's treatment. Otherwise, he maintained his newfound independence (or perhaps pseudoindependence) in all areas of his life and even consolidated his gains. He had been promoted on his job and given even broader responsibilities which he was able to carry through quite effectively. At the time of follow-up his wife experienced a relapse in her psychotherapy which required brief hospitalization, and he was able to carry on as usual. The only hint of a possible regression from his termination state was some return to drinking which, however, was still within the limits of social drinking. His global change score remained at 4 and HSRS residual change scores were essentially unaltered (59.6 and 61.4).

The split which occurred in his psychotherapy between the

good mother-therapist toward whom he could comply and the bad mother-wife against whom he could become assertive with the support of the therapist had apparently remained intact over the follow-up period. Undoubtedly this adaptive split had been reinforced by the rewards and gratifications of a more masculine and assertive stance in terms of both social rewards and his own sense of mastery.

FENCER

The *Fencer* had made a number of remarkable gains, at least in her overt adjustment, at the end of her three-year treatment course. Her barbiturate addiction was a thing of the past, she had married (albeit to a man with addictive and sexual problems), and she had completed her college degree. She was more clear and definite about her feminine goals, wanting to be a wife and mother, and she was no longer the lonely, isolated individual she had been at the start of treatment.

Although the therapist had made an effort to point the treatment in an expressive direction, both the patient's character resistance and the therapist's own problems in dealing with this patient had made him back away from consistent interpretation of the transference, particularly the hostile and sexual elements. Rather, the therapist accepted the role of the kindly and interested father assigned to him by the patient. This longed-for appreciation and respect from a man which she had never been able to experience from her own father appeared to be the catalyst for a number of changes which the patient was able to accomplish in her treatment. She did not resolve her angry, competitive conflicts with men nor did she uncover her poorly accepted strivings for oral nurturance.

Rather, her marriage represented a compromise formation for these needs: a pseudohetereosexual marriage in which a phallic woman marries a castrated male and attempts to be more successful in his cure than his therapist had been; at the same time she becomes the all-giving, nurturant mother and thus vicariously fills a deep-seated void.

The follow-up period reflected an even more adaptive combination of the patient's overt gains. Even though the patient showed a disquieting degree of denial and avoidance of problems in her life, she spoke glowingly (perhaps protesting too much) of her happiness and fulfillment in her marriage. She was attempting to get pregnant and she was working very hard to help her husband over some difficult academic hurdles. The research team's questions and doubts about the stability of the marital relationship revolved mainly around her husband's fragility and his capacity to cope with the increasing demands of his life (as he moved to get a higher degree and when a child arrived in the household). The tensions in the marriage from the husband's standpoint consisted of mounting irritation with the wife's dominance and control in their relationship although this was counterbalanced by his appreciation for her concern about him. Despite the marital problems, the patient's active, competent stance in dealing with her life problems reflected a consolidation of her treatment gains: her global change score remained at 4 while her HSRS adjusted ratings moved from 64.0 to 75.1.

With the help of treatment, the patient had been able to strike some important life compromises which were potentially gratifying and adaptive for her. Within the limits of the two-year follow-up period, she had seemingly achieved stability in her therapeutic gains, but her choice of spouse, a fragile and unstable man, at least made the marital relationship of questionable durability.

THESPIAN

The *Thespian* completed four years of psychotherapy, with decided gains mortgaged, however, to a firmly entrenched homosexual way of life. She gave up her wildly promiscuous self-destructive relationships in favor of more discreet liaisons and an outwardly conventional pattern of life. She settled into stable employment and carried out her responsibilities in an orderly fashion without the temper tantrums, histrionics, and chaotic behavior that characterized her life at the outset of treatment. In retrospect, at the follow-up point the patient described her pretreatment existence as going downhill and probably leading to suicide. At termination she was resigned to the limited gratifications of a homosexual way of life. Her earlier interest in theater and dramatics had waned based upon her recognition of not possessing sufficient talent.

Her treatment was essentially supportive in the sense that the therapist made no effort to work with transference manifestations. He maintained and used as a therapeutic agent the patient's view of him as a benign, interested, and concerned parent figure. The obvious depreciation of men expressed in her homosexual behavior was not interpreted in terms of its negative transference implications. The patient's liking for the therapist and her wish to please him was a major therapeutic agent in fostering the development of a more organized life.

This transference cure proved to be quite stable without continuing contact with the therapist after termination. The patient stated that on occasion she had a desire to speak with the therapist, but only because she enjoyed her contacts with him, not because she needed help with any specific problem. The patient settled in another city and carried on a life similar to that she had during the latter part of her psychotherapy. She found stable employment and had a small circle of woman friends, all homosexual, who provided her with social and sexual outlets. At follow-up the interviewers noted her aloofness and distance combined with an air of resignation concerning her anhedonic existence. There was a depressive cast to her life and the prospects for greater fulfillment (through marriage and a family) seemed remote indeed. But the good-parent image represented by the therapist had apparently stabilized and crystallized within the patient's psychological makeup so that she could at least maintain the partial gains of her treatment both in leading a stable existence and in avoiding involvement in destructive relationships. Her global change score remained at 4 and her HSRS change score remained essentially unaltered at 65.0 and 65.1.

These five cases of predominantly supportive psychotherapy maintained or improved their therapeutic gains without continuing therapeutic contact, illustrating that supportive treatment, at least for some patients, is capable of inducing stable psychological change. Factors which might have contributed to the relatively enduring gains were:

1. Three of the five cases acquired new spouses either during the treatment or shortly thereafter. In at least two of the cases, the appropriateness of marital choice contributed to the stability of change. Unquestionably the therapeutic process helped these patients understand better the nature of their needs and thus influenced them toward a wiser choice. The third patient (*Fencer*) made a choice strongly colored by her unresolved phallic competitive conflicts and her uninterpreted competitive strivings with her therapist as well as her hus-

band's therapist. Although this patient was maintaining her gains at follow-up and no serious problems had surfaced in the marriage, the stability of the marriage was in question.

2. All of these patients had either implicitly or explicitly been encouraged by their therapists to engage in new, more adaptive life behaviors. One therapist modeled the role of the responsible and conscientious physician, another patient had been helped to see how her self-destructive behavior prevented ultimate gratification, a male patient was helped to assume a more masculine, assertive role. These behaviors were originally initiated within the context of a "transference cure," an effort by the patient to please the therapist and to express gratitude for the therapist's interest and concern. But an important facet of the stability of such change was the built-in gratification which ensued from these new styles of living. To paraphrase an old proverb, "Adaptive behavior is its own reward." Thus, the *Obedient Husband's* newfound masculine assertiveness, although not based upon conflict resolution, was sufficiently gratifying and pleasing to be self-reinforcing.

3. All of these patients reported a continuing and durable positive feeling toward their therapists. In some instances there were expressions of gratitude for having been through a lifesaving process. We believe that these conscious, overt attitudes of friendliness and appreciation are, to a greater or lesser extent, the surface manifestations of significant shifts in the patients' inner world of object relationships. The fact that they all had achieved stability without significant contact with the therapist suggests that an internal alteration had occurred in the patients' conceptions of themselves in relation to others. It is, of course, theoretically possible to explain these changes and their stability simply in terms of certain adaptive changes which were initiated in treatment and were maintained by a combination of reinforcement and favorable environments. The

internalization of a strengthened positive parental image, however, was suggested by the research team in some cases as an explanatory factor, and this conception will be further developed in the final chapter.

STABLE CHANGE WITH CONTINUING THERAPEUTIC CONTACT

Four patients were able to maintain the change they had achieved at termination but required some degree of contact with either the therapist or a therapist surrogate during the follow-up period. Two required partial or irregular contact, and two others required fairly regular contact, albeit on a much less frequent basis.

Partial Irregular Contact

PHOBIC GIRL

The *Phobic Girl* presented a special problem for the research study because of the lengthy eight-and-a-half-year course of her psychotherapy. The time constraint of the study required an artificial cutoff after six years, and the follow-up study was done at the actual termination point. Hence, the only real follow-up data available were the therapist's notes on the contacts the patient had with him during the follow-up period.

When the patient was studied at the completion of her treatment, she showed quite significant changes in her functioning. She had been married for three years, and the gratifications in marriage far exceeded the difficulties. She had recently given birth to a child, and it was this pregnancy which made both patient and therapist decide to delay termination. Her masochistically colored sexual and social behavior had largely disappeared. "I no longer feel like a clown. I have a much greater respect for myself." Her phobias had largely disappeared, and she was now capable of making long trips, although with some degree of apprehension. Her infantile, orally fixated functioning had now progressed to a higher phallic-hysterical level. The HSRS change score remained stable, shifting only from 73.5 to 75.1 Her global change rating, however, moved from 4 to 5 expressing the judges' view that her substantial gains were in part based upon a partial resolution of her sadomasochistic conflicts.

Although the patient's treatment had contained some expressive elements in offering interpretations about her extratransferential masochistic behavior, essentially the treatment had been conducted without eliciting, uncovering, and resolving the transference. A positive transference attachment was maintained throughout the treatment and was utilized as a vehicle through which suggestions, manipulations, and reeducative efforts were funneled toward the goal of better reality orientation and reality adjustment. After the patient married there was active encouragement toward greater independence from the therapy and toward transfer of her emotional attachments to her husband. The therapist was primarily a teacher educating to reality rather than an uncoverer or resolver of unconscious conflict. To a great extent, the changes had the earmarks of a transference cure within the maintained, uninterpreted symbiotic transference of dependent child to caretaking parent; the patient improved her controls and modified her behavior in adaptive directions, doing it for her caring therapist on the basis of the at least partial gratification of her hitherto unmet oral-dependent needs.

Further postfollow-up information is available concerning this patient's adjustment after the *actual* termination of treatment. For more than one year, there was no contact with the therapist. Then, following a miscarriage which awakened her fears of being a bad mother, incapable of producing a sound, healthy baby, she resumed regular weekly interviews with the therapist. She was experiencing some depressive symptoms as well as a partial return of her phobic difficulties. This renewed contact lasted for a year and a half, during which time the patient became pregnant and had her second child. She regained her previous level of functioning and by mutual consent this second series of interviews was terminated. At this writing, some three years later, the patient has had no further contact with the therapist, even though she is free to contact him when necessary.

INVOLUTIONAL WOMAN

The *Involutional Woman* responded favorably to the ministrations of supportive psychotherapy with two different therapists over a six-year period. Not only did she overcome her involutional depression, but she was able to establish a more accommodating relationship with her husband and a busy, active daily schedule despite the encroachment of a chronic somatic problem. Her treatment had helped her to deal with all facets of her life more effectively primarily by helping her loosen her rigid denials and reaction formations against hostility. Her Pollyannaish denials and brittle constriction which had resulted in depression, somatization, and occasional eruptions of temper were all considerably softened.

Neither the first nor the second therapist attempted to uncover the orally deprived and phallic competitive roots of these angers. Rather, they maintained a friendly, supportive relationship with her, encouraging her to assert herself when her demands were reasonable, and counseling her to find sublimatory channels for the expression of her talents and capabilities. The major vehicle of change was formulated as the introjection of the therapist's more benign and accepting superego attitudes toward aggression.

The predictors wondered how durable and stable these supportive changes would be after termination. Because of the time constraints of the study, only a one-year follow-up period was available. She not only maintained her gains but the follow-up period found her even more satisfied with her life, filled as it was with various volunteer and civic responsibilities as well as careful attention to and successful management of her investments, something which she had previously left to her husband's judgment. These gains are consistent with a maintained global change of 4 and an essentially stable HSRS residual change score, moving only from 59.1 to 61.1.

Although the patient felt free to contact her ex-therapist whenever she chose, she did not indulge this permission. But the research team felt that her frequent and regular visits to her internist for the treatment of a chronic somatic problem were to some extent a substitute for her relinquished weekly psychotherapeutic interviews. Thus, it is possible that the stability of therapeutic change in this case

was at least partially dependent on a continuing psycho-
therapy-like contact with a therapist surrogate.

Patients Requiring Regular Therapeutic Contact

The two patients who were switched from psychoanalysis to
supportive treatment made slight gains during the follow-up
period but each maintained some form of regular contact with
his therapist.

HISTORIAN

The *Historian* was in a lengthy analysis which became
stalemated but finally was culminated in a temporary
psychotic regression. The therapist shifted the treatment
modality to supportive psychotherapy, and the patient
became more productive in his academic career, his
psychosomatic symptoms decreased, and his homosexual
preoccupations lessened. Although his paranoid propensities persisted in a somewhat attenuated form, he broadened his social life with his colleagues. Relationships with
women, however, remained an unresolved problem and he
was unable to establish an enduring heterosexual relationship.

The termination study (artificial cutoff) was done almost ten
years after he started treatment, and a partial termination
occurred about a year afterward. When the patient was
seen at follow-up, he was continuing to maintain a steady,
regular contact with the therapist, although the frequency

of appointments was reduced in part because of a move to a more distant location. He corresponded regularly with the therapist, reporting his day-to-day problems and listing the problems he wished to discuss at their next therapy appointment. Both patient and therapist had accepted the likelihood of his becoming a therapeutic "lifer." His global change score remained at 4, and his HSRS adjusted change rating moved upward from 42.4 to 59.1.

The basis for his significant, but limited, improvements seemed to be largely a "transference cure." Within the context of enduring dependent gratifications, the patient compliantly accepted the therapist's recommendations for more realistic appraisals of his environment and for more constructive and assertive behavior, at least in his professional life. The patient felt grateful and indebted to the therapist for his unswerving interest and saw the relationship as the only one he had ever had which was completely dependable and trustworthy. Unlike some other borderline patients in this study, like the *Playboy*, he seemed unable to internalize the good-therapist image sufficiently to draw upon its nurturant and protective qualities without a steady, personal contact to reinforce this internal image. Perhaps the crucial difference between the two patients, consistent with the greater instability of the good internal image, was the *Historian's* greater proneness to paranoid distortions.

TRAVEL PHOBIA WOMAN

The *Travel Phobia Woman* was hospitalized for prolonged addiction to drugs and alochol, phobic withdrawal, and a generally chaotic and disorganized life. Psychoanalysis was tried as a "heroic" measure, but her first analyst soon became convinced that she lacked the ego resources for this procedure, and began using supportive techniques. After the death of the first therapist, a second analyst attempted more intensive work with her but also shifted to a more supportive procedure. Throughout both treatments the patient showed significant gains, always limited by an excessively dependent attachment to her therapist. She overcame her addiction, took a relatively routine secretarial position, and progressively overcame her phobia for driving in unfamiliar places within the city. Though she functioned better than she had for many years prior to treatment, she remained unmarried and led a life of limited gratification.

An artificial cutoff study was done after eight years of treatment and again two years later. The frequency of appointments had decreased to once-a-week but a real termination was nowhere in sight. Like the preceding case, she appeared to be developing into a therapeutic "lifer." Her global change score remained at 4, but her HSRS adjusted rating had moved upward from 66.2 to 72.4.

The major vehicle of change was again a "transference cure" in which the patient expressed her gratitude for the therapist's sustained effort and interest by making efforts to please him through control of her addictive and phobic symptoms while widening her social and vocational activity, although very slightly. The stability of the outcome seemed to be dependent upon a continuing actual relationship; symbolic internalized gratification could not be achieved. Why such internalization was not possible for this woman while available to others with similar psychopathology remains an important unresolved question.

The coincidence of these two patients being the only ones in the series who were unable to reach a suitable termination and also having been in a relatively long five-day-a-week contact with an analyst suggests that possible iatrogenic effects may occur with such a procedure on people with weak egos and intense oral fixations. Both patients were described initially as showing a propensity for intense oral dependent strivings; and the regressive pull of the analytic process, for these people who were unable to resolve their dependency by interpretive methods, may have set up a process which was difficult to reverse.

Another factor these two patients shared which differentiated them from the others was that they were unmarried. Helpful as their supportive treatment was, it did not make possible their establishing a stable heterosexual relationship. A compatible spouse who could cater to their dependency needs would probably have made it easier for these patients to have given up the need to cling to a lifelong therapeutic relationship.

THE UNSTABLE TRANSFERENCE CURE

The only patient in this series who did not maintain his therapeutic gains during the follow-up period was the *Claustrophobic Man*. Following a series of successful operations for cancer of the larynx, he developed severe anxiety attacks, phobias about being alone or in strange, closed places, and a need to have his wife almost constantly by his side. In the course of a relatively brief period of treatment he had overcome most of these crippling symptoms even though he gained no insight into their origin. He had in part transferred his dependency onto the therapist but was able to terminate with the understanding that the therapist was available if needed.

During the follow-up the patient had a partial recurrence of his phobic anxieties. His anxiety level increased, and he attempted to avoid crowds and closed places or business meetings in strange locations. He found it difficult to cope with his father's criticisms about his handling of the family business, and during the follow-up period he visited the therapist for a series of five interviews for help with this problem. His relationship with his wife did not revert to its former state, since he was now more tolerant of his dependency needs. These partial symptomatic regressions resulted in a global change decline from 4 to 3, and a decrease from his adjusted HSRS of 73.2 to 66.6.

The transference cure with minimal reinforcement by actual contact with the therapist helped the patient avoid a full return to his old symptoms. However, he was also assisted by the dwindling threat of cancer, the original conflict trigger, which by now was well past the five-year cure point without recurrence. One might speculate that the reason this transference cure was less durable than those described previously was related to the brevity of the psychotherapy—only eighteen months and a total of forty-six therapy hours. The limited frequency and duration may have been insufficient to permit the patient to internalize the good-parent image which the therapist represented. This alteration seemed to have been started in that there was an implicit understanding between therapist and patient that he would always be available in time of need. The patient held an exalted view of the therapist's skill and became an avid spokesman in his community on behalf of mental health. But the patient's inability to take a forceful stand toward his troublesome and nagging father indicated that the fear of abandonment and castration—the intrapsychic conflicts which underlay his original illness—were not sufficiently neutralized by the therapeutic relationship. One could speculate that for the internalization process of the good-parent figure to reach its optimal point, even with relatively well integrated neurotics as this man was, required more time and more sustained contact than was available to him.

FOLLOW-UP IMPROVEMENT IN TWO ADDITIONAL CASES

All ten cases presented in this series have shown significant gains at termination with nine of them either maintaining or extending their improvement. There are two other cases which deserve mention in this chapter because the patients reached the category of 4 on the absolute global change scale at the follow-up point, even though they had either shown no particular change or had become worse at termination point.

COVERT ADDICT

The *Covert Addict*, a thirty-three-year-old divorced man, was hospitalized because of severe alcoholism, sexual perversion, and a generalized inability to manage responsibility. His global change score of 1 at termination reflected no improvement, indeed some deterioration, during the first phase of his supportive treatment. In that first phase (discussed in detail in Chapter 7), the patient's paranoid transference disposition combined with the therapist's "detective-prosecutor" countertransference reaction to produce a highly impaired therapeutic alliance.

However, in the second phase of treatment, after the patient had suffered a serious life-threatening illness which necessitated complete cessation of drug intake, the patient entered into a kind of marital counseling with the therapist in which considerable progress began to occur. Also important was the fact that his newly acquired wife was now an important part of the treatment process and her active concern and intervention helped to stabilize it. The progressive ego decompensating process was reversed: the patient's defenses were restabilized, his primary process thinking sealed over, his anxiety was now adequately coped with, and his addiction to tranquilizing medication was totally given up. His improvement was shown quantitatively in both ratings. He jumped from 1 to 4 on global change, and from 53.6 to 62.3 on the adjusted HSRS change score.

Thus, due to two new external circumstances—a life-threatening illness and firm pressure and support from his wife—he was able to reenter therapy and make use of it. The marital counseling process occurred during the research follow-up period and hence there is insufficient data on the length and stability of the second treatment, but there was every indication that such treatment would be continuing for an indefinite period.

MOVIE LADY

The *Movie Lady* was in a mainly supportive treatment for four and a half years during which time the treatment was filmed for research purposes (though not specifically part of the present study). The therapist stopped doing classical psychoanalysis after the first six months because he felt the patient was too sick. Although she made some treatment gains in terms of symptom improvement, her character structure was essentially unaltered. Her phobia for closed places and for driving had diminished, she experienced a significant reduction in anxiety, she no longer hyperventilated, and her somatic symptoms essentially ceased. Rage attacks, mainly at her husband, had significantly diminished.

More than any other treatment in the study, this psychotherapy was explicitly conducted along the lines of a "mutual friendship" model. Not only did the therapist convey a warm, genuine, and concerned attitude, but he attempted to engender a free, two-way expression of feeling. The therapist was open, honest, and direct in stating his own emotional responses and in answering all questions frankly, even questions about his personal life. The patient's improvement was at least partly based on her success in defeating the therapist. She had been able to get him to alter his therapeutic plan from classical psychoanalysis to supportive psychotherapy, had been able to sit up rather than lie on the couch, had decreased the frequency of her appointments, and had pulled the neutral therapist into a socially interactive position. In addition to this kind of gratification, a corrective emotional experience in which the therapist acted differently from how the introjected, unconsciously hated mother would have acted, had also occurred. On the basis of these considerations, the predictors expected that the follow-up period would result in an eroding of treatment gains and that the therapeutic change, to be sustained, needed a continuation of the ongoing gratification she had experienced in the treatment.

Actually, rather than relapse, the patient made further gains during the follow-up period. Her symptoms were further diminished and her problems in relationships were attenuated. The patient's competitive, belittling attitudes toward her husband were even further reduced. And, at an intrapsychic level, there was evidence of more smoothly functioning defensive apparatus. Global change at follow-up moved from 2 to 4 and HSRS change score was up from 61.2 to 67.6.

To what extent was this consolidation of a transference cure based on continuing therapeutic support or other situational factors? The patient and her family returned to their home city and once again lived close to her mother and other members of her family. Also important was the therapist's continuing contact with the patient through regular correspondence—three to four letters per year from each party. On one occasion when the therapist had not heard from the patient for some time, he placed a long-distance call to inquire how she was faring. Thus, there were two supporting features of the follow-up period: her new closeness to her mother and family, and her continuing correspondence with her concerned and devoted therapist. But the striking feature of this period was that the patient was able to maintain her symptomatic improvement even though her contact with the therapist was neither in person nor very frequent. At least one could say that whatever change was dependent on the gratification of defeating the therapist did not require continuing reinforcement.

SUMMARY

1. A major assumption of the project was that supportive psychotherapy produces relatively unstable changes, since relapses are prone to appear under the pressure of situational stress or conflict triggers. Also, therapeutic changes of this kind tend to require long-term continuing support in order to be maintained.

2. In this chapter we scrutinized the stability of change of the ten patients who, at termination, had shown at least moderate improvement. Judged quantitatively, the two overall change scores (absolute global change and HSRS) were consistent in showing that nine of the ten patients had either maintained their changes or showed further improvement during the two-year follow-up period.

3. Five patients had little or no contact with their therapist and all of them stabilized or further improved. The factors which seemed to contribute to the stability of change were (a) supportive environmental factors, (b) positive reinforcement for their new, more adaptive behaviors, and (c) a continuing and durable positive feeling toward the therapist.

4. Two patients required some degree of contact following their actual termination of treatment. One patient experienced a partial return of symptoms and had a brief second course of treatment, while a second seemed to depend on frequent, regular contacts with a therapist surrogate.

5. Two others, both ex-psychoanalytic patients, seemed destined to become therapeutic "lifers" in that they needed a continuing therapy contact, albeit on a much less frequent basis. They were both unmarried with rather limited social-sexual lives. Both were characterized by strong passive dependent needs.

6. The one patient whose gains were unstable and who showed a definite (but partial) relapse from termination to follow-up had the briefest course of treatment in this group (only forty-six hours over an eighteen-month period).

7. Two patients whose changes were not remarkable at termination showed considerable gains during the follow-up period. In one instance, situational factors helped to reverse a downward course. In the other, an apparently unstable transference cure surprisingly consolidated during the follow-up period. The therapist maintained a long-distance correspondence which undoubtedly contributed.

8. If we include the *Phobic Girl* (about whom we have postfollow-up information during which she briefly resumed treatment but was then able to terminate without further contact), as well as the *Movie Lady*, whose improvement was not clearly evident until the follow-up point, there were seven patients in this group who maintained or consolidated their gains after termination without any significant, face-to-face contact with the therapist or therapist-surrogate.

CHAPTER 11

THE CURATIVE PROCESS: SUMMARY AND REFORMULATION

An examination of the theory of psychoanalytic psychotherapy, using tested predictions on each of forty-two cases, has been described in detail in the preceding chapters. We may now ask whether the explanatory concepts used in the psychoanalytic theory of psychotherapy and applied by the predictors require further modification in order to encompass the observations and conclusions of the research team. An overview of both the starting assumptions of the study as well as its major findings should provide us with the basis for developing a modified conceptualization of the curative process.

WORKING ASSUMPTIONS OF PSYCHOANALYTIC PSYCHOTHERAPY

The hierarchically organized set of assumptions used in this study, both major and minor, is to be found in Appendixes 1 and 2. The theory of psychotherapy being tested was one which prevailed in the 1950s, the time the predictions were made and treament started. Almost two decades have elapsed since the initiation of these studies, and certain shifts in psychoanalytic thinking have occurred; but it is doubtful that any major changes have taken place in the psychoanalytic theory of psychotherapy. Let us first examine the major assumptions held by the predictors regarding the *curative process of treatment*.

The predictors believed that psychoanalysis was the most thoroughgoing procedure of the psychotherapies, ideally suited for extensively modifying and altering symptoms and character traits. Changes expected from psychoanalysis would be both more extensive and more stable than with other psychotherapies. The uncovering process was expected to occur by means of the development of a transference neurosis which the analyst would attempt to resolve by interpretation. The insight thus acquired, rather than being the cause of change or the effect of change, was considered a mutually interacting concomitant of such change. The unconscious intrapsychic conflicts resolved by this process would constitute a structural change in the ego.

In contrast, the psychotherapies operated curatively by means of a more diverse and heterogeneous set of mechanisms. Expressive psychotherapy comes closest to the transference model described above, differing only in degree (the depth of regression, and reliance on interventions other than interpretation of the transference). The psychotherapies, moving on a continuum from expressive to supportive, rely to a greater or a lesser extent upon so-called supportive vehicles of treatment.

These include gratification of certain psychological needs which the patient cannot achieve himself, mainly dependency strivings; a corrective emotional experience in which the patient's pathological and distorted expectations of a response from another person do not occur (like retaliation for one's aggressive wishes); a transference cure in which more adaptive behaviors are acquired for the purpose of pleasing (or displeasing) the therapist; internalization of the therapist's ego and superego attitudes. The adaptive changes which ensue as a result of one or more of these processes were considered by the predictors as likely to be less extensive and less stable than those produced by the expressive aspects of psychotherapy, particularly analysis, because the underlying unconscious conflicts will not have been uncovered and insight not acquired.

In capsule form, the above constituted the orientation of the predictors regarding the curative processes involved in the various modalities of treatment. We have seen in the previous chapters that these assumptions were partly confirmed, but also partly disconfirmed, particularly those propositions regarding the limitations of change associated with the supportive aspects of psychotherapy.

MAJOR FINDINGS OF STUDY BEARING ON CURATIVE FACTORS

The major postulates concerning psychoanalysis and psychotherapy as described above represented the thinking of the Initial Study Group (and presumably of analysts at large) in the mid-1950s. During the following decade of data collection, the Prediction Study team became impressed with a few major findings which gradually emerged from our completed cases.

These findings were not solely influenced by the examination of variables and concepts that characterized our beginning design. The research teams at termination and follow-up began to think about these cases also in terms of two new conceptions which were then being introduced into the psychoanalytic literature.

First, the idea of therapeutic alliance became increasingly important in psychoanalytic circles during the 1950s and 1960s. Introduced by Zetzel (1956) and Greenson (1960), it referred to a basic ingredient of the therapeutic relationship, the ability of the patient to perceive the "real" nature of his relationship with the therapist: the fact that the therapist is committed and concerned in attempting to help him with his difficulties in living. Despite the vicissitudes of the transference and the distortions that may occur at various times, the patient with a good therapeutic alliance is able to experience a protective envelope surrounding the relationship which permits the therapeutic work to proceed satisfactorily. This therapeutic alliance tends to become strengthened in a favorable therapeutic process. In psychoanalysis, it permits regression to intensify and deepen; in psychotherapy it probably contributes to significant changes per se.

The second modification in analytic conceptualizing was the increased influence of Kleinian thinking. This effect was partly a general phenomenon insofar as writers like Winnicott, Jacobson, Fairbairn, and Segal were having a more significant influence in psychoanalytic circles. But it was even more pronounced in Topeka and in the project when Otto Kernberg began his studies of borderline personality organization and applied this thinking to the understanding of many of the project's cases. The original design and early write-ups of the study were based on psychoanalytic ego psychology of the mid-1950s, but the later conceptualization of cases was also significantly weighted with object relations theory.

In what follows three major findings of the project will be

described which significantly contributed to a revised perspective concerning the dynamics of therapeutic change.

Therapeutic Alliance. In Chapter 8 on therapeutic alliance, we attempted to present evidence concerning the significance of this variable in both psychoanalytic and nonanalytic cases. In the analytic cases we observed how a psychotic potential interfered with the development and maintenance of a stable alliance. And in the nonparanoid patients, a low tolerance for frustration in two cases (*Good Son, Silent Woman*) prevented these analysands from overcoming their chronic sense of dissatisfaction with their analysts. We furthermore saw that certain patients (*Bohemian, Playboy, Thespian*) established a stronger therapeutic alliance than had been expected by the predictors, presumably because their capacity to perceive a good object had been underestimated. Also, among the psychotherapy cases, therapeutic alliance was invoked to explain the difference between two addictive cases (*Fencer, Covert Addict*) who achieved a successful result as opposed to two (*Addicted Doctor, Salesman*) who had failed in treatment.

Since the variable of therapeutic alliance was not a part of the study at the outset, we do not have systematic data which would permit us to form a generalization based on every case. But we were impressed with the importance of this variable in the above cases in explaining treatment successes and failures. Psychoanalysis requires a substantial therapeutic alliance to exist at the outset, and hopefully to continue growing, in order that the analytic uncovering process may proceed. Psychotherapy, especially of the supportive variety, may only require the growth of this therapeutic alliance over a period of time for personality change to occur.

We presented data to demonstrate that there are two major factors which permit a therapeutic alliance to develop—one in the patient and the other in the treatment. The patient must possess a sufficient core or disposition to perceive a benign object on which to build a strengthened internal conception of a good "significant other." Within the treatment, there must be sufficient need gratification in order to foster the perception of the therapist as a helping person. The therapist's role in this regard varies with the needs of the patient—his regressive potential, his age, his need for protection, etc. We have seen patients whose psychotherapy failed because more hospitalization was needed than was offered and therefore a sufficient alliance could not be formed. We have also seen patients who were considered by the termination research team to have been incapable of forming a therapeutic alliance despite a satisfactory treatment effort, because of the patient's weak potential for developing an internalized good object. On the other hand, when the potential for perceiving a good object is joined with a need-gratifying therapeutic regimen over a sufficient period of time, the patient shows significant adaptive change.

The Stable Effect of Supportive Psychotherapy. We have shown that there were ten patients who showed substantial improvement at termination, along with two additional patients at follow-up, under a predominantly supportive regimen of psychotherapy. These treatments were so described because the therapeutic work included little or no uncovering or interpreting of the transference, either negative or positive. They were cases which mostly accomplished more in therapy than the predictors expected, explicitly or implicitly, under supportive treatment. Furthermore, seven of the twelve maintained these gains at the follow-up point without any regular contact with the therapist. One patient did not maintain his gains and the four others required varying degrees of therapeutic contact in order to continue their improvement.

These cases showed a well-developed therapeutic alliance in the form of a clear, prevailing positive relationship between patient and therapist. Uniformly, the patients reported feelings of liking, respecting, and at times adulation for their doctors. Some spoke in loving terms, others referred to the lifesaving process they had experienced.

But just as the variable of therapeutic alliance was not explicitly examined or measured, so another variable of great importance emerged as the data was collected (but unfortunately was not systematically scrutinized). It was the variable of *internalization*—the process by which the representation of this new, more benign, and more gratifying relationship between the self and a significant other becomes assimilated into the individual's inner world of object relations.[1] The stability of change for certain of our patients, particularly those who did not undergo insight-giving treatment, suggests that such a process took place.

In addition to the factor of stability, there is more direct data in these cases which indicate that such an internalization process did indeed occur. One patient (*Bohemian*) reported imaginary conversations with the therapist long after the therapy had ended in which the therapist would help clarify an existing dilemma. Another (*Playboy*) continued to use the therapist, often consciously, as a model for appropriate behavior, professionally and in his close relationships after therapy had ended. Still another patient (*Obedient Husband*) was judged by the researchers to have benefited from his treatment by having internalized the "white magic" of the therapist-good mother as opposed to the "black magic" of the wife-bad mother. A drug-addicted young woman (*Fencer*) who had suffered long-standing feelings of rejection and unacceptability from her family, presumably because she was "only a woman,"

[1] The concepts of internalization and identification used in the discussion follow Schafer's (1968) definitions: *"Internalization* refers to all those processes by which the subject transforms real or imagined regulatory interactions with his environment, and real or imagined characteristics of his environment, into inner regulations and characteristics." (p. 9) *"Identification* refers to modifying subjective self or behavior, or both, in order to increase one's resemblance to an object taken as a model . . ." (p. 16)

began to see herself in a new and more favorable light as a result of the therapeutic relationship. A chaotic and rebellious existence in one patient (*Thespian*) subsided into a more orderly life-style, ostensibly in an effort to please the "good therapist."

Supportive Aspects of Expressive Cases. The dynamics of change find further elaboration in a number of expressive cases where the therapeutic relationship per se loomed large as a vehicle of therapy. Perhaps the outstanding instance is the college professor (*Prince*) who underwent analysis because of his inability to form a gratifying relationship with one woman. His limited capacity to tolerate narcissistic hurt severely handicapped analytic progress, but he substantially overcame his presenting symptom largely on the basis of his identification with his perseverant and committed analyst. Another analytic case (*Adoptive Mother*) had been unable to adopt a child, but in her analysis was able to achieve a partial resolution of the conflicts impeding the assumption of a feminine, maternal role. She became more tolerant of her passivity and aggressive impulses. But, in addition, the researchers believed that she showed a very clear wish to please the good mother-analyst—a marked impetus to the successful overcoming of her presenting symptom. Likewise, a woman (*Heiress*) with a low sense of self-esteem about her femininity, and unable to profit from a classic analytic technique that was proffered because of her borderline features, derived considerable benefit from the relationship in which she came to feel that she could be regarded as a significant valued person by another individual.

The above are instances of therapeutic change based in large measure upon the curative factors inherent in the therapeutic relationship per se. This is not to diminish the value of interpretive, uncovering work whose special contribution will be discussed later. But we believe that a major contribution of this study is the indication that the therapeutic alliance is not only a prerequisite for therapeutic work, but often may be the main vehicle of change.

INTERNALIZATION OF THERAPEUTIC ALLIANCE

We are proposing to account for the numerous observations of stable change associated with the development of a favorable therapeutic relationship as due to the internalization of the therapeutic alliance. From the outset of this study, the predictors espoused the idea that *one* of the factors leading to therapeutic change in supportive treatment was an identification with the therapist's ego and superego values and attitudes. This identification process took its place as coordinate with other factors—like transference cure and corrective emotional experience—which contributed to modifications in the patient.

But the considerations described in the preceding section led us to propose that an internalization process is the central feature in supportive treatment and often plays a significant role in expressive treatment as well. That is, a structural alteration occurs in the patient's internal world of object relations based upon his experience of a good therapeutic relationship which contributes to more adaptive functioning in his environment. This dynamic is not unlike the ordinary maturation and developmental process of infancy and childhood when crucial internalized self and object representations become imprinted upon the personality. Psychotherapy attempts to achieve a "reprinting" of psychological reactions and, when successful, a significant change of the inner object world occurs.

In the previous section we described some of the preconditions for the development of an effective therapeutic alliance.

We emphasized the disposition to perceive a good object as well as the factor of need gratification in the therapy geared to the patient's personality organization. A further factor of duration should also be mentioned. All of these changes occurred in relatively long-term treatment—practically all of them at least two years in length. It was striking that the least stable of the cases in our supportive series was also a case of the briefest duration in total hours and time span (forty-two hours over a period of less than eighteen months).

Internalization has a number of part-processes which act in a reciprocally enhancing manner with the therapy relationship; they both contribute to the growth of a therapeutic alliance and, conversely, tend to be enhanced by a growing positive relationship. For example, in the corrective emotional experience the therapist behaves differently than expected by the patient, e.g., retaliation is not forthcoming after the patient's display of hostility. Such an experience contributes to the growth of the alliance; it engenders trust in the therapist's intentions and fosters hope that this relationship will fare better than others in the past. But the growing alliance in turn contributes to the patient's capacity to experience and perceive these benign and helpful therapeutic responses for what they really are. They enhance the climate of the treatment by contributing to the growth of a good internalized self-object relationship.

We are proposing four factors as part-processes which both contribute to the growth of the therapeutic alliance and are, in turn, the effects of a growing positive relationship. These part-processes (enhanced self-esteem, corrective emotional experience, transference cure, and identification with the therapist's ego and superego) are separate but interrelated. The therapist's acceptance and tolerance of the patient's hostility helps the patient to modify his overstrict superego by identification but it also raises his self-esteem, since his weaknesses have not alienated a significant person. In addition, it partakes to some extent of a corrective emotional experience insofar as it constitutes an unexpected response from the therapist.

Enhanced Self-Esteem. The research team observed that every patient who improved with treatment had more positive feelings about himself, a greater self-respect and self-regard. In supportive treatment these changes were clearly related to the experience of the therapist's interest, concern, and valuing of him. In object relations terms, the affective bond between self and object became strengthened, ideally at all levels of genetic development. The love of the good parent that was inadequately experienced in the patient's development was reexperienced, at least to some degree, and hence the patient's self-love and self-regard were enhanced. The case of the *Playboy* who considerably exceeded the gains expected by the predictors illustrates the potency of such a process. The research team believed that the enhanced internalized image of the good parent was the most important facet in helping him overcome deep-seated and disturbing feelings of emptiness and deprivation which had been at the basis of his cyclic mood disturbances.

This heightened self-esteem is even more intense when experienced in the context of being accepted and valued despite the expression of socially unacceptable instinctual wishes. Some patients had such a great conviction that a direct expression of angry feelings toward the therapist would result in dire consequences that they strove to keep this important relationship "untainted" by base desires or motives. On the other hand, the exposure of these angry, demanding, and childish behaviors accompanied by the therapist's continuing and sustained interest further consolidated the patient's self-esteem.

The therapist's ability to accept the "badness" of the patient's instinctual drives also reduces the pressures of the patient's superego which, in turn, heightens self-esteem. In effect, the patient has the opportunity to internalize the therapist's superego attitudes regarding these drives, he begins to regard them more benignly and tolerantly as a part of the human condition, and therefore does not have to expend psychic energies defending himself against the awareness of such feelings in consciousness.

Corrective Emotional Experience. The therapist's commitment to his patient and the patient's capacity to perceive his concern will not only produce a heightened self-esteem, but will also modify the patient's special conflicts. A corrective emotional experience refers to a therapist responding differently to certain aspects of the patient's behavior than the latter had expected. The patient gradually learns that his neurotic expectations are unrealistic and, with or without insight, modifies his misperceptions as well as his usual defenses against them. Usually this experience occurs without benefit of an interpretive approach by the therapist. One type of corrective emotional experience in our population occurred in the cases of several women who believed that the therapist could not really respect them because of their sex. They clearly rejected their own femininity and expected others to see them as inferior and unacceptable. When the reverse of this expectation occurred (and reoccurred) over a period of time, these patients (*Fencer, Bohemian, Heiress, Involutional Woman*) began to view their femininity in a more favorable light. As we see, a clear-cut differentiation between corrective emotional experience and enhanced self-esteem is not really possible, except that the former refers to a specific facet of the self (like femininity), while the latter encompasses more generalized feelings about the self.

Transference Cure. Another concomitant of an internalized good relationship is the patient's effort to please the therapist by engaging in improved, adaptive behavior. Transference cure is often used depreciatingly by analysts ("only" a transference cure) to convey the expectation of a fleeting and transitory result. Such changes may indeed be temporary and unstable when they are not based upon a sufficiently strong, positive internalization. For example, a few patients (*Suspended Student, Rebel Coed, Covert Addict*) experienced a predominantly mistrustful transference during the course of their treatment, and attempted to comply with the perceived demands of the therapist mainly out of fear. They had the conviction of being unacceptable and feared that failure to make at least some token changes would result in further alienation, or even open rejection. One such patient (*Rebel Coed*) kept a number of secrets from her therapist, mainly concerning her homosexuality. Superficially she presented herself as showing improvement because she thought that the "bad parent-therapist" would abandon her if she confessed to perverse sexuality. But, when a transference cure develops in the context of a trusting relationship between patient and therapist, one should expect the change to persist. Thus, the transference cure aspects of the change which occurred in the case of the *Movie Lady* were surprisingly stable, to the surprise of the research team. The stability of the change was partly a function of the correspondence between therapist and patient during the follow-up period, but there also seemed to be a built-in, stabilized internalization of a therapeutic alliance which helped the patient maintain her gains.[2]

Identification. Another product (and cause) of the internalization process is an identification with the therapist's "ego and superego attitudes." A patient's relationships may take on the characteristics which the therapist has demonstrated

---

2. Another factor which increases stability of change is the positive reinforcement and feedback which adaptive change induces. The patient may begin a new and more adaptive form of behavior out of a wish to please the therapist. But frequently, the internal and external rewards of such behavior may become an equally potent force in maintaining it. The *Obedient Husband* became more assertive and masculine in compliance with the expectations of his therapist. But he continued this new behavior pattern because he found that the rewards of such behavior, from others and from himself, were gratifying and fulfilling.

toward the patient. Often, the identification is based on the therapist's sense of commitment, his feelings of responsibility and concern for the patient. These essential ingredients of the therapeutic relationship are absorbed and assimilated, to a greater or lesser degree, both consciously and unconsciously. The process of identification is a basic ingredient of normal development in childhood, and when it occurs in psychotherapy it represents an acquisition in an area where normal development failed either because of conflictual relationships with the parents or because the parents presented inferior models.

Two cases will illustrate this process. The therapeutic gain made by the *Prince* via uncovering of unconscious conflict was nil in a four-year-long analysis mainly because the patient was unable to tolerate the narcissistic threats involved in facing weakness and inadequacy in himself, but he made significant gains in overcoming the central problem which had brought him to treatment: his inability to form a stable commitment to another person, particularly a woman. The analyst's devotion, over a long period of time, to the task of patiently listening and attempting to understand became the model for the patient's major gain. These attitudes made it possible for him to get married during his treatment and to effect a reasonably successful relationship with his wife. In a similar way, the *Playboy* was not only able to become more considerate of his wife's needs, but he was also able to become more like his therapist in discharging his professional responsibilities. A person with serious problems in wholeheartedly devoting himself to his professional work, the patient acquired a new professional perspective which was helpful both to him and to his clients.

This process of identifying with certain specific attitudes exemplified by the therapist is another by-product of a more basic and generalized internalization process of a strengthened affective bond between self and other. The development of this internal alteration is initiated by the growth of a therapeutic alliance which, in turn, may result in some or all of the effects which have been described above. One of the well-accepted axioms of developmental psychology is that a libidinal tie between parent and child forms the matrix within which major developmental tasks are accomplished. Psychotherapy, whether supportive treatment or psychoanalysis, provides a second chance to make up for past developmental failures.

The foregoing ideas have, to a great extent, been represented in the revised hierarchical organization of assumption statements devised by the author and his co-worker, Dr. Ann Appelbaum (Appendixes 1 and 2). A schematized version of these views is presented in the accompanying diagram.

Need Gratification in Therapy			Transference Disposition to Experience a Good Object
	Internalization of Therapeutic Alliance		
Identification with Therapist's Values	Heightened Self-Esteem	Corrective Emotional Experience	Transference Cure

The diagram represents the view that the necessary prerequisites for internalization of the therapeutic alliance reside partly in the patient and his transference dispositions and partly in the need-gratifying aspects of the therapeutic process.

Another feature of the diagram is the relegation of identification to being a part-process of the more general internalization effect, consistent with the view that identification is one type of internalization. Identification refers to the process of becoming like an external object, in this instance taking on certain ego and superego qualities of the therapist. But the most general kind of change, we suggest, is one in which a new self-object representation based upon the therapeutic alliance becomes an intrapsychic structure. This means that an altered

262 The Curative Process: Summary and Reformulation

view of the self in relation to an altered view of a significant other, as well as the affective bond between the two representations, becomes assimilated into the person's internal world. The latter involves not only new and more accepting perceptions of the self, including those based on identifications, but also includes more realistic and benign views of the attitudes of others. Identification involves a modification of the self-representation; the internalization of a new self-other representation involves a modified view of the person's introjects as well.

NEGATIVE TRANSFERENCE AS A BARRIER TO INTERNALIZATION

A point of view commonly held in analytic circles is that the negative transference will prevent a therapeutic alliance from developing unless it is explicitly and systematically interpreted in the psychotherapy. Otherwise, it will constitute a barrier to the development of accurate and realistic perceptions of the therapist as a helping figure.

The evidence in this study, however, is that certain patients are capable of responding to the benign effects of a therapeutic relationship without interpretive work done on the negative transference. At least in the twelve successful cases described in the sections on supportive psychotherapy (Chapters 9 and 10), we saw varying degrees of internalization without such interpretive efforts. This is not to say that these cases might not have been even more successful if such work had been attempted. In the next section, in fact, we propose to account for varying degrees and stability of change at least partly in terms of the uncovering of negative transference. The research team expressed the view that in at least two of these cases

(*Thespian* and *Fencer*) more explicit interpretation of the patient's hostility, fear, and competitiveness with the therapist might have eventuated in a better result.

Also relevant to this question were the psychotherapy cases who were relatively unsuccessful. How many of these did not achieve therapeutic goals because of the therapist's failure to use a more interpretive mode? Of the twelve cases who made either minimal or no change, only one (*Grandson*) was felt by the research team to have failed for that reason. He interrupted treatment prematurely because the growing relationship presented him with the threat of a homosexual submission which was not clarified or interpreted by the therapist.

From the data available we are unable to offer a differentiation between those patients who are able to profit from a supportive approach and those who require more expressive work in order to succeed. The only clear conclusion we can offer is that a substantial number of patients treated by a predominantly noninterpretive approach were able to benefit from their psychotherapy.

This finding also raises the question of why a "good friendship" cannot produce the same results we found in our successful cases. A supportive therapy relationship, without interpretations and confrontation, shares much in common with the relationship which ideally transpires between close friends: the friend feels valued and appreciated, he experiences support in times of stress, he is aware of considerable interest in his welfare. However, these ideal relationships are the very things which elude the patient with emotional disturbances. If they were able to establish such friendships, they would not be seeking treatment. Through his training, understanding, and commitment to his patient, the therapist tolerates and works with the patient's hostility, unreasonable demands, and narcissism which would ordinarily alienate another party to a relationship.

DEGREES OF SUCCESSFUL INTERNALIZATION

We have already detailed our findings on the ingredients, both in the patient and in the therapy, necessary for the formation of a therapeutic alliance. The patient must bring to the therapy a sufficient nucleus of a good parental image and relationship to permit the therapy to build upon and strengthen this kind of libidinal attachment. Conversely, the internalized bad object must not be so potent as to "overpower" the good, and thus prevent the development of a therapeutic alliance. From the standpoint of the treatment, there must be sufficient need gratification, depending upon the patient, in order to engender a therapeutic alliance and its by-products.

We propose the general hypothesis that varying degrees of stable structural change occur in all successful treatments depending upon the extent and quality of the internalization process. We would like to describe three degrees and kinds of internalization of therapeutic processes in ascending order of stability and structural change. The first two are associated with supportive treatment, while the last is based on expressive aspects.

Splitting of Good and Bad Images. Splitting between the good and bad internal object is a pathological defense associated with primitive and borderline personality organization (Kernberg, 1966). The patient's failure to integrate feelings of love and hate toward one individual constitutes a serious developmental defect, and gives rise in therapy to attitudes which remain unintegrated and uninfluenced by the positive therapeutic relationship.

There were at least two cases in our study of patients where the splitting phenomenon was pronounced. The *Thespian* maintained a polite and respectful distance from her therapist, excluding all sexual and aggressive feelings from the relationship. At the same time, she was engaging in active homosexual relationships which expressed the infantile and "bad" wishes. The patient protected the integrity of the therapeutic relationship by overidealizing the therapist and herself in relation to him. It was as though contaminating the pure by the impure would have rendered it completely unusable. Similarly, the *Loner* took an even more extreme stance in distancing himself from his therapist. He tolerated no probing from the therapist, and when the latter got too "personal," the patient raised his eyebrows as a signal to cease and desist. He has maintained a long-term relationship with his therapist, and is probably a therapeutic "lifer," but he must maintain almost absolute control over the relationship in order to extract the good from it. The therapist's (projected) violence and sadism had to be actively curtailed and split off from the good which the therapist had to offer.

In both of these cases, there was clear evidence that primitive aggression had to be isolated from the positive relationship with the therapist by active, strenuous measures. In the more extreme instance of this process, the *Loner* could not really internalize the therapist as a person. He could only engage in an imitative process, accepting advice and recommendations about the techniques of living much as a client receiving counsel from his attorney would make use of legal advice. In other words, there seemed to be a minimum of good image internalization since it was so constantly threatened by the potential incursions of malevolent forces. Hence, the changes in therapy were limited and depended for survival upon continuing therapeutic contact.

The *Thespian*, on the other hand, did indeed establish and maintain a positive image of the therapist during and after the treatment. In the follow-up interviews she expressed strong feelings of appreciation and liking for him and felt that he had rescued her from a downward sweep that would have resulted in suicide. However, the positive changes and the resulting stability were cast into the constricting mold of a homosexual way of life with its attendant loneliness, need for discretion, and threat of disclosure. Her relationships with other women were less self-destructive and more gratifying than they had been before treatment, but they were far from stable and tranquil. The splitting process had probably facilitated considerable change but not without a costly limitation.

Repression of Bad Object Representation. There were a number of other cases in our supportive psychotherapy series in which the good object was strengthened, but without clear evidence of extensive splitting. In all of these cases there were varying degrees of dependent, angry, and sometimes sexual feelings expressed within the therapeutic relationship. In none of them did the therapist attempt to elicit such feelings, nor to work with them interpretively. But the dominant transference was warm and friendly while negative transference feelings were avoided by both patient and therapist.

The patients in the splitting group, in contrast to the repressors, showed two differentiating characteristics: the need for distance and tendencies toward overidealization associated with a poor tolerance for ambivalence. The patients in this group were not described as exhibiting polite, respectful distance nor excessive control. Rather, the patients' hostile feelings and angry demands and critical attacks could, and often would, occur from time to time despite the prevailing friendly atmosphere. Furthermore, the overidealization of the therapist, so characteristic of defensive splitting, was not present to the same degree. All of these patients were appreciative and, to some extent, one might say that they endowed their therapist with unrealistically positive qualities. But they also tended to see the therapist as he actually was. Thus, the *Bohemian* saw her therapist as a benignly interested and benevolent figure, but she did not endow him with the brilliance which one might expect from a narcissistic person like herself who valued intellectual and cultural attainments so highly. The *Fencer* enjoyed jousting with her therapist and often won debating points; she valued the relationship highly and respected his human qualities without unduly exaggerating his characteristics.

One might hypothesize, therefore, that the process involved in the strengthening of a good object representation in individuals where splitting is not predominant results in a repression and partial neutralization of the bad object. One might think of the splitting process as involving a thick, impermeable barrier between good and bad which essentially prevents one region from influencing the other.[3] Where this barrier is relatively permeable, as in the case of repression as opposed to splitting, the enhancement of the good introject results in a relative diminution of the bad. For example, the *Fencer's* feelings of oral deprivation, as well as her sense of depreciation as a woman, were substantially alleviated because she felt valued and respected by her therapist. Her enhanced self-esteem helped her undertake relationships and activities which she previously had avoided. The good self view flourished, causing the bad self representations to become less potent and virulent.

Judged according to the dimensions of distance and over-idealization, one would have to view the two categories of splitting and repression as points on a continuum. In two of the cases in which repression appeared to be dominant, there was still some degree of splitting. The *Obedient Husband* was described by the research team as having become more assertively masculine on the basis of the "therapist's white

---

3. Like all analogies, this one involves a possible source of confusion. The "thick impermeable membrane" applies to the separation between good and bad object representations but is not applicable more broadly with respect to instinctual derivatives. Raw, untamed, and primitive contents emerge more easily into consciousness in the "splitters" than in the repressors.

magic substituting for his wife's black magic." He had been unable to rid himself of the fear that asserting himself against his wife's wishes would result in a serious loss or abandonment. The therapist's encouragement of this man to become more manly and less submissive counteracted this bad introject. But to some extent the research team saw this process as endowing the therapist with overly strong and benevolent powers (white magic), and hence some degree of splitting may be presumed. Furthermore, despite his appreciation and respect for the therapist, he was not without some fear and awe of her "power." In a setting where long-term psychotherapy is the rule, he terminated after the relatively brief period of eighteen months. Both he and the therapist were satisfied with his progress, but his discomfort in the relationship seemed to have contributed to his readiness to stop. Though he substantially maintained his gains during follow-up, there was some reversion to reliance on alcohol (still within the limits of social drinking) to deal with his anxieties.

The ingredients of distance and overidealization are also to be found to some degree in the case of the *Involutional Woman*. The research team described the arrangement with her as one involving a "gentlemen's agreement" in which she would behave in ladylike fashion and the therapist would reciprocate by not disturbing the polite atmosphere of the treatment by exploration or confrontation which might run counter to the patient's wishes. Also, the patient described with some exaggeration her second therapist as "one of the outstanding psychiatrists in the country." Recall that the research team believed that her posttreatment gains were maintained in part by a shift in her dependency from therapist to an internist whom she saw regularly for treatment of a chronic somatic condition.

Thus, it is likely that both splitting and repression will be used concomitantly in the course of supportive treatment, but the dominance of one over the other is likely to have important effects on the stability of change.

Integration of Good and Bad Object Representations. In splitting, the good self-object relationship is enhanced in the context of a thick impermeable boundary between good and bad; in repression the good relationship flourishes in a more fluid context and helps repress or neutralize the bad elements. In contrast, the process of "integration" involves eliciting the hostile, dependent, and sexual impulses within the protective envelope of the therapeutic alliance in such a way that the bad self-object representations are diminished through a process which we may call "experiential dissonance."

We are essentially describing what happens in the expressive psychotherapies, especially psychoanalysis. Various aspects of the analytic situation, including free association, use of the couch, the neutrality of the therapist, and consistent interpretation of transference, induce a regression in which the patient's infantile fears and wishes are brought into the open. Analysis is a treatment which maximizes in consciousness bad as well as good object relationships occurring at various levels of the patient's psychosexual development. Unlike the processes of splitting and repression, the "integration" method is characterized by actively uncovering and making conscious the neurotic defenses used to cope with the patient's bad internal objects. One might describe the outcome of the ideal analytic treatment as one in which the boundaries between good and bad object representations are dissolved. The patient is confronted with inner conflicts between love and hate toward the same object, becomes better able to deal with his ambivalences, and attains a reasonable security concerning the predominance of love over hate.

To illustrate, the analytic patient on the basis of a strong therapeutic alliance, recognizes that the analyst is devoted to the task of being as helpful as possible, that he is fair-minded and objective and, despite his human shortcomings, he is using his skill to help the patient overcome his neurotic distortions. Yet, unaccountably, the patient is often inundated with feelings of rage and fear concerning the analyst's presumed callousness as, for example, in relation to treatment interruptions. It is this dissonance between the rational and the irrational, between the therapeutic alliance and the transference neurosis, between the observing ego and the experiencing ego, or between the good introject and the bad introject—each equally exposed to consciousness—which is the major curative factor in psychoanalytic treatment.

Experiential dissonance seems to be the most felicitous term to describe this process. It is not the cognitive dissonance of the simultaneous presence of two contradictory *ideas*. Rather, it is the simultaneous presence of two contradictory sets of experiences, two currents of disparate feelings, which is the matrix of this therapeutic process. Although insight is useful in furthering this process, it is not the central factor, nor is it primary. It is actually a by-product of a potent emotional experience which is interpreted, worked through, and hopefully resolved.

This formulation is consistent with the differentiation described by Gill (1954) between the patient who resolves a conflict and one who achieves better control over troublesome impulses. He distinguishes the two processes in terms of repression or suppression leading to better control as opposed to the patient who experiences, works through, and ultimately renounces the infantile wish. Analytic work would lead to the latter and could be subsumed under the concept of "integration."

The extensiveness and stability of therapeutic change associated with psychoanalysis may be understood in terms of its being the most thorough process of integrating good and bad internal objects when the experiential dissonance between therapeutic alliance and regressive transference neurosis gets resolved.

CRITIQUE OF THE STRUCTURAL CHANGE CONCEPT

This Prediction Study started with two broad conceptions of change which were clearly differentiated from each other. One was the change in impulse-defense configurations and referred to the person's handling of instinctual drives, including the patterning, range, flexibility, and appropriateness of the ego-defensive operations. The primary focus was on the change in the quality and adaptiveness of overt behavior, and such "alterations in the techniques of adjustment" were judged to be nonstructural (relatively impermanent) as long as they did not derive from conflict resolution in expressive psychotherapy or psychoanalysis. The predictors recognized that such change might develop from a variety of sources, most of which have been mentioned in our discussion of mechanisms of supportive psychotherapy. Almost parenthetically, in a handful of cases, they allowed for the possibility of stability in those instances where identification with the therapist occurred.

But the analytic ideal was the vaunted "structural change in the ego." It was distinguished from impulse-defense change linking the observed change to the uncovering treatment processes which produced it and by determining whether verbalizable insights could be elicited. There was a very clear conception that reliable and stable alteration in symptom or character trait required the uprooting of the underlying unconscious conflict by making it conscious.

In the Manual of the Initial Study, written in 1954 by the analysts involved in making the predictions, they stated: "To the extent that these newer, more adjustive means of adaptation are not just altered techniques of adjustment through transference effects or shifts in defensive patterns, but are more permanently different ways of coping with stresses based on resolution of the older, inhibiting, conflict-bound ways, they represent actual structural changes in the ego." (p. 41) The authors clearly viewed those changes as nonstructural which could not be associated with a process of uncovering, insight, working through, and ultimately, conflict resolution.

A shift away from this dichotomous thinking first appeared in 1964 when a committee of project members collaboratively defined the key terms used in the assumption statements. In this Glossary of Terms (Appendix 3), the agreed-on definitions of impulse-defense and structural change had shown a clear shift. There was now a conception of a *continuum* of change with structural change representing greater stability based on a resolution of infantile impulses while the impulse-defense change involved a persistence of similar drives, perhaps, but a shift in the ego's (or superego's) mode of dealing with these impulses. The alterations could be relatively stable and were no longer characterized as "*just* altered techniques of adjustment."

The significance of this historical note is that the new formulation occurred at a time when the data-collection phase of the project was coming to an end. It is probable that as the results of the study were becoming known, there was a shift toward crediting the supportively based changes with greater stability and permanence than had previously been accorded them.

Now, with all of the data collected and analyzed, the trend adopted by the authors of the Glossary seems entirely justified. Those supportively treated cases that made significant gains and maintained them during the follow-up period without continuing therapeutic contact compelled us to revise the original hypothesis. Any alteration which seems to be relatively permanent is entitled to an appellation like "structural," since the term denotes a process of a slow rate of change.

But it is now questionable whether the concept of structural change has any useful meaning when broadened to include a whole variety of mechanisms of change. It is now fairly certain that such diverse phenomena as the wish to please, the corrective emotional experience, and the introjection of the therapist's ego and superego attitudes are capable of producing permanent or relatively permanent changes. We also have observed that once a change has been set in motion, by whatever mechanism, there are certain situational reinforcers which tend to perpetuate it. Adaptive changes are often self-reinforcing in terms of rewards from others, not to speak of the self-fulfillment which often accompanies socially valued behavior. Also, a benign environment (frequently made possible by treatment-induced changes) will tend to enhance and strengthen a new behavior pattern.

We have proposed that there are degrees of structuralism or permanence of change to be found both in supportive and expressive treatments and that the crucial determinant of stability is the degree of strengthening of the internalized self-object representations. Expressive treatments like psychoanalysis provide the maximal opportunity for such strengthening, while the limiting factor in supportive treatment is most often that posed by the patient's potential to develop a useful therapeutic alliance. Here we assume, of course, that the treatment modality necessary to foster this alliance is applied with the requisite skill.

Finally, any change based on an internalization of altered self-object representations is potentially stable according to the quality and degree of the internal realignment. Whether this alteration results in the oft-belittled transference cure, or the equally depreciated corrective emotional experience, or "just" enhanced self-esteem, the permanence of the change may only be assessed by investigating the alteration in the inner object world. To the extent that the therapeutic process has induced a strengthened affective bond between the internalized self and object, the attendant change will be stable. Our present methods for precisely assessing such internal restructuring still need much refinement, but the importance of these processes have been strongly suggested by the Prediction Study.

APPENDIXES

Appendix 1. Diagrams of the Hierarchical Organization of
          Assumptions
          A. Expressive Aspects of Psychotherapy
          B. Supportive Aspects of Psychotherapy
          C. Common Core
Appendix 2. Predictive and Postdictive Assumptions
Appendix 3. Glossary of Terms

APPENDIX 1

Diagrams of the Hierarchical Organization of Assumptions

    A. Expressive Aspects of Psychotherapy
    B. Supportive Aspects of Psychotherapy
    C. Common Core

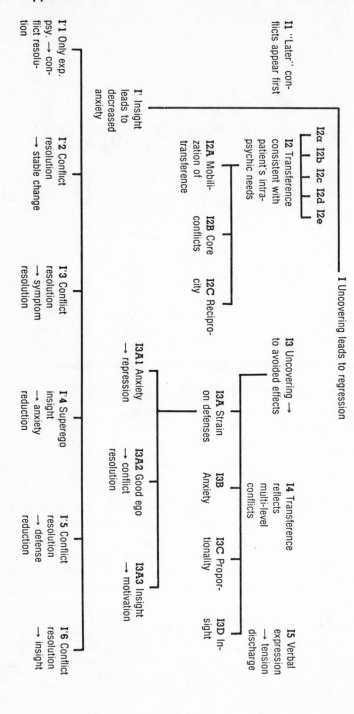

Diagram 1
HIERARCHICALLY ORGANIZED ASSUMPTION STATEMENTS
EXPRESSIVE ASPECTS OF PSYCHOTHERAPY

I Uncovering leads to regression

I1 "Later" con-
flicts appear first

I2 Transference
consistent with
patient's intra-
psychic needs

I2a I2b I2c I2d I2e

I2A Mobili-
zation of
transference

I2B Core
conflicts

I2C Recipro-
city

I3 Uncovering →
to avoided effects

I3A Strain
on defenses

I3A1 Anxiety
→ repression

I3A2 Good ego
→ conflict
resolution

I3A3 Insight
→ motivation

I3B
Anxiety

I3C Propor-
tionality

I3D In-
sight

I4 Transference
reflects
multi-level
conflicts

I5 Verbal
expression
→ tension
discharge

I' Insight
leads to
decreased
anxiety

I'1 Only exp.
psy. → con-
flict resolu-
tion

→ stable change

I'2 Conflict
resolution

→ symptom
resolution

I'3 Conflict
resolution

→ anxiety
reduction

I'4 Superego
insight

→ defense
reduction

I'5 Conflict
resolution

→ insight

I'6 Conflict
resolution

Diagram 2

**HIERARCHICALLY ORGANIZED ASSUMPTION STATEMENTS
SUPPORTIVE ASPECTS OF PSYCHOTHERAPY**

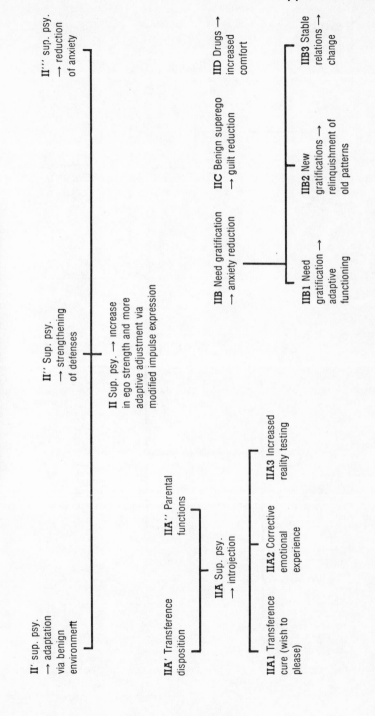

II′ sup. psy. → adaptation via benign environment

II′′ Sup. psy. → strengthening of defenses

II′′′ sup. psy. → reduction of anxiety

II Sup. psy. → increase in ego strength and more adaptive adjustment via modified impulse expression

IIA′ Transference disposition

IIA Sup. psy. → introjection

IIA′′ Parental functions

IIA1 Transference cure (wish to please)

IIA2 Corrective emotional experience

IIA3 Increased reality testing

IIB Need gratification → anxiety reduction

IIC Benign superego → guilt reduction

IID Drugs → increased comfort

IIB1 Need gratification → adaptive functioning

IIB2 New gratifications → relinquishment of old patterns

IIB3 Stable relations → change

Diagram 3
HIERARCHICALLY ORGANIZED ASSUMPTION STATEMENTS
COMMON CORE

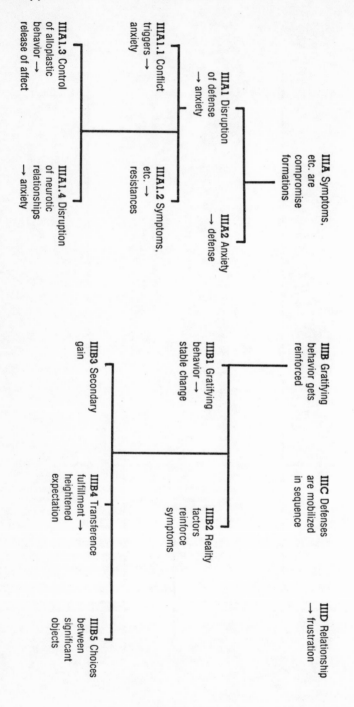

APPENDIX 2

Predictive and Postdictive Assumptions[1]

I—The uncovering aspects of psychotherapy facilitate regression by encouraging and requiring the verbal expression of repressed impulses, affects, and ideas.

I 1—Treatments which uncover unconscious conflicts work with genetically later layers of conflict first, and the earlier layers later.

I 1 A—Expressive psychotherapies, particularly psychoanalysis, eventually lead to the verbal expression of infantile wishes and fantasies in the transference.

(I 1 A1)[2]—To the extent that a patient has an internalized good, protective parental image, and to the

1. The predictive assumptions were written as part of the initial study of the case by the Prediction Study team.
2. The postdictive assumptions were written to explain a predictive error and are indicated by parentheses.

extent that the therapist avoids a regressive transference development, the relationship with the therapist is predominantly positive and friendly.

I 1 B—Patients in psychoanalysis with a predominantly hostile identification with a parent figure first reveal the negative aspects of the identification and only later display the deeper more positive longings.

I 1 C—The more intense the fixation at a genetically earlier psychosexual level, and the less the fixations at genetically later levels, the sooner in treatment will the genetically earlier conflicts determine the character of the transference.

I 1 D—Reality aspects, both of the treatment situation itself and of the patient's current difficulties, play a more prominent role early in expressive psychotherapy and become subordinated later to the more internal, fantasy dictated and genetically prior aspects of the patient's conflicts.

I 1 D1—In expressive treatment, transference attitudes toward one particular sex are experienced earlier toward a therapist of that sex.

I 2a—To the extent that reality cues are minimized, transference reactions are fostered.

I 2a1—In a situation in which reality cues are minimized, those reality factors which are present are particularly effective in mobilizing transference reactions.

(I 2a2)—The more supportive the treatment mode,

the greater is the tendency of the transference to conform to the actual personality attributes of the therapist.

I 2b—The more infantile wishes have been fulfilled, and the reality of infantile fears confirmed, the more peremptory are these wishes and fears in psychotherapy.

I 2b 1—To the extent that the parental figures were in reality estranged and at cross-purposes, the therapeutic task of coming to terms with the ambivalently held parental introjects is more difficult.

I 2c—Patients whose infantile needs are not gratified within the transference respond to this frustration with regressive and/or resistive reactions, and/or painful affects.

(I 2c1)—To the extent that a patient's infantile wishes are gratified in the treatment situation, the negative side of the transference will not emerge.

I 2d—Transference wishes represent a longing for a regressive reexperiencing of less conflict ridden ego states along with the associated object attachments.

(I 2e)—Interpretation facilitates the emergence of unconscious wishes.

(I 2e1)—To the extent that interpretations are focused upon one level of conflict, the expression of the patient's strivings toward the therapist, related to other psychosexual levels, is inhibited.

(I 2e2)—To the extent that the therapist overlooks the

transference meanings of the patient's behavior, the patient's intrapsychic conflicts will not be uncovered.

(I 2)—To the extent that treatment aims consistently to uncover unconscious conflict, transference distortions override the realities of the treatment situation (i.e., patient's reactions to the therapist are more consistent with genetically determined intrapsychic needs which are active at a given time than with the actual behavior and intentions of the therapist).

I 2 A—To the extent that "reality" factors in the therapeutic situation fulfill transference expectations, a particular transference reaction is mobilized.

I 2 A1—Female patients with strong repressed passive longings toward mother eventually display toward a male therapist a seemingly heterosexual wish which has an underlying homosexual component.

I 2 A2—When the same reality factor in the treatment situation can be experienced with equal ease by the patient as either positive or negative, transference patterns corresponding to these contradictory experiences will alternate with one another during psychotherapy.

(I 2 A3)—To the extent that the therapist's attitude toward a patient is persecutory, the patient's paranoid and masochistic mechanisms are intensified.

(I 2 A4)—Patients with an expectation to be gratified and indulged by the therapist experience the permissiveness to talk freely as encouragement to relinquish to the therapist responsibility for their actions.

I 2 B—The core conflicts and their associated defensive patterns give rise to the *major* transference paradigms.

I 2 B1—Patients with marked oral fixations cling to the idea that change, favorable or unfavorable, will come about by means of an external force.

I 2 B2—Intellectualized pseudoinsights are used by patients who are intellectually competitive to establish the feeling of superiority over the therapist.

I 2 B3—Patients with strong masochistic needs experience therapeutic interventions as aggressive acts.

I 2 B4—Patients with a marked distrust of the therapist's attitude toward them have difficulty in expressing their wishes in relation to the therapist lest they be hurt or disappointed.

I 2 C—There is a reciprocal relationship between the intensity of wishes directed toward the therapist and the fulfillment of psychological needs in the patient's life outside the therapy.

I 2 C1—Patients treated by psychoanalysis with marked ambivalent ties to significant others, who experience a loss of this object after a transference neurosis has been established, intensify the transference ties.

I 2 C1.1—Patients treated by psychoanalysis who have ambivalent ties to significant others, who cannot tolerate the conscious recognition of the hostile side of the ambivalence and who experience loss of the object of the ambivalence after the development of an effective transference neurosis, avoid the otherwise expected depression or some equivalent thereof.

I 2 C1.2—Patients treated by psychoanalysis who have ambivalent ties to significant others and who cannot tolerate the conscious recognition of the hostile side of the ambivalence and who experience a loss of the object prior to the development of an affective transference neurosis develop a depression or some equivalent thereof.

I 2 C2—To the extent that a patient displaces affects and attitudes onto the therapist, these become less disruptive to the patient's life outside of treatment.

(I 2 C3)—When the hospital environment gratifies the patient's needs for nurturance and comfort in ways which are impossible in the psychotherapeutic relationship, a highly alloplastic patient is helped to develop a therapeutic alliance in psychotherapy.

(I 2 C4)—When expectations based upon infantile conflicts are fulfilled by a patient's current reality, it is difficult for him to achieve insight into the intrapsychic sources of these expectations.

I 3—As the underlying conflicts are uncovered, patients experience the affects which were avoided and which gave rise to symptom formation.

I 3 A—The regression involved in the uncovering of repressed impulses, affects, and ideas, places a strain upon the patient's defenses and arouse anxiety and other unpleasurable affects.

I 3 A1—The arousal of anxiety stemming from the imminent awareness of unacceptable impulses leads to an increased effort at repression of infantile fantasies.

I 3 A1.1—The arousal of anxiety in response to the uncovering process leads to increased reliance upon characteristic symptoms, characteristic patterns for defenses as a way of augmenting resistance to the conscious recollection of infantile fantasies.

I 3 A1.11—Patients in expressive psychotherapies who are extremely compliant, or who rely upon denial and avoidance, when affects and anxieties associated with the emergence of underlying conflicts begin to arise, resort to premature behavioral change without the resolution of unconscious conflict.

I 3 A1.111—Patients who use strivings toward independence as a defense against passive wishes seek to terminate psychotherapy prematurely.

I 3 A1.12—Intellectualization serves as a defense against a fuller affective recognition of unconscious impulses.

I 3 A1.121—Patients in expressive psychotherapies who rely upon intellectualization, when affects and anxieties associated with the emergence of underlying conflicts begin to arise, develop intellectualized insights in advance of affective reactions or behavioral changes.

I 3 A1.1211—To the extent that patients in expressive psychotherapies rely heavily upon intellectualization they show a wide contrast between the extent of behavioral change and of intellectual understanding of their dynamics.

I 3 A1.122—Patients in expressive psychotherapy with marked passive compliant tendencies develop intellectualized insight as a means of gratifying the therapist.

I 3 A1.123—Patients in whom ideational modes of binding anxiety are not prominent do not use intellectual insights as a defense against further insightful understanding.

I 3 A1.13—Patients in expressive therapies will reveal a fluctuating symptom picture concomitant with the mobilization of the corresponding conflicts within the transference.

I 3 A1.14—Patients more readily give up specific symptoms in response to the transference wish to please (or displease) the therapist than in response to treatments attempting to uncover the underlying unconscious conflicts.

I 3 A1.15—Patients who are confronted with reality stresses in their life situation that seriously endanger their psychic equilibrium require a predominantly supportive therapy during the period of reality stress.

I 3 A1.16—To the extent that a patient's denial of internal conflict is dependent upon his neurotic life situation, he resists insight into the true nature of the life situation.

I3 A1.2— The uncovering of resistances is a prerequisite to the bringing about of insight.

I3 A1.21—To the extent that the therapist overlooks resistances, intrapsychic structural changes do not occur.

I3 A1.211—Treatment in which the patient's strong unconscious guilt is overlooked by the therapist will founder.

I3 A1.212—The more socially acceptable and rewarding certain adaptive behaviors are, the more readily may they be used as a resistance in expressive psychotherapy.

I3 A1.2121—Independence as a defense against passive strivings is generally mistaken for autonomy in patients with good ego strength.

I3 A1.2122—The neurotic components of religious beliefs tend to be less thoroughly explored than are the neurotic components of other attitudes and values, and this sets limits to the completeness of otherwise successful treatments.

I3 A1.21221—The quality of a patient's religious attachments is not altered as a result of conflict resolution unless treatment is specifically addressed to these attachments.

(I 3 A1.2123)—Adaptive behavior that is developed and consolidated in the course of expressive psychotherapy with the aim of preventing a conflict from developing further in the transference—with all the attendant anxiety —is "transference acting out," and serves as resistance to further uncovering the relevant unconscious conflicts.

I 3 A1.21231—Adaptive changes that occur in expressive psychotherapies as a result of transference effects or introjection of the therapist's ego or superego attributes are investigated with the aim of uncovering unconscious conflicts.

I 3 A1.3—The capacity of the therapist to understand a patient is limited by his countertransference predisposition and neurotic distortions and level of skill.

I 3 A1.31—To the extent that a therapist understands the patient exclusively in terms of a single guiding transference paradigm, manifestations of other transference predispositions will be overlooked.

(I 3 A1.32)—To the extent that the therapist possessed the same character traits and defensive makeup as his patient, changes in these characteristics will not occur.

(I 3 A1.33)—To the extent that the patient's behavior in therapy is regressive, the therapist's behavior is more in accord with his countertransference dispositions.

(I 3 A1.331)—Patients with marked ego weakness, yet able to display a facade, however brittle, of adequate functioning, produce diagnostic confusion and hence inconsistent treatment approaches.

(I 3 A1.34)—Highly competitive patients with equivocal symptoms (i.e., equally understandable as a manifestation of severe or mild disturbances) who evoke strong countertransference feelings in the therapist are treated as more seriously ill than they actually are.

I 3 A2—To the extent that patients have good ego strength to effect psychological change in themselves, they are able in expressive psychotherapies to resolve their intrapsychic conflicts with a concomitant remission of symptoms as well as characterological changes.

I 3 A2.1—To the extent that character structure is rigid, the resolution of conflict and consequent behavioral change are limited.

I 3 A2.11—Patients in expressive psychotherapy whose character structure contains marked elements of passivity, dependency, and/or masochism, are able to attain only limited resolution of conflict and consequent behavioral change.

I 3 A2.12—Patients with a predominantly anal character which is rigidly organized to minimize conscious affect are able to attain only limited resolution of conflict and consequent behavioral change.

I 3 A2.13—Patients with markedly rigid character structures who terminate treatment prematurely and do not become involved in another treatment continue their lifelong mode of adjustment essentially unchanged.

I 3 A2.14—Patients in psychoanalysis whose character structure is markedly rigid require a long period of
treatment (five years or more) to achieve that degree of
conflict resolution possible to them.

I 3 A2.141—Patients in psychoanalysis with deep-
seated passive-compliant attitudes and/or masochistic
needs to endure discomfort require a prolonged period of
treatment to achieve that degree of conflict resolution
possible to them.

I 3 A2.15—Patients with good ego strength who are
in expressive psychotherapies and who begin by denying
serious difficulty, either internal or external, eventually
are able to give up these denials.

I 3 A2.16—The less consolidated the character
structure at the onset of expressive psychotherapy, the
more marked the alteration of character in response to
successful treatment.

(I 3 A2.17)—To the extent that patients in expressive
psychotherapy are limited in their capacity to tolerate the
anxiety associated with the full impact of their aggressive
and libidinal strivings, they are able to achieve at best a
partial resolution of their conflicts.

I 3 A2.2—The more primitive the fixations and the
less adequate the defensive structures, the less capable
is the patient in psychoanalysis of integrating and using
what emerges in his free associations.

I 3 A2.21—To the extent that behavior is dictated by intense infantile fixations, it is particularly resistant to modification.

I 3 A2.211—Patients with good ego strength whose major conflicts are at the phallic-Oedipal level are capable of achieving a high degree of conflict resolution.

I 3 A2.212—The length of expressive psychotherapy needed to reach therapeutic goals is directly proportional to the extent to which conflicts are rooted in genetically early (pregenital) disturbances in psychological development.

I 3 A2.2121—Patients whose symptoms reflect deepseated characterological problems, who undertake expressive psychotherapies in adolescence require either prolonged treatment, or additional treatment after reaching maturity for the full resolution of conflict.

(I 3 A2.213)—Patients who are dominated by a need to be admired based upon intense oral fixations have great difficulty acknowledging unpleasant aspects of the self, and hence are unable to take this essential first step toward uncovering unconscious conflict.

I 3 A2.2131—Markedly narcissistic patients obtain insight in expressive psychotherapies into the nature and consequences of this aspect of their character which permits them to modify their behaviors without fully giving up their narcissistic orientation.

I 3 A2.214—Patients with marked oral fixations

particularly resist giving up their fantasies of being gratified by the analyst, and hence are prone to insoluble transference neuroses.

I 3 A2.22—To the extent that patterning of defenses is primitive, conflict resolution is limited.

I 3 A2.221—Patients with marked oral fixations who rely primarily upon externalizing defenses such as projection, somatization, and denial are unable to achieve major intrapsychic change.

I 3 A2.222—To the extent that patients with the capacity to develop psychological mindedness develop increased ego strength and impulse control in response to the supportive aspects of psychotherapy, they can be treated more expressively.

I 3 A2.23—The more primitive the fixations and the less adequate the defensive structures, the more likely is a patient to experience an uncontrolled ego regression in response to the uncovering of unconscious conflicts.

I 3 A2.231—The more primitive the fixations and the less adequate the defensive structures, the more difficult it is for patients to develop and resolve an adequate transference neurosis.

(I 3 A2.2311)—Patients who enter the psychotherapy situation with the fantasy of being cared for by a benevolent parent, who experience the permissiveness and dependability of the psychotherapy as consistent with this fantasy, and who are able to ward off their instinctual demands toward the therapist, can experience psychotherapy, even psychoanalysis, as gratifying.

(I 3 A2.2312)—Patients in expressive psychotherapies with a fear of closeness based on the fear of losing a clear definition of ego boundaries are unable to achieve more than a limited degree of conflict resolution and consequent personality restructuring.

(I 3 A2.232)—Treatments in which the therapist fails to recognize the patient's ego weakness and need for support will founder.

(I 3 A2.233)—The more primitive the fixations and the less adequate the defensive structures, the greater the tendency of alloplastic patients in psychoanalysis to disrupt the treatment to ward off impending ego regression.

I 3 A2.24—The effort to bring about insight into any impulse defense configuration is contraindicated when such insight will not lead to more adaptive ego functioning.

I 3 A2.241—The supportive aspects of psychotherapy lead to limited insights into the maladaptive solutions the patient has been using, less so into the content of the unconscious conflicts, and even less into the underlying mechanisms and early determinants of his conflicts.

I 3 A2.2411—Patients with limited ego strength in supportive psychotherapy achieve at most a very limited insight into the relationship between their conflicts and their symptoms.

(I 3 A2.25)—Patients who suffer from an intense distortion of object relations are unable to profit from psychoanalysis because the anonymity of the analyst prevents correction of their distorted transference perceptions.

I 3 A2.3—To the extent that reality gratifies needs and provides support against impending impulse discharge, affective impact of emerging insight is modulated.

I 3 A2.31—When necessary ego strength is lacking for expressive psychotherapy, it will be compensated for by certain supportive factors in the environment.

I 3 A2.311—When adequate ego strength is lacking for utilizing the expressive aspects of psychotherapy a patient will derive sufficient support and control from the hospital structure to be treated expressively to some extent.

I 3 A2.3111—Patients who suffer from a severe impulse disorder require that expressive psychotherapies be carried on with concomitant hospitalization until the symptoms of the disorder have come under internal control.

I 3 A2.31111—Patients with alloplastic symptoms who are discharged from the hospital before establishing a firm therapeutic alliance with their therapist resume their acting out in an unchecked fashion.

I 3 A2.312—Life circumstances that enhance a patient's self-esteem by providing opportunities for better functioning expand the patient's capacity to tolerate the expressive aspects of psychotherapy.

I 3 A2.32—To the extent that ego strength is limited, it is necessary to introduce supportive aspects into the psychotherapy itself in order to enable the patient to tolerate expressive treatment.

(I 3 A2.321)—Patients whose ego strength and impulse control are somewhat below the minimum level needed for successful psychoanalytic treatment but whose conflicts are to a large extent at the phallic level and who are hospitalized during the early phase of psychoanalysis are able to resolve their major conflicts.

I 3 A2.322—Patients in expressive psychotherapies who can tolerate the frustration of transference wishes eventually are able, through interpretation alone, to uncover and work through their neurotic conflicts.

I 3 A2.33—Patients with limited ego strength in expressive psychotherapies who are not able to control alloplastic symptoms and self-destructive behavior require adjunctive supports for a considerable period of time until at least a partial resolution of conflict has occurred.

I 3 A2.4—Patients with adequate ego strength for expressive psychotherapies who begin with a predominantly supportive treatment for whatever reason (financial, diagnostic unclarity, low motivation) when the deterrent circumstances improve can be treated more expressively.

(I 3 A2.5)—Patients who are significantly lacking in psychological mindedness are unable to use the expressive aspects of psychotherapy to uncover unconscious wishes and conflicts.

I 3 A3—To the extent that a patient experiences anxiety and other painful affects and sees them as due to his inner conflicts, the patient is motivated to endure the discomfort of the uncovering process.

I 3 A3.1—To the extent that patients gratify their infantile needs in reality, motivation for change in psychotherapy is reduced.

I 3 A3.11—Patients in treatment who initially lack motivation for change but whose life circumstances render untenable their previous mode of adjustment are forced to revise their conscious treatment goals.

I 3 A3.12—To the extent that neurotic life circumstances are present there will be a proportional limitation of the amount of intrapsychic change that can be effected in expressive psychotherapies.

I 3 A3.13—Patients whose neurotic object relationships are significantly altered, and who are capable of tolerating insights into unacceptable facets of themselves, achieve enhanced understanding of the neurotic needs previously fulfilled by the neurotic relationship.

I 3 A3.2—The more ego syntonic a manifestation is, the less useful it is as a motive force for psychological change, and therefore the less likely to be given up.

I 3 A3.21—Patients in psychotherapy who do not become motivated for a major personality change will achieve in treatment at most the development of, or restoration to, a more satisfactory state of equilibrium.

I 3 A3.211—Patients who seek psychotherapy because of some disruption of their life situation and who do not become motivated for major personality change achieve in treatment only a restoration of the previous equilibrium or a comparable one.

I 3 A3.212—Patients who seek psychotherapy because of symptoms precipitated by a severe conflict-triggering and/or stressful reality and who had made a satisfying premorbid adjustment achieve insight and resolution of conflict limited to the extent necessary for the reestablishment of the premorbid adjustment.

I 3 A3.213—Patients whose presenting symptoms are reactive to a severe conflict-triggering and/or stressful reality and have good ego strength can achieve a resolution of the relevant conflict sufficient to return them to their premorbid adjustment through supportive-expressive psychotherapy without recourse to psychoanalysis.

I 3 A3.22—Patients with good ego strength who seek psychotherapy because of some disruption of their life situation and who are not motivated for major psychological change who become more comfortable while in psychotherapy do not seek more thoroughgoing reconstructive expressive psychotherapy.

(I 3 A3.23)—When shifts (however slight) in impulse-defense configurations lead to marked relief of symptoms and/or marked increase in comfort and gratification in a patient's life, he does not seek a more thoroughgoing reconstructive psychotherapy.

I 3 A3.231—Patients with limited ego strength and deep-seated characterological problems, who become comfortable through a predominantly supportive treatment, do not seek a more thoroughgoing reconstructive expressive psychotherapy.

I 3 A3.24—To the extent that a patient's oral strivings are within moderate limits of ego dystonicity, he successfully avoids an insoluble transference neurosis.

I 3 A3.25—To the extent that patients recognize the maladaptive nature of their life patterns, they become more motivated to achieve a change in their lives.

I 3 A3.251—Patients who never in the course of treatment acknowledge their difficulties, internal or external, fail in treatment.

I 3 A3.252—To the extent that a patient is able to give up his denial of psychological illness, insight into the maladaptive nature of his symptoms and character traits is facilitated.

I 3 A3.253—Patients who gain insight into the fact that certain behaviors do not lead to the expected gratification are able to modify those behaviors to some extent without resolution of the underlying conflict.

I 3 A3.26—When insight into the infantile origins of a

behavior does not lead to painful affects, patients do not renounce that behavior.

(I 3 A3.261)—Patients with good ego strength, for whom behaviors that interfere with the psychoanalytic process are ego-syntonic, cannot be induced to give up these behaviors by interpretation alone, but require supportive interventions.

(I 3 A3.2611)—Behaviors (for instance affect storms) that prevent a patient from participating in the interpretive process must be interrupted by supportive measures in order for insight to develop.

I 3 A3.27—To the extent that a patient's sexual feelings are peremptory and ego syntonic, erotization of the transference becomes a significant resistance.

I 3 A3.3—The duration of expressive psychotherapy needed to restore the previous equilibrium is short in the presence of a combination of acute symptoms, intense precipitating stress, adequate premorbid personality, and ample future life opportunities available to the patient.

I 3 A3.4—Since patients whose symptoms and character traits are primarily determined by masochism experience their analysis as particularly productive of suffering, they are prone to insoluble transference neuroses.

I 3 A3.5—To the extent that insight into the relationship between a patient's inner life and his life difficulties generates expectations of increasing gratifications, the patient is motivated to seek further insight.

I 3 A3.6—The extent of verbalizable insight achieved in psychotherapy is a function of the patient's investment in self-observation.

I 3 A3.61—Patients who rely heavily upon intellectualization need to put the self-understanding they achieve in psychotherapy into words.

I 3 A3.62—Patients who are not especially psychologically minded nor especially intellectualizing tend to forget the insights they achieved in their psychotherapy.

I 3 A3.7—Patients with brain damage manifested by impairment of symbolic functioning are limited in their capacity to make the connections among intrapsychic events necessary to develop anxiety and achieve insight into unconscious motives and conflicts.

I 3 A4—Patients in treatment who begin to become aware that aspects of their personality structure or of their relationship to their life situation are unacceptable to them react depressively or anxiously.

I 3 A4.1—The intensity of the reaction to insight is proportional to the degree of ego dystonicity of the content.

I 3 A4.2—Patients in psychotherapy, who become aware that certain ego syntonic wishes are not capable of being gratified, react depressively or anxiously.

I 3 B—To the extent that the uncovering of the unconscious material proceeds too rapidly to permit the development and consolidation of new impulse-defense configurations, patients experience excessive anxiety.

I 3 B1—To the extent that a patient possesses a wide repertoire of defenses against depression and well-developed channels for the expression of aggression, he does not experience severe depression in expressive psychotherapy.

I 3 B2—Insight into unconscious contents is useful to patients only to the extent that such awareness is accompanied by tolerable guilt and anxiety, and can be integrated into more gratifying modes of functioning.

I 3 C—The more extensive the defensive efforts of a patient against a given unconscious content, the more discomfort he experiences in the process of the material being brought into awareness* in expressive psychother-apy.

I 3 C1—The wider the range of defensive functions performed by a particular resistance, the more difficult it is for a patient in expressive psychotherapy to give up that resistance.

I 3 C1.1—To the extent that masochism is a part of the character structure, patients derive gratifications from the uncovering of unacceptable aspects of the self.

I 3 C1.2—To the extent that a patient's alloplastic defensive modes effectively relieve anxiety, he strongly resists giving up these behaviors.

I 3 C2—Patients in expressive psychotherapies who overcome a persistent long-standing symptom or inhibition react initially with anxiety.

(I 3 C3)—To the extent that pathological defenses become crystallized, affording gratification and/or relief from anxiety, the possibility to deal with these mechanisms expressively is diminished.

I 3 C3.1—The more recent the onset of the symptom the more readily it is relinquished.

I 3 C4—Patients who rely upon avoidance and suppression to bind the anxiety associated with intrapsychic conflict experience difficulty in talking freely in the therapeutic situation.

I 3 C4.1—The more strongly the conflicts, attitudes, and wishes are defended against, the more slowly are they uncovered in expressive psychotherapy.

I 3 C4.2—Patients who rely upon suppression and repression are slow to verbalize their perceptions of the therapist.

I 3 C5—The more deeply repressed a mental content, the more difficult it is to achieve the relevant insight.

I 3 D—Patients who rely upon repression of affects to deal with unconscious conflict experience the relevant affects as they gain insight into the unconscious conflict.

I 3 D1—Patients with a history of hostile and destructive behavior eventually experience a conscious sense of guilt based upon both the real destructiveness they have wrought and upon the guilt feelings associated with earlier hostile impulses.

I 4—Whatever the predominant level of conflict manifested in a given transference reaction, elements of conflict at other levels will be present as well.

I 4 A—Before conflicts of a genetically later psychosexual level are completely resolved it is necessary that the major conflicts at an earlier level be worked through.

I 4 A1—Treatments which encourage the expression of unconscious conflicts go through, in their entirety, movement from conflicts reflecting genetically later levels of psychosexual development to earlier level conflicts and then back for ultimate resolution to the later level.

I 4 A2—The more intense the fixation at any given psychosexual level, the more will conflicts referable to that level reappear and require repeated working through in the course of expressive psychotherapy.

I 4 B—Patients in whom an attitude of passive compliance serves as a defense against rebellious feelings behave rebelliously during expressive psychotherapy as a means of denying their passivity as well as expressing their aggressive impulses.

I 4 B1—Patients in whom an attitude of passive compliance serves as a defense against rebellious feelings experience in expressive psychotherapy the therapist's permission to talk freely as permission to behave rebelliously in their lives outside of treatment.

I 4 C—Patients with a number of readily available

transference modes present the technical problem to the therapist in expressive psychotherapies of accurately identifying and interpreting which aspect of the transference relationship is in the foreground at any given time.

l 4 C1—Patients with dominant and active unconscious conflicts on multiple levels of psychosexual development, whose resistance takes the form of silence, make it difficult for a therapist to understand the nature of their conflicts at that time.

l 4 D—Resolution of the core neurotic conflict facilitates uncovering and resolution of conflicts at other levels.

l 4 E—To the extent that the core conflicts are pregenital, when they are resolved the residual impulse defense configurations will be colored by phallic conflicts.

l 5—The verbal expression of feelings in psychotherapy constitutes an alternative channel for impulse discharge that renders other tension-relieving devices less necessary.

l 5 A—The tendency toward impulse discharge through action, stimulated by regression induced by uncovering, is diminished to the extent that a patient is able to express impulse in words.

l 5 A1—To the extent that impulses are discharged in action so quickly that they are not represented ideationally, they are not brought within the scope of interpretive work.

I 5 A1.1—To the extent that the patient's infantile needs are gratified in the treatment situation (either explicitly or by promises of future fulfillment), insight and intrapsychic structural change do not occur.

I 5 A1.11—Predominantly transference-based wishes in expressive psychotherapies are not fulfilled by the therapist for the sake of attaining higher therapeutic goals, e.g., the resolution of conflict.

I 5 A1.111—Expressive psychotherapies in which the therapist wittingly or unwittingly fulfills transference expectations without subsequent interpretive working through do not achieve more than a limited resolution of underlying conflict.

I 5 A1.1111—When the overt behavior of the therapist strongly and/or continually reinforces the transference expectations of the patient, then the treatment will fail.

I 5 A1.11111—Treatment in which the therapist's expectations for change exceed the patient's capacities to respond will founder.

I 5 A1.112—In psychoanalysis, interpretation is the primary mode of intervention, and all other kinds of intervention are subsidiary thereto in the sense of being designed to facilitate interpretive work; whereas in other expressive psychotherapies interventions other than interpretation may be introduced for other purposes as well.

I 5 A1.1121—The therapist's greater neutrality in

psychoanalysis than in other expressive psychotherapies is important in facilitating a more intense transference, a deeper regression, and a fuller uncovering of the patient's unconscious fantasies.

I 5 A1.11211—Treatments other than psychoanalysis for patients who are capable of participation in psycho-analysis and whose symptoms reflect lifelong deeply rooted characterological problems are not able to facili-tate the resolution of all of these intrapsychic conflicts and their attendant symptoms as fully as psychoanalysis can.

I 5 A1.11212—The recumbent position of the analy-sand and the basic rule of psychoanalysis evoke particu-larly strong resistances in patients with a major conflict concerning domination and submission.

I 5 A1.11213—The greater degree of free associa-tions of patients in psychoanalysis, in contrast to psy-chotherapy, make more readily possible continuous enlargement of the therapist's understanding about the patient's subjective experience.

I 5 A1.11214—If the full unfolding of the transference risks the danger of an insoluble transference neurosis, then psychoanalysis should not be used.

I 5 A1.11215—Patients in psychoanalysis who expe-rience diffuse distress rather than crystallized symptoms of neurotic conflict begin to experience the latter as the transference neurosis unfolds.

I 5 A1.11216—Patients with good ego strength who

are in supportive-expressive or expressive psychotherapy are able to develop insight into the relationship between their symptoms and inner conflicts, without necessarily recognizing the infantile roots of their conflicts.

I 5 A1.11217—Patients who develop an insoluble transference neurosis in psychoanalysis require that the therapist introduce treatment vehicles other than interpretation.

I 5 A1.12—Those transference wishes which impede effective participation in expressive psychotherapy must be worked through before other problems can be dealt with.

(I 5 A1.13)—Patients with peremptory needs for reassurance and acceptance are severely limited in their ability to gain insight into intrapsychic conflicts.

(I 5 A1.14)—When the treatment situation renders it feasible (ego syntonic) for a patient to sacrifice his reality attachment in favor of transference fantasies (e.g., by involving separation from family and/or work), it is more difficult for these transference fantasies to be resolved.

I 5 A1.2—Patients with verbal skill that they can use to describe their inner life have an advantage in expressive psychotherapies over those who lack this ability.

I 5 A1.3—Patients with limited ego strength and limited anxiety tolerance develop only a minimal explicit understanding of the nature of the transference situation.

I 5 A2—Patients in expressive psychotherapies with low anxiety tolerance and prominent alloplastic tendencies require a long period of treatment (four to five years) for the full resolution of conflict.

I 5 A3—To the extent that a patient's feelings toward the therapist are not verbalized and interpreted in expressive psychotherapy, they will be expressed in action inside or outside the treatment.

I 5 A3.1—To the extent that patients in expressive psychotherapies have good ego strength and high anxiety tolerance, they are able to confine their transference struggles to the therapeutic situation.

I 5 A4—Patients with alloplastic tendencies and good ego strength respond to the therapist's interpretations concerning the relationship between their feelings and their behaviors with reduction of acting out and a concomitant increase in reflectiveness.

I'—When a patient is enabled to recognize an unconscious wish or prohibition as belonging to infancy and thus inappropriate to current reality, that wish is no longer a potential source of anxiety.

I'1—Only the expressive aspects of psychotherapy have the possibility of resolving unconscious core conflicts which underlie symptoms and/or pathological character traits.

I'1.1—Symptoms, character traits and life-style which are rooted in lifelong deeply repressed intrapsychic conflict are significantly altered only on the basis of a full working through of the conflict.

I'1.11—Symptoms that express multiple conflicts do not change unless all the component unconscious determinants are worked through.

I'1.12—To the extent that symptoms and attitudes and life-styles are deeply rooted in the character structure, they are modified only slowly in psychotherapy.

I'1.13—Patients who begin psychotherapy without prominent alloplastic patterns of relieving tension or evident defenses against them do not develop such patterns except as an expression of major intrapsychic change.

I'1.2—The introjection of the therapist's ego and superego attributes, while leading to more adaptive behavior, does not resolve the pathogenic infantile conflicts to the extent of leading to mature and gratifying object relationships nor to full relief of symptoms associated with the unconscious psychological conflicts.

I'2—To the extent that conflict resolution and insight are achieved, the resultant psychological changes are stable; insights not only reflect but also help to consolidate psychological change.

I'2.1—Patients treated by expressive psychotherapies who subsequently manifest relief of symptoms and shift in behavioral patterns based upon conflict resolution maintain these improvements even under the impact of external stress.

I'2.11—Patients whose symptoms are reactive to a specific external stress who resolve the conflicts triggered by this event show an abatement of symptoms at least in proportion to the degree of resolution of conflict despite the continuance or recurrence of the external stress.

I'2.111—Patients who successfully work through the conflicts triggered by a specific external stress and who then experience a repetition of the original stress either late in treatment or after treatment is over react at most with a temporary flare-up of the original symptoms.

I'2.12—Patients who successfully work through conflicts and defenses triggered by a specific external stress handle these conflicts and defenses more effectively after treatment than they did premorbidly.

I'2.2—Patients with weak egos who are not hospitalized during at least part of their treatment and thus are not able to work expressively on their intrapsychic conflicts fail to achieve stable changes of personality.

I'2.3—Patients who are successfully treated by psychoanalysis gain insight into the nature and origin of their major repressed infantile wishes.

(I'3)—The partial resolution of unconscious conflict frees energy for the adaptive functions of the ego (e.g., maintaining repression of the remnants of the conflict).

I'3.1—To the extent that a resolution of unconscious conflict occurs via the acquisition of insight, there is at least a proportional change in symptoms, character traits, and character structure.

I'3.2—To the extent that conflicts are resolved, the patient's capacity to delay and sublimate instinctual gratifications is increased.

I'3.21—To the extent that resolution of unconscious conflict occurs, there are shifts in impulse defense configurations which are reflected in behavioral changes.

I'3.22—To the extent that conflicts are resolved, patients are enabled to use their capacities for productive work more effectively.

I'3.23—Psychological change through conscious renunciation of a mode of gratification rather than conflict resolution necessitates the use of other channels for the discharge of tension.

I'3.3—Patients who show primary and secondary symptomatic expression of the same core conflict, as this conflict and the primary symptoms are resolved, show an abatement of the secondary symptoms without special working through in the course of treatment.

I'3.4—To the extent that conflicts are resolved, there is at least a proportional modification of the patient's neurotically determined initial goals.

I'3.5—Patients who develop insight into the unconscious determinants of their behavior are able to recognize in themselves those behaviors which are maladaptive.

I'3.51—To the extent that patients are able to work through those transference wishes which impede active participation in the psychotherapy, they cease to seek gratification of these wishes, to the detriment of the therapy.

I'3.52—To the extent that unconscious conflict is resolved, a patient gains the freedom to find the most advantageous reality setting for his own needs and for the needs of the significant others in his life.

I'3.521—To the extent that resolution of conflict leads to a modification of a neurotic life circumstance, a patient is able to use his new freedom to establish a more gratifying way of life.

I'3.522—Patients who gain insight into the meaning of certain situational factors which they previously denied make realistic and appropriate modifications in their lives.

I'3.6—Somatic manifestations of unconscious conflict that have not produced irreversible body changes disappear when the underlying conflicts are resolved in expressive psychotherapy.

I'3.61—Somatic expressions of unconscious conflict that are of long standing are particularly resistant to change in expressive psychotherapies even though underlying conflict has been resolved.

I'3.611—The symptom of frigidity persists to some extent despite successful resolution of the related unconscious conflicts (actuarial assumption).

I′3.7—Patients successfully treated by expressive psychotherapies are disposed by the remnants of conflict to life choices and character traits which continue to express the conflict in attenuated form.

(I′3.8)—Patients whose ego capacities and resources combine to constitute a high level of ego strength but who lack the capacity to tolerate anxiety are able to develop anxiety tolerance in expressive psychotherapy.

(I′3.9)—Markedly ego-dystonic symptoms which are rooted in lifelong deeply repressed intrapsychic conflicts are attenuated when other related but less deeply repressed conflicts are sufficiently resolved to permit a redeployment of psychic energies such as to maintain the core conflict in repression.

(I′3.10)—The continued use of psychotropic drugs after termination of psychotherapy is a reflection of conflicts left unresolved by the treatment.

I′4—Patients who gain insight into unrealistic superego prohibitions are able to entertain previously unacceptable impulses without undue anxiety.

I′4.1—Patients treated successfully by expressive psychotherapies come to recognize the discrepancy between the conscious and unconscious aspects of the superego.

I′4.2—Behaviors which afford an appropriate discharge for aggressive drives become more gratifying when patients are relieved of infantile guilt about aggression in expressive psychotherapies.

I'4.3—Patients who gain insight into unrealistic superego prohibitions experience relief of depression.

I'4.4—To the extent that a patient becomes less frightened of his hostile impulses and their potential destructiveness, he is capable of more intimate and gratifying object relationships.

I'5—To the extent that instinctual strivings are attenuated as a result of conflict resolution, reactions to frustration of these strivings and the associated defenses become less prominent.

I'5.1—Those defenses which form a prominent part of the symptom complex are used in a more stereotyped way at the outset of the treatment and are used more flexibly and appropriately to the extent that the underlying conflict is resolved.

(I'5.2)—Patients who perceive themselves as helpless victims of their symptoms experience an alleviation of their symptoms when they come to understand their own role in producing them.

I'6—Patients with good ego strength in the expressive psychotherapies as they reexperience and work through a principal life conflict in the transference relationship acquire insight into their modes of relating themselves to others.

I'6.1—Patients with a distorted view of themselves and others, when treated successfully by expressive psychotherapies, correct these distortions.

I'6.11—To the extent that conflict is resolved in expressive psychotherapies, the quality of a patient's object relationships improves.

I'6.111—To the extent that related conflict resolution occurs, there is a favorable modification of the patient's sexual life.

I'6.12—Patients who externalize their conflicts when successfully treated by expressive psychotherapy achieve insight into their own contribution to their difficulties.

I'7—The degree of the conflict resolution is proportional to the depth of the genetic insight.

II'—Supportive aspects of treatment achieve the result of more adaptive functioning by providing an external environment conducive to realization of a patient's potentialities for maturation.

II'1—Patients with limited ego strength manifested by poor impulse control and poor anxiety tolerance can check their most flagrant symptoms when the environment offers controls and sanctions appropriate alternative modes of impulse expression.

II'1.1—A serious exacerbation of destructive, alloplastic behavior or of incapacitating symptoms during psychotherapy requires an increase of external controls, even in the form of increased hospital structure or hospitalization, to help preserve the psychotherapeutic situation.

(II'1.2)—Patients with primarily alloplastic defensive modes who show a capacity to give up their denial of psychological illness, whose need to resort to destructive behavior is reduced while adjunctive supports are provided, become more aware of their need for treatment when such supports are withdrawn.

II'1.3—Adjunctive supports concomitant with psychotherapy provide support to the patient in engaging in constructive activities and provide control against destructive activities.

II'1.31—Patients who are unable to lead a stable organized life require family care and/or day hospital during their psychotherapy.

II'1.32—Patients with limited ego strength and whose symptoms are alloplastic and destructive require that supportive psychotherapy be carried on with concomitant adjunctive supports until controls have been internalized.

II'1.321—Patients with limited ego strength and anxiety tolerance, and destructive behaviors who are treated by psychotherapy in conjunction with hospitalization and who begin to modify their destructive behavior require gradual transition to full outpatient status (through day hospital and/or foster home placement).

II'1.322—The rechanneling of impulses away from destructive behavior into more socially acceptable activity results in a decreasing need for hospitalization.

II'1.323—Patients with low anxiety tolerance and destructive alloplastic defensive modes who lie about their feelings and behaviors require hospitalization concomitant with psychotherapy in order that the therapist be provided with accurate information upon which to base his interventions, and thus prevent the disruption of treatment.

II'1.33—To the extent that patients with limited ego strength and a predominantly alloplastic orientation are provided with situational supports, they are able during psychotherapy to maintain their participation in psychotherapy.

II'1.331—The less frequent the contacts with the therapist, the more readily can avoidance, denial, and lying be rationalized, when used in the service of resistance.

II'2—A patient's level of anxiety is reduced by removing him from a conflict-triggering environment.

II'2.1—Patients removed from the pressures of a stressful and/or a conflict-triggering environment become better able to engage in pursuits that they were previously unable to manage.

II'2.2—Patients who undertake treatment away from their homes where they had hostile and destructive relationships experience a considerable reduction in the need for symptomatic expression.

(II'2.3)—The duration of supportive psychotherapy needed to restore the previous equilibrium is shortened by the diminution of the reality stresses that precipitated the illness, and the provision of new gratifications by the environment.

II'3—Patients whose interpersonal contacts are few require adjunctive activities as a source of real experiences upon which psychotherapeutic work can be based.

II'4—Patients whose intrapsychic conflict is expressed in, and reinforced by, their life-style, require an alteration of their habitual patterns, even by a hospital regimen, in order to make them accessible to psychotherapy.

(II'4.1)—Patients with low anxiety tolerance and alloplastic defensive modes who rely heavily upon lying, and who experience therapy as giving license to the free expression of impulse cannot be treated successfully outside of the hospital.

(II'4.2)—To the extent that the hospital reinforces pathological mechanisms (e.g., sadomasochistic patterns), a patient is unable to develop concern about such mechanisms as to seek to change them.

(II'5)—To the extent that the hospital experience gratifies the need to be degraded and mistreated, development of ego resources will be impeded.

II''—To the extent that a psychotherapy is supportive, it involves a strengthening of certain defenses.

II''''—Certain supportive measures lead to the reduction of anxiety.

II—Supportive aspects of psychotherapy are capable of leading to a relative increase in ego strength and hence more gratifying and adaptive adjustment via modifications in the intensity or channeling of impulse expression and not via the uncovering and resolution of conflict.

II 1—Supportive aspects of psychotherapy lead to better interpersonal relationships and a greater capacity to work productively.

II 2—Supportive psychotherapy leads to a decrease in the patient's self-destructive behavior.

II 3—Supportive aspects of psychotherapy do not alter the infantile fantasies which underly symptoms.

II 3.1—Supportive psychotherapies do not lead to the integration of infantile instinctual aims and objects into a mature personality organization.

II 3.2—Patients in supportive psychotherapy with limited ego strength, low anxiety tolerance, and limited psychological mindedness but with a strong motivation for change are unable to achieve major intrapsychic change but can achieve more socially acceptable modes of expression of unconscious conflict and therefore an improved life adjustment.

II 3.3—Patients who achieve at most a minimal resolution of conflict in response to the supportive aspects of psychotherapy effect a more adaptive adjustment, but continue to show behavioral evidence of the unresolved core conflicts.

II 4—To the extent that the adaptive capacities are enhanced, there is a proportional increase of anxiety tolerance.

II 4.1—As anxiety tolerance increases so does the capacity for self-reflectiveness.

II 5—Patients with limited ego strength require a predominantly supportive psychotherapy in order to achieve a more adaptive mode of functioning.

II 5.1—Patients with profound neurotic conflicts, inadequate defensive mechanisms, low anxiety tolerance, and limited psychological mindedness require prolonged supportive treatment in order to achieve even partial freedom from painful or destructive symptoms.

IIA'—A transference predisposition to experience the therapist as a significant object promotes the development of a therapeutic alliance and the internalization of the therapist's attitudes and values.

(IIA'1)—Experiencing the therapist as capable of fulfilling one's needs is a necessary condition for the formation of the therapeutic alliance.

(IIA'1.1)—To the extent that defects in ego strength impair a realistic view of the therapist as a potentially helpful figure, the development of a therapeutic alliance is hampered.

(IIA'1.11)—To the extent that a patient is expecting to be disappointed and frustrated by the therapist, the establishment of a therapeutic alliance is hindered.

(IIA'1.111)—Patients with weak egos, intense oral aggressive wishes, and primarily projective and masochistic defenses have great difficulty in forming a therapeutic alliance.

(IIA'1.112)—Patients whose major defense is externalization, and whose major transference is depreciation of helping figures, and who make the therapist feel incapable of helping them fail in treatment.

(IIA'1.12)—Patients whose character is dominated by the expectation to be disappointed and frustrated, and who consistently perceive the therapist as unfriendly, are unable to internalize benevolent aspects of the therapist.

(IIA'1.2)—To the extent that a patient is able to overcome feelings of inferiority and shame toward the therapist, a therapeutic alliance is fostered.

(IIA'1.21)—Patients with weak egos and intense conflicts over dependency, who are unable to permit themselves to become dependent upon the therapist, are unable to benefit from psychotherapy.

(IIA'2)—To the extent that a patient's self-concept is uncrystallized and his identifications are fluid, the proportion of change achieved in psychoanalysis due to identification with the therapist will be greater, as opposed to change via insight and conflict resolution.

(IIA'3)—Patients whose conflict over sexual identity takes the form of independence (masculine) vs. dependence (feminine) are able to overcome their dependent behavior through solidifying their masculine identification (i.e., identifying themselves with what they perceive as the aggressive and masculine aspects of the therapist).

IIA''—Introjection of figures in the treatment situation is facilitated by their performing parental functions (need fulfillment, providing controls, clarifying reality).

IIA''1—In psychologically immature patients, the provision of suitable identification figures in the treatment situation makes possible the unfolding of normal maturational sequences without concomitant conflict resolution necessarily occurring.

IIA''1.1—Patients in a predominantly supportive psychotherapy who lack an adequate identification with a figure of their own sex require such an identification model as part of the total treatment situation, preferably in the person of the therapist.

IIA''1.2—Patients who undertake psychotherapy in adolescence, and whose illness is in a major way related to deprivation of adequate identification figures, require an opportunity to form stable identifications as well as to achieve insight into neurotic conflicts.

IIA''2—Patients who have had a paucity of satisfying relationships in the past and who experience a strong need to communicate their distress to a helping person eventually develop a positive relationship to their therapist, i.e., the therapist becomes internalized as a positive helping figure.

(IIA''3)—Patients who are unable to internalize aspects of the therapist may nevertheless achieve improved adaptation through imitation of the therapist (e.g., following specific instructions, etc.) thus acquiring more successful techniques without intrapsychic change, related to a rudimentary identification with the therapist (feelings of trust).

(IIA''4)—To the extent that the hospital structure promotes delay of impulse discharge, it becomes possible for a highly alloplastic patient to develop a therapeutic alliance in psychotherapy.

IIA''5—Introjection of therapist's ego and superego attributes is facilitated by the direct giving of advice and the expression of the therapist's opinions regarding the patient's reality problems in the context of a positive relationship.

IIA—Supportive aspects of psychotherapy lead to the patient's introjection of the therapist's ego and superego attributes and to a modification of the patient's internal view of the self in relation to others.

IIA 1—Supportive aspects of psychotherapy achieve the result of more adaptive functioning by means of the development of a patient's wish to please, or sometimes to displease, the therapist.

IIA 1.1—When a positive transference prevails, certain of a patient's defenses and character traits will be used to further the goals of treatment.

IIA 1.11—Transference reactions that cause the patient to see their therapist as potentially friendly and helpful facilitate the development of a therapeutic alliance.

IIA 1.2—Patients with limited ego strength manifested by poor impulse control and poor anxiety tolerance but who are passive and dependent respond positively to the appropriately controlling aspects of supportive psychotherapy by engaging in more adaptive behavior.

IIA 1.3—Symptomatic manifestations change in psychotherapy in accordance with patient's perceptions of what will please or displease the therapist.

IIA 1.31—Passive, compliant patients attempt to please the therapist particularly in the early phases of treatment by modifying their symptomatic behavior.

IIA 1.32—To the extent that a patient finds significant gratifications in the treatment situation, he is able to govern symptomatic behavior in such a way as to prevent it from disrupting treatment.

IIA 2)—Some capacity to internalize loving aspects of the therapist is a prerequisite for the corrective emotional experience.

IIA 2.1—Supportive aspects of psychotherapy achieve the result of more adaptive functioning by means of a corrective emotional experience which modifies a patient's attitudes by means of the therapist and the treatment situation responding in a manner different from the patient's expectations based upon projections of his early introjects.

IIA 2.11—Patients in psychotherapy react to appropriate fulfillment of their need for understanding, acceptance, and appreciation with enhanced self-esteem.

(IIA 2.111)—The internalization of a protective, nurturing object helps the patient reinforce denial of depressed affects related to early oral deprivation.

IIA 2.12—Patients respond to the corrective emotional experience of psychotherapy by becoming more realistic in their expectations of others.

IIA 2.13—Patients whose behavior is motivated by rebellion against parental introjects eventually are able to curtail their rebellious, self-destructive behavior by means of a corrective emotional experience.

IIA 3—Patients whose perception of reality is distorted by denial and projective thinking are able to improve their reality testing by means of introjecting ego attitudes of persons in the treatment situation.

IIA 3.1—To the extent that a patient finds reality in the therapy situation different from his habitual way of distorting it, he finds it necessary to entertain alternative views of himself and others in order to bring these contradictory experiences into orderly synthesis.

IIA 4—Patients who introject the therapist's ego and superego attributes respond to the therapist's implicit or explicit interest in their feelings by becoming more sensitive to the affective aspects of their inner life.

(IIA 4.1)—Insight in psychotherapy cannot take place unless a patient is able to internalize helpfully observing aspects of the therapist.

(IIA 4.11)—Patients who maintain a consistently negative attitude toward the therapist as a rejecting, depriving person cannot achieve insight in psychotherapy.

IIA 5—To the extent that a patient finds support and control in his relationship with his therapist, his need for adjunctive supports (hospitalization, drugs, etc.) diminishes.

(IIA 6)—Patients respond to the supportive aspects of psychotherapy by modifying their own treatment goals in the direction of conformity with those of the therapist.

(IIA 7)—A patient's object relationships become more stable and gratifying to the extent that he is able to internalize the benevolent interest the therapist has maintained in him.

IIB—To the extent that the more ego syntonic derivatives of unacceptable needs are gratified in the treatment situation, the anxiety stemming from the need pressure is reduced.

IIB 1—Supportive aspects of psychotherapy achieve the result of more adaptive functioning by means of gratifying some of the patient's psychological needs which he otherwise is unable to gratify.

IIB 1.1—Intellectualized or incomplete insights or

even erroneous beliefs reduce anxiety and feelings of confusion by making the patient's inner life appear to him less chaotic.

IIB 1.2—Schizoid patients whose ego weakness prevents them from overcoming their severe isolation from others utilize psychotherapy to fulfill needs for human contact but not for the bringing about of change in themselves.

IIB 2—The availability of new sources of need gratification in the treatment and/or life situation enables patients gradually to relinquish older patterns of need fulfillment.

IIB 2.1—Patients who derive gratification of infantile needs from the supportive aspects of the treatment situation experience a modulation of symptoms and character traits associated with this gratification without a resolution of the conflicts.

IIB 2.11—The rechanneling of hostile impulses into acceptable aggressive behavior leads to diminished conscious guilt and/or depression.

IIB 2.12—The rechanneling of impulses toward more narcissistically gratifying socially acceptable behaviors leads to a diminished need to engage in destructive behaviors.

IIB 2.13—Patients with an alloplastic orientation, who in therapy realize significant gratifications, show a diminution of alloplastic behaviors.

IIB 2.14—Patients in psychotherapies who find grati-fications, conscious or unconscious, realistic or unrealis-tic, in the therapy show improved interpersonal relations without full resolution of conflict, as long as the gratifica-tions continue.

IIB 2.141—Patients in expressive psychotherapy are able to give up neurotic object relationships without experiencing depression or some equivalent thereof once they have established a firm positive transference.

(IIB 2.142)—Patients become able to relinquish an inappropriate marital partner when the therapist consti-tutes an interim object that fulfills the infantile needs the gratification of which was sought in the marriage.

IIB 2.15—Patients whose presenting symptoms are reactive to a relatively recent precipitating stress experi-ence a diminution of these symptoms as they develop a positive relationship with the therapist.

IIB 2.16—To the extent that changes in symptoms or behavior are dependent upon continued gratification of infantile psychological needs, these changes are unsta-ble (fail to be sustained when significant conflict-trigger-ing alteration of the patient's life situation occurs).

IIB 2.161—To the extent that a patient is enabled to come to terms with the ambivalently held parental introjects, the psychological changes achieved in psy-chotherapy are stable.

IIB 2.1611—To the extent that changes resulting from introjection of the therapist's ego and superego attributes are consolidated into identifications, the resulting improvement is stable.

(IIB 2.1612)—To the extent that patients in a predominantly supportive psychotherapy are able to internalize the therapist's attitudes, the adaptive changes resulting from the psychotherapy are stable.

IIB 2.162—Patients with limited ego strength and poor impulse control require frequent contacts with the therapist in order to sustain transference reactions that effectively delay impulse expression.

(IIB 2.163)rev—Patients with limited ego strength and long-standing symptoms require some long-term contacts with a therapist or therapist-surrogate in order to maintain changes brought about by the supportive aspects of psychotherapy.

IIB 2.164—Patients who achieve changes in symptoms and character traits based upon the supportive aspects of psychotherapy maintain these gains by substituting the dependence on symbolic representations of the therapist for dependency on the therapist.

IIB. 2.165—Patients who achieve at most a minimal resolution of conflict in a predominantly supportive psychotherapy effect a more adaptive adjustment, but are vulnerable to some continuing life difficulties consistent with the unresolved conflicts and may require further treatment after termination.

(IIB 2.166)—Patients with good ego strength whose symptoms are reactive to a temporary reality stress

maintain the gains they make in response to the supportive aspects of psychotherapy.

(IIB 2.17)—Patients whose symptoms are reactive to
unacceptable wishes to be dependent give up these
symptoms as soon as they permit themselves to become
dependent upon the therapist.

(IIB 2.18)—The regularity of psychotherapeutic sessions exerts a stabilizing influence via the gratification of
infantile needs, particularly the need for predictability.

IIB 2.2—Adjunctive activities provide an opportunity
for patients with limited ego resources to try out more
adaptive and gratifying new behaviors.

IIB 2.3—Patients who are unable to renounce infantile needs experience greater comfort in their relationships with significant others as the latter become more
capable of gratifying those needs.

IIB 2.4—The verbal expression of feelings in psychotherapy constitutes an alternative channel for impulse
discharge that renders other tension-relieving devices
less necessary.

IIB 2.41—Patients with low anxiety tolerance and
poor impulse control in supportive psychotherapies
require frequent contacts (two to three times a week) with
the therapist in order to prevent development of excessive tension between therapy sessions.

IIB 2.411—Patients with low anxiety tolerance and
alloplastic defensive modes who have demonstrated

some ability to control their destructive behavior can be treated in supportive psychotherapy without hospitalization provided they are seen sufficiently often (at least two to three times a week).

IIB 2.5—Patients with perverse sexual behavior experience diminished need for the direct expression of the perverse impulses while in the hospital.

IIB 2.6—To the extent that a patient's interests and life goals represent efforts to gratify psychological needs that are more adequately fulfilled by the supportive aspects of psychotherapy, these interests and goals will be given up in the course of supportive treatment.

(IIB 2.7)—As his life situation becomes more supportive to a patient's self-esteem, he is able to relinquish fantasy as a source of narcissistic gratification, and hence experience less of a discrepancy between reality and his expectations of it.

(IIB 2.8)—Patients with major conflicts over dependency can be protected against severe depressive reactions, or other anxiety equivalents, at termination by making the termination process a gradual one.

IIB 3—To the extent that patients with limited ego strength and limited anxiety tolerance develop a stable, positive relationship with their therapist, they become able to tolerate some partial insights into the nature and meanings of their symptoms and maladaptive behaviors.

IIB 3.1—Patients with limited ego strength and limited anxiety tolerance cannot tolerate a clear picture of their ego operations, particularly early in treatment before a close positive relationship with the therapist has been established, without being overwhelmed by anxiety and/or guilt.

IIB 4—Patients with markedly ambivalent object relations and fear of affects require that the therapist maintain distance until a firm therapeutic alliance is established, or else they institute distance devices of their own that prevent the achievement of therapeutic goals.

IIB 4.1—Patients who devalue others and are aloof and cold in their relationships require a considerable period of time to establish a stable therapeutic alliance.

IIC—The introjection of a more benign superego leads to less fear of instinctual pressures, and therefore a reduction of guilt feelings.

IIC 1—The introjection of the therapist's more realistic ego and superego attributes leads to lessened constriction of the patient's ego and thus to a greater flexibility of behavior, and a wider range of instinctual gratifications.

(IIC 1.1)—The introjection of the therapist's ego and superego attributes in a compliant patient leads him to accept the therapist's suggestions for more assertive behavior.

IIC 2—The introjection of a more benign superego leads to increased self-esteem.

IIC 2.1—Symptoms, character traits, and defensive patterns linked to faulty development of self-esteem are favorably altered as a more benign superego is internalized.

IID—Supportive aspects of psychotherapy achieve the result of more adaptive functioning by means of somatic agents (drugs, ECT, etc.) which physiologically induce changes manifested on a psychological level as increased comfort.

IID 1—Patients who develop a marked and prolonged depression in reaction to the treatment require somatic intervention (drugs or ECT) in order to facilitate the therapeutic process and to protect the patient against self-destructive behavior.

IID 2—The earlier the fixations and the less adequate the defensive structures the more likely is a patient to require somatic agents as a supplement to the supports provided by hospitalization.

IID 3—Patients who are unable to internalize aspects of the therapist may nonetheless achieve improved adaptation through imitation (e.g., following specific instructions, etc.) thus acquiring more successful techniques without intrapsychic change.

IIIA—Symptoms, character traits, and character structure are crystallizations of compromise solutions for unconscious conflicts and are therefore efforts to cope with anxiety or other unpleasurable affects which would otherwise be generated by these conflicts.

IIIA 1—The disruption, threatened or actual, of any defensive pattern mobilizes anxiety.

IIIA 1.1—To the extent that external factors trigger intrapsychic conflicts there is a proportional enhancement of painful affects and defenses.

IIIA 1.11—To the extent that there is a residue of still unresolved intrapsychic conflicts, patients will experience a reactivation of anxiety and/or characteristic defenses in the process of termination.

IIIA 1.111—Patients who are markedly masochistic and who fail to achieve consciously held goals in psychotherapy react to the failure with an accentuation of their masochistic behaviors.

IIIA 1.112—Patients with strong dependency conflicts which have not been fully resolved in treatment manifest a reactivation of anxiety, depression, and/or characteristic defenses during the termination phase of treatment.

IIIA 1.113—Patients whose conflicts involve the fear of success behave self-destructively during the termination phase of psychotherapy in which some success has been achieved.

IIIA 1.114—Patients for whom the loss of an ambivalently held object has constituted a major trauma react depressively during the termination process.

IIIA 1.115—Patients who find gratification of their infantile wishes in the treatment situation and experience this gratification as ego-syntonic are unable to give up treatment without experiencing a recrudescence of symptoms.

IIIA 1.1151—Patients with strong masochistic tendencies which are largely ego-syntonic attempt to cling to treatment and resist termination.

(IIA 1.1152)—Patients who find gratification of their infantile wishes in the treatment situation but who also must maintain vigilance lest their closeness to the therapist threaten their sense of identity in feelings of ego integrity experience *both* feelings of loss and a sense of relief during termination.

(IIIA 1.1153)—Patients who do not experience the therapist as a need-fulfilling object do not react to termination with depression, anxiety, or regressive behavior.

(IIIA 1.11531)—Patients whose paranoid fears of the therapist persist throughout psychotherapy do not seek to prolong the termination phase.

(IIIA 1.12) rev—To the extent that a patient with major conflicts over dependency is permitted to experience dependent wishes in the treatment situation, he reacts depressively during the termination phase of psychotherapy.

IIIA 1.121—Patients with persistent strong passive dependency yearnings directed toward the therapist attempt to cling to the treatment and resist termination.

IIIA 1.13—Treating patients away from their homes fosters the tendency to avoid, disavow, and repress material relevant to problems involved in the home situation.

IIIA 1.131—Patients whose symptoms involve their families in pathological interactions and who do not have ongoing contact with them during treatment are unable to integrate their insights into a stable new adjustment.

IIIA 1.1311—Patients treated successfully while living away from home whose family relationships had been damaged by chronic hostility and destructiveness experience difficulty in creating a new adjustment to the home situation.

IIIA 1.14—To the extent that a patient must deny and repress strong passive wishes, hospitalization mobilizes anxiety and reduces self-esteem.

IIIA 1.15—Patients with well-structured alternative modes of behavior for the achievement of unconscious goals shift between these modes during the course of treatment.

IIIA 1.16—Patients react to aspects of treatment they perceive as ego alien with anxiety and characteristic defenses.

(IIIA 1.161)—Patients with poorly developed defenses against aggressive impulses experience marked anxiety in association with negative transference developments.

(IIIA 1.162)—Patients with a disposition to split their good and bad introjects are capable of idealizing their relationship with their therapist, thus preventing negative feelings from intruding.

IIIA 1.17—Patients with intense contradictory instinctual strivings are beset by much frustration in psychotherapy as either of these strivings comes closer to conscious expression.

IIIA 1.171—Patients in psychotherapy who wish to comply with the expectations of the treatment and for whom compliance runs counter to other needs experience great discomfort in their treatment.

(IIIA 1.1711)—Patients in psychotherapy geared to the suppression of symptoms, whose major response is a strained effort to please the therapist, do not react to termination with an exacerbation of symptoms.

(IIIA 1.172)—Patients who establish a positive relationship with their therapist, in which the therapist is seen as an overidealized person toward whom negative feelings may not be expressed, fail to derive more than a limited gratification from the relationship.

IIIA 1.18—Patients in expressive psychotherapies who have resolved their core conflicts successfully nevertheless experience a reactivation of some aspects of their symptoms during the termination phase of treatment.

(IIIA 1.19)—Denial that is called upon to ward off an

external threat is relinquished when that threat actually diminishes.

(IIIA 1.110)—Patients with intense competitive wishes and who view termination mainly as a defeat of the therapist's efforts do not react depressively to the termination process.

IIIA 1.2—Symptoms, defenses, and character traits are brought into play during treatment as resistances to prevent the fulfillment of consciously held treatment goals.

IIIA 1.21—Patients who are dependent upon others for support of treatment use the potential withdrawal of the support as resistance to the psychotherapy.

IIIA 1.211—Patients who are dependent upon others for the support of treatment and who have strong resistance to treatment attempt consciously or unconsciously to disrupt treatment by provoking the withdrawal of this support.

IIIA 1.22—Patients for whom masochism is a major determinant of symptoms and life-style seek forms of treatment that will either be ineffectual or harmful.

IIIA 1.23—To the extent that patients rely upon role-playing as a defense, the therapist will have difficulty in sorting out reality and fantasy in the patient's productions.

(IIIA 1.24)—Masochistic patients strive to defeat the goals of treatment.

IIIA 1.3—To the extent that alloplastic behaviors come under control in psychotherapy, patients experience the disturbing affects and ideation formerly warded off by that behavior.

IIIA 1.31—To the extent that alloplastic behaviors are interfered with, whether by interpretations, prohibitions, or external controls, anxiety is mobilized.

IIIA 1.311—Patients who use alloplastic behaviors to avoid experiencing disturbing affects develop autoplastic symptoms as the alloplastic behaviors are curbed.

IIIA 1.4—The disruption of neurotic object relationships mobilizes anxiety.

IIA 1.41—Patients whose symptoms are reactive to a threatened loss of a neurotic object relationship experience an exacerbation of symptoms when the threatened loss becomes actual.

IIIA 1.5—Patients whose self-esteem depends largely upon denial of psychological illness resist such treatment measures as would render such denial difficult to maintain.

IIIA 2—The arousal of anxiety stemming from any source leads to an increased use of the patient's characteristic defensive operations.

IIIA 2.1—Increments of anxiety induced by the therapeutic process produce increased reliance upon characteristic symptoms and behavior in the patient's life outside the therapy.

IIIA 2.11—Displacement of transference wishes to a patient's relationships outside the treatment is facilitated by preexisting neurotic interactions.

IIIA 2.2—To the extent a patient must defend against unacceptable perceptions of himself, he must establish and maintain neurotic object relationships.

IIIA 2.21—Patients whose symptoms are reactive to a threatened loss of a neurotic object relationship are able to regain their previous equilibrium when the situation shifts in such a way as to permit the patient to again find gratification of his infantile needs.

IIIA 2.22—Patients whose symptoms are reactive to a threatened loss of a neurotic object relationship enter treatment with the goal (explicit or implicit) of being helped to restore their previous neurotic life situation.

IIIA 2.23—Patients whose symptoms are reactive to the threatened loss of a neurotic interaction act directly to minimize the alteration of the defense patterning embodied in the relationship.

IIIA 2.3—Patients in psychotherapy who find relief from their presenting symptoms on the basis of having their needs fulfilled in the treatment situation experience a periodic return of these symptoms as their conflicts are mobilized.

IIIA 2.4—Patients who are unable to tolerate their intensely ambivalent object attachments are able to develop and maintain a positive attachment to the therapist only by displacing hostile feelings from him to other objects.

IIIA 2.5—To the extent that alloplastic patients are uncertain about the therapist's attitudes or intentions they resort to provocative behavior as a means of testing the therapist.

IIIA 2.6—Patients with marked alloplastic tendencies are able to ward off painful affects by their actions.

IIIA 2.7—Patients whose conflicts include the fear of a father-figure, and unconscious guilt feelings based upon unacceptable aggression toward him, present symptoms involving self-destructiveness and the need to fail.

IIIA 2.8—In patients with strong self-destructive trends and somatizations, the somatizations are a vehicle for the expression of the self-destructive impulses.

IIIA 2.81—To the extent that a patient relies upon somatization to express self-punitive impulses, he does not experience guilt and depression.

(IIIA 2.9)—Symptoms that express multiple conflicts do not change unless all the component determinants are worked through.

IIIB—To the extent that any behavior pattern brings about gratification, it is reinforced.

IIIB 1—To the extent that patients obtain gratification

from their adaptive achievements, psychological changes are reinforced.

(IIIB1.1)—Patients with good ego strength who make favorable modifications in their life circumstances during psychotherapy are then able to maintain the psychological change they achieve in the absence of conflict resolution.

IIIB 2—The reality factors in the therapeutic structure reinforce the primary or secondary gain of a symptom or character trait.

IIIB 2.1—To the extent that a patient is dependent and/or masochistic, prolongation of hospitalization reinforces these pathological impulse-defense configurations.

IIIB 2.2—Patients treated away from their homes and who use this separation as a socially acceptable means of expressing aggression toward their families suffer a marked disadvantage in their treatment because the treatment contributes to gratification of neurotic needs.

(IIIB 2.3)—Patients who characteristically respond to instinctual tensions with prompt alloplastic discharge, and who enter psychotherapy with the fantasy of being magically protected by the therapist, become even more prone to alloplastic behavior.

IIIB 3—To the extent that patients find a strong secondary gain in their illness, they resist giving up symptoms.

IIIB 4—Transference expectations are intensified by being partially fulfilled by the therapist.

IIIB 4.1—Patients experience in treatment a reactivation of those transference attitudes which have been reinforced in previous treatment.

IIIB 4.11—Patients whose passive dependent or addictive behaviors have been strongly reinforced in previous psychotherapies cannot subsequently be successfully treated by the same therapeutic modality.

IIIB 4.2—Patients with strong dependency needs who are permitted to gratify these needs in their treatment and are not encouraged to use their own independence and initiative fail to achieve desirable growth.

(IIIB 4.3)—Psychotherapy conducted concomitant with business or social interaction between patient and therapist will founder.

IIIB 5—Patients under pressure (internal or external) to choose between the therapist and significant others will choose (transiently or definitively) the relationship in which there is more positive cathectic involvement.

IIIB 5.1—Patients will abandon treatment even after developing a strong therapeutic alliance when external pressures to discontinue treatment occur in conjunction with a period of strong negative transference.

IIIB 5.2—Patients who have developed a strong therapeutic alliance, even under external pressure to discontinue treatment, will not give up treatment until termination is indicated.

(IIIB 5.3)—Patients under pressure to choose between the therapist and significant others will abandon treatment even after the development of a therapeutic alliance when the pressure coincides with the imminent mobilization of conflicts associated with excessive anxiety.

(IIIB 6)—Patients with symptoms of sexual perversion do not give these up when substitute gratifications are available to them.

IIIC—Defenses are mobilized in response to increments of anxiety in a sequence, characteristic of the individual, from those involving the least to the greatest reality abrogation.

IIIC 1—Patients with good ego strength, who expect significant gratifications in the treatment situation, are able to govern symptomatic behavior in such a way as to prevent it from disrupting the treatment.

IIIC 2—Patients with limited ego strength who perceive aspects of treatment as extremely threatening mobilize characteristic defenses in such a way as to disrupt treatment.

IIIC 3—The less elaborate the defensive structures and the more insistent the instinctual strivings, the more intense the reaction to the frustration of wishes in psychotherapy.

IIIC 3.1—The earlier the fixations and the more primitive the defenses, the greater the range of objects upon which transference wishes can be displaced.

IIIC 3.2—Patients with intense oral needs and the fantasy of eventually finding a magical and omnipotent parent react to the inevitable frustration of this wish with regressive and/or resistive reactions and/or painful affects.

IIIC 4—Patients whose symptoms are predominantly autoplastic and whose overt behavior has been fairly appropriate make few changes in overt behaviors as an outcome of successful treatment.

IIIC 5—Patients with good ego strength who attempt to maintain conventional behavior give vent to stormy affects only in the presence of those with whom they are on intimate terms.

IIID—Establishing and maintaining an interpersonal relationship involves inevitable frustration and deprivation.

IIID 1—A certain minimum of ego strength and motivation are required for any degree of favorable response to psychotherapy.

IIID 1.1—Patients in supportive psychotherapy with limited ego strength, low anxiety tolerance, and limited psychological-mindedness, and with weak motivation for change are able, at best, to be helped to keep their destructive tendencies under control.

(IIID 2)—Markedly narcissistic patients need to devaluate potential sources of support and gratification and are unable to experience concern for their objects.

(IIID 2.1)—Markedly narcissistic patients with limited ego strength do not develop guilt in psychotherapy.

(IIID 2.11)—Patients who do not develop concern for their objects concomitant with gaining insight into their destructive effects upon these objects do not develop motivation to change themselves in psychotherapy so as to bring about more mature object relations.

(IIID 2.2)—Markedly narcissistic patients cannot internalize helping figures.

(IIID 2.3)—Patients who feel omnipotent and who fail to develop concern about the therapist's opinion of them do not attempt to rationalize behavior that is contrary to the goals of the psychotherapy.

(IIID 3)—Borderline patients in analysis set up distance devices (such as withholding, paranoid fears) which permit them to accommodate themselves to the stress of the treatment situation.

IIIE—Patients, whose primary symptoms are reduced in intensity, experience a reduction in intensity of the associated secondary symptoms.

IIIE 1—Patients whose maladaptive behavior engenders secondary symptoms and who are able to achieve a favorable modification of such behavior experience an abatement also of the attendant secondary symptoms.

APPENDIX 3

Glossary of Terms[1]

Acting out: We use this term in its original technical sense; that is, the expression in behavior, outside the therapeutic session, of an unconscious fantasy, often a transference wish, without the individual's full awareness of the nature of the impulse being expressed. We do not use this term, as many people do, to connote alloplasticity in general.

Adaptation or adaptive behavior: The appropriate fitting into and mastery of a changing environment resulting in the maximal attainment of individual and societal objectives. Adaptive behavior is geared to the requirements of external current and future reality.

Adjunctive supports: *see* Supports, adjunctive.

Affect, repression of; repressed affect; unconscious affect: Since affect is a process of discharge it is not theoretically meticulous to speak of "repressed affect." In repression, ideas are kept from awareness. Repressed affect is a verbal shorthand implying that impulse discharge through certain channels is blocked. Uncon-

1. The authors of this glossary were Drs. A. Appelbaum, L. Horwitz, O. Kernberg, G. Murphy, I. Rosen, R. Siegal, and R. Wallerstein.

scious affect exists only as a disposition to impulse discharge through certain channels. The associated ideas may or may not be repressed.

Alloplasticity: Although this was originally defined by us (Wallerstein, R. S., *et al.*, 1956, 20:243) as "the nature and extent of the expression of the illness on the environment and the deleterious consequences to the environment," we have found its useful connotations somewhat broader. By alloplasticity we mean an individual's characteristic tendency to attempt to dispel or ward off consciousness of an affect (particularly anxiety) and its associated ideas through motoric action (whether leading to adaptive or maladaptive consequences). The individual may be entirely unaware of the connection between the threatening affect and his behavior.

Anxiety: We conceive of anxiety as a subjective experience, an inferred experience, and an observable phenomenon. We categorize it in terms of its intensity, how it is evident (expressed, dealt with, or avoided), and the degree of awareness of it. For details of this classification see Wallerstein, R. S., *et al.* (1956), 20:241.

Anxiety tolerance: Elsewhere (*see* Siegal, R. S., and Rosen, I. C., 1962) we have suggested that in applying this concept of anxiety tolerance it is necessary to consider both the nature and intensity of the anxiety to be experienced (whether still "signal" or "traumatic") and also the ego's style of reacting to it (whether autoplastic or alloplastic). Within the framework of these considerations anxiety tolerance is defined as the ego's capacity to experience and utilize signal anxiety. This is a revision and extension of our original definition (Wallerstein, R. S., *et al.*, 1956, 20:245).

Autoplasticity: Autoplasticity, in contrast to alloplasticity, indicates an individual's characteristic tendency to attempt to dispel or ward off consciousness of an affect (particularly anxiety) and its associated ideas, through perceptual and cognitive means alone. This generally implies the functioning of one or more of the classically described mechanisms of defense. An individual psychic phenomenon may function alloplastically or autoplastically or both. This can only be determined with full knowledge of its psychological meaning and context.

Change: An alteration in a psychological state or attribute, transient or enduring. Judgment of change implies no commitment to (value-influenced) judgments of improvement or of degrees of mental health or illness. (See Wallerstein, R. S., 1963, 44:31–41.) (*See also* Characterological change; Stable change; Structural change.)

Change in impulse-defense configuration: A change in impulse-defense configuration is a shift in intensity, direction, or nature of the impulse and/or defense against it as represented in any aspect of symptom, behavior, or character. *For example*, an individual is now more accepting of his dependent strivings, he need no longer defend against them so vigorously (lessened use of denial and reaction formation), and he can now allow them more ego-acceptable expression. Thus the individual may give up a conflict-ridden struggle to be an independent businessman and accept employment in someone else's business. He is not necessarily less dependent (i.e., there is not necessarily conflict resolution), but he need not defend against his dependency so intensely (the denial and the reaction formation), at such psychic cost, and with the attendant concomitant intensification of the repressed dependent strivings.

Character (or character structure): The overall organization of the habitual modes of response of the ego to environmental and intrapsychic demands. It is the quasi-stable organization of all character patterns and traits.

Character pattern: A group of dynamically integrated character traits organized in accord with the principle of multiple functions (Waelder).

Character trait: A relatively fixed, only slowly changing disposition to a particular behavioral configuration comprising varying admixtures of adaptive, defensive, and automatized functions.

The above definitions imply a hierarchical organization, within which character is the superordinate principle, character patterns are the major substructures, and character traits the "atomic" components. For example, the rubric "oral character" would imply the description of the overall character organization. "Inordinate dependency" would represent one character pattern within this character.

"Greediness" and "subserviency" would be character traits which form part of the character pattern mentioned.

Characterological change: A stable change in an aspect or attribute of character.

Conflict, core: *see* Core conflict.

Conflict resolution: Like structural change, this is a relative term covering degrees of an intrapsychic process along a continuum. The maximal degree of conflict resolution (full conflict resolution) results in a full structural change as defined by Gill (Gill, M. M., 1954, 2:771–797) and as reflected in a sustained alteration of behavior valid not simply in a specific context or for a particular interpersonal relationship, but with a more general applicability. An example Gill cites is ". . . dependent behavior is given up not because he has learned that if he acts too dependent he will be punished by a loss of therapy hours, but because despite the invitation to regress and the maintenance of the frequency of his hours he has come to feel and understand his dependency in such a way that he no longer needs it or wants it."

Conflict trigger: Those environmental factors which, through their resonance with the idiosyncratic repressed conflicts of the individual, disturb the intrapsychic equilibrium.

Constriction of the ego: Ego constriction defines an intrapsychic situation in which the ego's available energy is so rigidly defensively deployed as to narrow its repertoire of adaptive and integrative capacities.

Core conflict: The nuclear intrapsychic conflict originating in the infantile situation manifest in the current life situation, re-created in the transference situation, and central to the determination both of the character structure and of the nature of the illness of the patient.

Corrective emotional experience: The modification of neurotic attitudes by means of the therapist responding in a manner different from the patient's expectations, namely, by the therapist's abstention from counterinvolvement in the patient's conflicts and distorted object relations. This abstention derives from and reflects a steady neutrality by the therapist in the face of the patient's conflicts combined with a sympathetic interest in helping in the resolution of those conflicts. We do *not* mean by the term the connotation given by Alexander of "manipulating the transference," through the therapist assuming a *deliberate* stance vis-à-vis the patient, different from and *in opposition to* the expected transference image.

Defense; defensive operation; defensive pattern: Defenses are behaviors, affects, or ideas which serve defensive purposes. Their functioning is explained in terms of the operation of the defense mechanisms. For example, an exaggerated sympathy is a defense against an impulse to cruelty; the operative mechanism by which this is explained is called reaction formation. Defenses range from discrete attributes or aspects explicable by reference to the simple operation of a single defense mechanism (as in the example just cited) to complex behavioral and characterologic constellations that are likewise specific, recurrent, and serve defensive purposes. These more complex configurations are variously called *defensive operations, patterns, maneuvers,* etc. They are made up of various combinations and sequences of behaviors, affects, and ideas, the operations of which are explicable by reference to a variety of classical defense mechanisms, admixed with other ego activities. "The Glossary of Defenses" published by Bibring, *et al.* (1961, 16:9–72), is the most comprehensive classification yet essayed. It encompasses both the most discrete defenses explicable by reference to a single defense mechanism and the more regularly recurring of the more complex defensive patterns as well.

Defense mechanisms as theoretical abstractions of ways of working of the mind cannot of course be conscious. [Freud made this same point about the psychical systems: ". . . the systems (which are not in any way psychical entities themselves and can never be accessible to our psychical perception) . . ." (*The Interpretation of Dreams*, Standard Edition, Vol. V, p. 611).] The contents of the defenses (the simple or complex behaviors, affects, and ideas) are usually unconscious; they may be conscious: "a specific content which is able to attain consciousness and, though it serves defensive purposes, is not *recognized* as a defense." (This last quotation is from Gill, M. M., 1963, 3:1–179). The definitions of defense mechanisms and defenses used here are consonant with, and influenced by, though not identical with Gill's position as stated in Chapter 5 of that monograph.

Defense mechanism: A defense *mechanism* is a construct that denotes a way of functioning of the mind. It explains how behaviors, affects, and ideas serve to inhibit, avert, or modulate unwanted impulse discharges.

Defenses, strengthening of: *see* Strengthening of defenses.

Depression: A subjective state, characterized affectively by sadness or apathy and/or ideationally by feelings of guilt, loss, or diminished self-esteem. Metapsychologically, depression has classically been thought of as a manifestation of regressively defused aggression directed against an ambivalently held introject, together with the regressive manifestations of oral aggressive impulse derivatives. Our use of the term, however, more broadly encompasses everything experienced by the ego as loss, thereby also including Spitz's ideas conerning anaclitic depression (Spitz, R. A., 1946, 2:313–342) and Bibring's concept of depression as a state of ego depletion (E. Bibring, 1953).

Depressive equivalent: Defenses against and alternate expressions of the depressive state, which function to avoid, deter, or reverse its psychological processes (described above). Such phenomena are, in varying degrees, guilt-expiating, self-punitive, reparative to others, or narcissistically restitutive to one's self-esteem. By "equivalence" to depression is meant some measure of dynamic relatedness, and we infer such relationship from the depression-deterring function of such behaviors.

Ego, constriction of: *see* Constriction of the ego.

Ego strength: The capacity of the ego to resist disorganization and to function adaptively in the face of internal and external pressure. This involves an assessment of defensive and integrative functioning, since optimal functioning and deployment of defenses would permit the individual to deal with inner and outer reality most effectively. The concept ego strength also embraces *ego resources* which we consider to be those distinguishable qualitative aspects of ego functioning (adaptive, integrative, and defensive) whose organization and interplay contribute to the overall assessment of ego strength.

Environment: The psychological environment or "life space" (Erikson) which includes, in addition to the usual connotations of the word, the somatic structures and experiences that impinge upon, and are perceived as external to, the self.

Externalization: For our conceptualization of externalization as a measure of an aspect of one's attitude toward his illness, in effect, a subcategory of insight, *see* Wallerstein, R. S., *et al.* (1956), 20:245.

Identification: A more differentiated form of introjection, taking place at a time when perceptual and cognitive capacities of the psychic apparatus have increased to the point of reacting to the role aspects of interpersonal interaction. Role implies the presence of a socially recognized function that is exerted by the object or by both participants in their interaction. The cluster of memory traces implicit in identification thus comprises: (1) the image of an object exerting a role in the interaction with the self, (2) the image of the self, more clearly differentiated from the object that in the case of introjection, (3) an affective coloring of the interaction, of a more differentiated, less intense and less diffuse quality than in the case of introjection (*see* definition of Introjection).

Impulse control: Impulse control is the generic term referring to the degree and manner of the ego's control over instinctual impulses. Weak impulse control implies maladaptive alloplastic impulse discharge in the search for gratification. Overly rigid impulse control implies severe inhibition of impulse discharge and consequent autoplastic symptoms or maladaptive character patterns.

Impulse-defense configuration: By this is meant a relatively stable combination of impulse (or impulses) with the defense (or defenses) that characteristically (for that individual) modulates or controls its expression.

Impulse-defense configuration, change in: *see* Change in impulse-defense configuration.

Insoluble transference neurosis; unanalyzable transference jam: A development in psychotherapy or psychoanalysis in which a regressively induced transference paradigm is of so intensely conflictual a nature or so intensely gratifying that its working through and resolution cannot be accomplished.

Insight: A process through which a person attains self-awareness. It involves three elements: (1) awareness, with its cognitive and affective components, of some aspect of the self (feelings, attitudes, behaviors, etc.); (2) a comparison between this awareness and a desired state which is more appropriate to the integrated expectations of the self; and (3) concern about the discrepancy that provides the conditions for change.

States of self-awareness that lack one or more of these components are "partial insights"; "intellectualized insights" are a special category of such partial forms of self-awareness. Partial insights represent steps in the process of attaining insight as defined here, but may also serve as resistances against that process.

Integration: The operation of the synthesizing function of the ego as defined by Nunberg (1931, 12:123–140). Infantile drives, aims, and objects have been subsumed in a set of behaviors and attitudes harmonious with one another. In an integrated personality, infantile components are available to contribute to goal-directed thinking and behavior. They need not be available to consciousness, but can operate automatically. In nonintegrated or disintegrated personalities, repressed infantile wishes and conflicts exert independent pressures, and do not contribute to, or may actually interfere with, the total functioning of the individual.

Introjection: A mechanism or function of the psychic apparatus which can be used for defensive purposes by the ego. It consists in the intrapsychic reproduction and maintenance of an interaction with the environment by means of an organized cluster of memory traces implying at least three components: (1) the image of an object, (2) the image of the self in interaction with that object, (3) the affective coloring of both the object and the self under the influence of a drive representative present at the time of the interaction.

Masochism: The conscious or unconscious seeking of painful affects and/or physical pain as a means to the gratification of repressed infantile wishes. The term thus applies both to a circumscribed behavioral manifestation such as a sexual perversion and to a pervasive orientation of the character. We distinguish masochism from the more general class of phenomena described as self-destructive or self-punitive by its special attribute of affording unconscious *pleasure* instead of, or in addition to, constituting a means of expiating guilt.

Motivation: A prevailing wish for change in the direction of escaping from pain and/or achieving gratification. It can have both realistic and unrealistic, conscious and unconscious components. It ranges from a relatively steady wish to achieve more adaptive modes of need fulfillment, combined with an expectation of being able to do so through changing the self, through desires for primitive and infantile gratifications and/or wishes to achieve such goals through bringing about changes in the environment. There are various gauges of motivation; these are categorized in our listing of patient variables under the headings of honesty, of willingness to pay for the help sought, of nature and extent of the consciously desired changes, and of secondary gains of the illness (or its treatment).

Narcissism: A quality of a person's relationship to himself and others in which the maintenance of a stable equilibrium is inordinately dependent upon a steady supply of gratification, whether this comes from the environment or from one's self. Other persons are thus valued predominantly for their capacity to fulfill current needs, and are readily abandoned in favor of other objects, or of self-absorption, when they fail to afford gratification. A pathological overvaluation of the self (conscious or unconscious) is an essential component of this orientation.

Neurosis; neurotic: Those compromise solutions of intrapsychic conflicts between unacceptable impulses and defenses against them which tend to be applied inflexibly are more determined by infantile experiences than by present reality, and are more in reponse to internal pressure than to external requirements. We are not here using the term to designate a nosological distinction, i.e., to differentiate neurotic from psychotic, but only to designate the compromise formation aspect of the phenomenon in question.

Neurotic life circumstance; neurotic life situation: A life situation which has largely resulted from the patient's psychopathology but which has become irreversible to a significant extent so that even the resolution of intrapsychic conflict will not necessarily modify the life situation itself. An example is a neurotically bound marriage held together by children or religious factors.

Psychological-mindedness: We mean this (as defined in Wallerstein, R. S., *et al.*, 1956, 20:246) as a *capacity*, and a readiness, to see psychological relationships. It is distinct from our definition of insight (*see* Insight), but is a necessary precondition for it.

Repression of affects: *see* Affect, repression of.

Schizoid; schizoid potential: A character style referring to the withdrawl of cathexes from the external object world and their reinvestment into the internal object world with some concomitant reality distortion.

Self-destructiveness: Self-destructiveness is used, in a very broad sense, to connote behaviors and attitudes which, wittingly or unwittingly, tend to destroy or weaken an individual's well-being, or the chances of his realizing important social, vocational, or personal objectives. Often this is manifested in behavior which tends to destroy the possibility of a successful outcome to the psychotherapy.

Somatization: We use this term to encompass the whole gamut of somatic expressions of psychological conflicts and/or the somatic end-states that eventuate from psychological conflicts. This range includes the following: (1) classical conversion phenomena, (2) physiological dysfunctions ("organ neuroses"), (3) physiological dysfunctions with structural organic alterations (psychosomatic diseases proper), (4) sexual inhibitions and dysfunctions, (5) hypochondriasis, and (6) somatic delusional experiences.

Stable change: The more stable a change, the more it is *both* enduring in time and independent of a particular situational context.

Strengthening of defenses: This term refers to the enhancement of control and mastery over impulse by defense. It is manifest in the lessening of stereotypy and rigidity in the development of defense, *pari passu*, in the enhancement of selectivity, flexibility, and appropriateness to context (i.e., in degree of adaptation to the requirements of reality). It occurs in both expressive and supportive psychotherapies, but is brought about by (by and large) different kinds of technical maneuvers in the two psychotherapeutic modes. In expressive psychotherapies it is brought about largely through the analysis of the defenses and of their operation, as a step toward an eventual reintegration. Gill (Gill, M. M., 1951, 20:62–71) spells out the techniques of strengthening the defenses in supportive psychotherapies as follows: (1) the encouragement of adaptive combinations of instinct and defense and the concomitant discouragement of maladaptive combinations, (2) refraining from uncovering or interpreting defensive constellations essential to the equilibrium of the patient, and (3) the offering of "inexact interpretation" (in Glover's sense) which offer a partial discharge of instinct derivatives, thus making the instinct relatively weaker and the work of defense against the remainder easier.

Stress: Noxious factors, external or internal, continuous or intermittent, which in their own right affect everyone adversely to some degree. (We recognize that this usage differs from that of Selye who defines stress as the organismic *response* to the stress-inducing environmental factor.)

Structural change (in the ego): This is a relative term covering degrees of an intrapsychic process (with its behavioral reflections) along a continuum. At its maximum it represents the kind and degree of change consequent upon full *conflict resolution* and is illustrated in the example included in the definition of that term. More limited structural change is represented by the kind and degree of shift illustrated under the definition of *change in impulse-defense configuration*. In both instances (full conflict resolution and change in impulse-defense configuration) there is a more or less enduring change in major ego functional alignments.

Supports, adjunctive: Those prescribed environmental factors provided within the total treatment situation which contribute to intrapsychic equilibrium and successful adaptation. This encompasses such planned and/or supervised factors as hospital management, activities programs, and in general a controlled and prescribed milieu.

Supports, life-situational: Those aspects of the environment, both human and material, which contribute to intrapsychic equilibrium and successful adaptation.

Symptom; symptomatic behavior: We mean a usage broader than that which covers the classical neurotic symptoms alone (cf., phobias, obsessions). We mean as well those traits, behaviors, etc., which represent compromise expressions of intrapsychic conflicts and which are sufficiently salient to be either (1) distressing to the patient and/or his environment, or (2) regarded as significantly restrictive of the patient's full range of adaptive functioning.

Tension: Tension has two meanings, one clinical, one theoretical. Clinically, tension is a physiological manifestation of anxiety reflecting chiefly autonomic or musculoskeletal hyperactivity. These manifestations may or may not be subjectively experienced. If they are, it is likely to be as a "nervous symptom" rather than as anxiety, which is a specifically mental state of apprehension. In this use, tension contrasts with relaxation or comfort. Used theoretically, the term tension contrasts with "discharge." Tension in this sense is the outcome of frustration consequent to the inability to discharge impulses, which inability is attributable, in a psychopathological context at least, to intrapsychic conflict. Intrapsychic tension may or may not be reflected in psychic discomfort. Tension reduction or discharge would include relief of anxiety, guilt, depression, subsiding of a manic attack, etc.

Therapeutic alliance (working alliance): Ideally, both patient and psychotherapist consistently know, believe, or feel—at some level of consciousness—that their primary goal in working together is to help the patient. The cognitive-affective attitudes which constitute this belief create the therapeutic alliance (Zetzel) or the working alliance (Greenson). Various vicissitudes of their relationship or personalities (principally transference and countertransference) may, temporarily or permanently, obscure, interfere with, or dissolve this alliance. The measure of its strength is the extent to which behaviors of both patient and therapist take it into account. (We see this as essentially the same as Freud's conceptualization of the "mild positive transference" necessary to the continuing progress of the analytic treatment.)

Transference neurosis, insoluble: *see* Insoluble transference neurosis.

REFERENCES

Appelbaum, A. (1972), "A Critical Re-examination of the Concept of 'Motivation for Change' in Psychoanalytic Treatment," *Int. J. Psychoanal.*, 53:51–59.

———, and Horwitz, L. (1968), "Diagnosis and Prediction." Unpublished.

——— (1969), "Correlates of Global Change in Psychotherapy." Unpublished.

Bakan, D. (1955), "The General and the Aggregate: A Methodological Distinction." *Percept. Motor Skills*, 5:211–212.

Bergin, A. E., and Strupp, H. H. (1972), *Changing Frontiers in the Science of Psychotherapy.* Chicago: Aldine-Atherton.

Bibring, E. (1953), "Mechanism of Depression," in *Affective Disorders*, ed. P. Greenacre. New York: International Universities Press, pp. 13–48.

Bibring, G. L., Dwyer, T. F., Huntington, D. S., and Valenstein, A. F. (1961), "A Study of the Psychological Processes in Pregnancy and of the Earliest Mother-Child Relationship." *Psychoanal. Study of the Child*, 16:9–72.

Eysenck, H. (1952), "The Effects of Psychotherapy: An Evaluation." *J. Cons. Psychol.*, 16:319–324.

Gill, M. M. (1954), "Psychoanalysis and Exploratory Psychotherapy." *J. Amer. Psychoanal. Assn.*, 2:771–797.

——— (1963), "Topography and Systems in Psychoanalytic Theory." *Psychological Issues*, Monogr. 10. New York: International Universities Press.

Greenson, R. R. (1960), "Empathy and Its Vicissitudes," *Int. J. Psychoanal.*, 41:418–424.

Harty, M., and Horwitz, L. (1973), "Therapeutic Outcome as Rated by Patients, Therapists, and Judges." Unpublished.

Horwitz, L. (1963), "Theory Construction and Validation in Psychoanalysis," in *Theories in Contemporary Psychology*, ed. M. H. Marx. New York: Macmillan, pp. 413-434.

———Appelbaum, A. (1966), "The Hierarchical Ordering of Assumptions About Psychotherapy." *Psychotherapy*, 3:71-80.

Kernberg, O. (1966), "Structural Derivatives of Object Relationships." *Int. J. Psychoanal.*, 47:236–253.

———, et al. (1972), "Psychotherapy and Psychoanalysis." *Bull. Menninger Clin.*, 36:3–275.

Luborsky, L. (1962), "Clinicians' Judgments of Mental Health: A Proposed Scale." *Arch. Gen. Psychiat.*, 7:407–417.

Nunberg, H. (1931), "The Synthetic Function of the Ego." *Int. J. Psychoanal.*, 12:123–140.

Pfeffer, A. Z. (1959), "A Procedure for Evaluating the Results of Psychoanalysis: A Preliminary Report." *J. Amer. Psychoanal. Assn.*, 7:418–444.

Rapaport, D. (1960), "The Structure of Psychoanalytic Theory: A Systematizing Attempt." *Psychological Issues*, Monogr. 6. New York: International Universities Press.

Sargent, H. D. (1961), "Intrapsychic Change: Methodological Problems in Psychotherapy Research." *Psychiatry*, 24:93–108.

———, et al. (1967), "An Approach to Quantitative Problems of Psychoanalytic Research." *J. Clin. Psychol.*, 23:243–291.

———Horwitz, L., Wallerstein, R. S., and Appelbaum, A. (1968), "Prediction in Psychotherapy Research: A Method for the Transformation of Clinical Judgments into Testable Hypotheses." *Psychological Issues*, Monogr. 21. New York: International Universities Press.

Siegal, R. S., and Rosen, I. C. (1962), "Character Style and Anxiety Tolerance: A Study in Intrapsychic Change," in *Research in Psychotherapy*, eds. H. H. Strupp and L. Luborsky. Baltimore: French-Bray.

Spitz, R. A. (1946), "Anaclitic Depression." *Psychoanal. Study of the Child*, 2:313–342.

Voth, H., and Orth, M. (1973), *Psychotherapy and the Role of the Environment*. New York: Behavioral Publications.

Wallerstein, R. S., *et al.* (1956), "The Psychotherapy Research Project of the Menninger Foundation: Rationale, Method, and Sample Use." *Bull. Menninger Clin.*, 20:221–278.

———(1958), "The Psychotherapy Research Project of the Menninger Foundation: I. Further Notes on Design and Concepts." *Bull. Menninger Clin.*, 22:117–125.

Wallerstein, R. S. (1964), "The Role of Prediction in Theory Building in Psychoanalysis." *J. Amer. Psychoanal. Assn.*, 12:675-691.

Wallerstein, R. S., and Robbins, L. L. (1954), "Manual of the Initial Study of the Psychotherapy Research Project." Unpublished.

Zetzel, E. (1956), "The Concept of Transference," in *The Capacity for Emotional Growth*. New York: International Universities Press, 1970, pp. 168–181.